Southern Fried Football

The History, Passion, and Glory of the Great Southern Game

Revised and Expanded Edition

Tony Barnhart

TRIUMPH
BOOKS

Triumph Books and colophon are registered trademarks of Random House, Inc.

Library of Congress Cataloging-in-Publication Data

Barnhart, Tony.
    Southern fried football : the history, passion, and glory of the great southern game / Tony Barnhart—Rev. and expanded ed.
    p. cm.
Includes bibliographical references.
ISBN-13: 978-1-60078-093-6
ISBN-10: 1-60078-093-8
    1. Football—Southern States—History. 2. Football—Southern States—Miscellanea. 3. Football—Records—Southern States. I. Title. II. Title: History, passion, and glory of the great southern game.

GV959.52.S9B37 2008
796.3320975—dc22

                                                                                2008023300

This book is available in quantity at special discounts for your group or organization. For further information, contact:

    Triumph Books
    542 South Dearborn Street
    Suite 750
    Chicago, Illinois 60605
    (312) 939-3330
    Fax (312) 663-3557

Printed in U.S.A.
ISBN: 978-1-60078-093-6
Design by Patricia Frey

To my mother, who taught me the love of reading and writing;

To my father, who taught me the love of athletic competition;

To Maria and Sara Catherine, who have given me all the wealth I have, and all that I will ever need.

TABLE OF CONTENTS

FOREWORD

College football, as played in the Southern region of the United States, defies absolute definition. The mechanics and techniques are much the same as in other regions. Hats, pads, and socks are the same. It's somewhere in that mysterious area of fervor that we probably should seek the difference.

But what is the point of doing that? Isn't it more fun to just enjoy it? Jump at every chance to be part of it?

If you are like me, with white growing under your cap, Tony Barnhart's *Southern Fried Football* will be a memory jogger.

If you're waiting for your first mortgage, you will learn something about the history of football in the South and the game's evolution.

Long before the Falcons, Dolphins, Jaguars, Saints, Panthers, Ravens, Redskins, Oilers, and Buccaneers came along, the old game was doing nicely down in Dixie.

Keith Jackson, ABC's voice of college football for 40 seasons (1966–2005), grew up in Roopville, Georgia. Photo courtesy of ABC Sports/ESPN.

Yale played Georgia. Vanderbilt was a powerhouse under McGugin. Centre and Sewanee took no guff from anybody. There was a Paladin over at Furman long before Richard Boone ever set a horse.

Folks were eating fried chicken, potato salad, and white cake under the shade tree long before Henry Ford's folks gave us the station wagon and created a new buzzword, *tailgating*! My Grannie never did trust that word!

Coaches were characters and at least feudal barons, if not kings. There has been one general who actually coached more wins when he was a mere major. He gave the profession a list of 10 basic principles of coaching, but I like the 11th unwritten one the best. On game day he reminded his troops that touchdowns follow good blocking, just as surely as night follows day.

There was a Notre Dame quarterback who was head coach at Alabama for 16 seasons.

There was the Auburn guy who coached forever at Georgia (Vince Dooley) and the Georgia guy (Pat Dye) who was a big winner at Auburn. In college football winning has always been the bridge over troubled waters...leading occasionally to forgiveness and acceptance.

For six decades I've lived and loved college football. Good games, bad games, good people, and bad people. I think I have heard every preachment and parable from the coaches. I think the best one defining the game of football came from Wallace Wade: "Nobody ever wins a football game...somebody loses it."

Enjoy!

—Keith Jackson

Editor's note: Keith Jackson, one of the most decorated announcers in television history, became the voice of college football for ABC in 1966. He officially retired after the 2006 Rose Bowl.

ACKNOWLEDGMENTS

A Toast to Friends No Longer with Us

As I was doing the research to update *Southern Fried Football* a couple of things quickly became clear: (1) a whole lot has happened in Southern college football over the past eight years, and (2) in that same span of time we have had to say good-bye to a lot of people who were responsible for making the game what it is today.

When *Southern Fried Football* was first released in 2000, I wasn't sure if I would ever write another book. I wanted to thank everybody who had ever helped me in my life and career. The list was long. I want those folks to know that I will always be grateful for their support.

This time I want to raise a toast to a number of people—players, coaches, writers, broadcasters, and sports information directors—who made a tremendous contribution to college football before they left us. Some of them left us much too soon.

This list is far from complete, but everyone on it helped to make college football the greatest game in the world. Many were my personal friends. All of them will be missed.

Ray Beck: An All-SEC guard on Georgia Tech's great 10–0–1 team of 1951. Beck was inducted into the College Football Hall of Fame in 1997 and died on January 10, 2007.

Bob Bradley: The longtime Clemson sports information director died on October 20, 2001, after a long battle with cancer. Mr. Bradley worked 502 consecutive football games for Clemson. He was 75.

Al Browning: Award-winning sports-writer whose books include *The Third Saturday in October*, which is the definitive work on the Alabama-Tennessee football rivalry. He died in April 2002.

Bob Bradley, seen here with a friend, served as Clemson's sports information director from 1955 to 1989. The press box at Clemson's Memorial Stadium is named in his honor. Photo courtesy of Clemson University/Sports Information.

"Coach" Bill Hartman was an All-American at Georgia who developed a generation of great kickers for the Bulldogs. Photo courtesy of the University of Georgia/Sports Information.

Kim King and his wife, Gail, were honored at Georgia Tech's October 2, 2004, game against Miami. His son, Beau, is in the background with athletics director Dave Braine. Just 10 days later King passed away. Photo courtesy of the Georgia Institute of Technology/Sports Information.

Otis Boggs: The radio voice of Florida football for 43 seasons (1939–81). He died in August 2002, at age 82.

Jerry Claiborne: Head coach at Virginia Tech, Maryland, and Kentucky. A member of the College Football Hall of Fame, Claiborne died in September 2000, at age 72.

Paul Eells: The radio voice for Vanderbilt and Arkansas football for a total of 39 seasons. Eells, 70, was killed in a traffic accident in July 2006.

John Ferguson: For the better part of 42 years Ferguson was the radio voice of the LSU Tigers. He died in December 2005, at age 86.

Jim Fyffe: He was the voice of Auburn football for 22 seasons (1981–2002) before his sudden death in May 2003. He was 57.

Marvin "Skeeter" Francis: Francis was the long-time director of media relations for the ACC and was given credit for moving that league into the modern era of communications. Francis died in July 2004, at age 82.

Bill Hartman: "Coach Hartman," as he was affectionately known, was an All-American at Georgia in 1937 and a member of the College Football Hall of Fame. He served as a volunteer kicking coach for Georgia and produced several All-Americans, including Kevin Butler. Hartman died March 16, 2006, on the day before his 91ˢᵗ birthday.

Kim King: One of Georgia Tech's greatest quarterbacks, King was tabbed "the Young Left-hander" by radio voice Al Ciraldo. King died in October 2004, after a long battle with cancer. He was 59.

Kathy Lumpkin: She was the first female member of the Alabama Sports Writer's Association and daughter of legendary sportswriter Bill Lumpkin. She died November 29, 2007. She was 63.

Banks McFadden: Three-year letter winner at Clemson in football, basketball, and track and a member of the College Football Hall of Fame, McFadden died June 4, 2005, from cancer. He was 88.

Van McKenzie: Longtime sports editor of the *Atlanta Journal-Constitution*, he gave me the biggest break of my career when he hired me on August 7, 1984. One of the most brilliant newspapermen who ever lived, Van died from cancer in January 2007. He was 61.

Tom Mickle: One of the smartest people ever involved in college football, a former sports information director at Duke, and associate commissioner of the ACC, Mickle drew up the original structure of the BCS on the back of a cocktail napkin. He was the executive director of the Capital One Bowl in Orlando when he died in April 2006, at age 55. He is survived by his wife, Jill, and his two children, Matthew and Holland.

Charlie McClendon: "Cholly Mac" was the head coach at LSU for 18 seasons. He died in December 2001, at age 78.

George Morris: Morris was one of Georgia Tech's greatest players and most noted ambassadors. A member of the College Football Hall of Fame, Morris died suddenly of a heart attack in December 2007. He was 76.

Clemson's Banks McFadden was an All-American in both football (1939) and basketball (1938–39). Photo courtesy of Clemson University/Sports Information.

Tom Mickle drew up the original structure of the BCS on the back of a cocktail napkin. Photo courtesy of the Atlantic Coast Conference.

Georgia Tech coach Bobby Dodd called George Morris (right) "the greatest player I ever coached." Photo courtesy of the Georgia Institute of Technology/Sports Information.

Tom Price was the sports information director at South Carolina for 31 years (1962–92). Photo courtesy of the University of South Carolina/Sports Information.

Jackie Parker: An All-America quarterback at Mississippi State, Parker died on November 7, 2006. He was 74.

Jim Phillips: Phillips had broadcast over 2,000 events during 36 seasons for Clemson University when he died suddenly in September 2003. He was 69 years old.

Barney Poole: A three-time All-America end who, because of unique eligibility rules during World War II, played seven years of college football at three different schools (Ole Miss, North Carolina, and Army). He died April 12, 2005, at age 81.

Tom Price: Price became the sports information director at South Carolina,

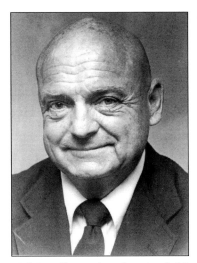

Erk Russell won three Division I-AA national championships at Georgia Southern. Photo courtesy of Georgia Southern University/ Sports Information.

Reggie White, known better as "the Minister of Defense," was only 43 at the time of his death. Photo courtesy of the University of Tennessee/Sports Information.

his alma mater, in 1962 and never left. He was the authority on the history of Gamecock athletics. Tom died February 1, 2008, at age 81.

Eddie Robinson: When "Coach Rob" retired after 57 years at Grambling he had won 408 games, more than any other coach. He died April 3, 2007, at age 88.

Erk Russell: For my money Erk was the greatest motivator of football players who ever lived. After 17 years as the defensive coordinator at Georgia, Russell won three Division I-A national championships. He died of an apparent stroke in September 2006. He was 80.

Chris Schenkel: A legendary voice of college football for ABC, Schenkel died September 11, 2005, at age 82.

John Vaught: Vaught built the Ole Miss program into a national power in his 25 seasons as the head coach. Vaught died February 3, 2006, at age 92.

Bob Ward: A Hall of Fame lineman from Maryland who was a two-time first-team All-American (1950–51). He died April 29, 2005, at age 77.

Reggie White: White was a Tennessee All-American and one of the greatest defensive linemen to ever play the game. Known as "the Minister of Defense," White died suddenly in December 2004. He was 43.

INTRODUCTION

2007: The Best Year Ever for Southern Fried Football

I should have known that the 2007 season was going to be something special. I got my first clue in August when I was on a conference call with Jerry Moore, the head coach at Appalachian State. The Mountaineers, who had won two straight Division I-AA national championships, were scheduled to open the season at Michigan on September 1. Michigan, with quarterback Chad Henne and running back Mike Hart returning, thought it could make a run at the national championship.

I asked Coach Moore if he had spent any time talking to his team about the aura of playing in Michigan's famed Big House, which seats over 100,000.

"We haven't talked a whole lot about aura," Coach Moore said in that wonderful Texas drawl. "We have talked a lot about what plays we think will work against their defense."

Uh-oh.

Appalachian State, whose Kidd Brewer Stadium seats just under 17,000, shocked the world by blocking a field goal on the game's last play to beat mighty Michigan, 34–32. With that stunning upset we were off and running on a season that none of us will ever forget.

When I decided to update *Southern Fried Football* for the fall of 2008, I hoped that the 2007 season would give us at least a few memories worth putting in the book.

Well, well, well. We got more than that. In fact, we got a lot more. What we got in 2007 was the wildest, most unpredictable college football season in my 30 years as a sportswriter.

I can't tell you how many times during the course of the 2007 season that people stopped me in airports and stadiums just to ask: "Is this the craziest college football season you've ever experienced?"

I would always say yes, and ultimately I could offer this as proof: In 2007 I went to Lexington, Kentucky, not once, not twice, but three times to watch college football. I saw three great games and all had a direct bearing on the SEC championship. One went into triple overtime. Another went into quadruple overtime.

It was a year that began with Alabama making one of the boldest statements in its football history—or anybody else's history, for that matter—by signing Nick Saban to an unprecedented eight-year $32 million contract to be its head coach.

A few days later Florida shocked college football by dominating No. 1 Ohio State, 41–14, in the BCS championship game in Glendale, Arizona. It gave the SEC its fifth national championship since its expansion in 1992.

Fast-forward to December 1, and the regular season ends with one of the wildest days ever for Southern college football. That Saturday began with LSU coach Les Miles holding a press conference two hours before the SEC championship game at the Georgia Dome in Atlanta. He was there to deny reports by ESPN's Kirk Herbstreit that he had agreed to become the next head coach at Michigan.

Miles's team began that day ranked No. 7 in the BCS standings. By midnight both No. 1 Missouri and No. 2 West Virginia had lost, and LSU was suddenly in the BCS championship game against Ohio State. On January 7, 2008, the Tigers beat the Buckeyes, 38–24, in New Orleans to give the SEC its second national championship in 12 months.

It was a year where LSU was ranked No. 1 twice during the regular season, only to lose the rankings both times by a total of eight points in six overtimes. When all the smoke cleared and all the games were played, LSU finished the season holding up the crystal football as the nation's No. 1 team.

It was a year where Georgia's entire team stormed the field after scoring its first touchdown against Florida in Jacksonville. It was a risky move by coach Mark Richt, but the Bulldogs won the game, made a bunch of Gators mad, and injected a big booster shot of life back into the rivalry.

It was a year where Auburn made history by beating Alabama for the sixth straight season.

It was a year where Houston Nutt decided he could not heal a fractured fan base and resigned at Arkansas. Four hours later he was the head coach at Ole Miss. Not only did he

LSU coach Les Miles holds up the BCS national championship trophy as quarterback Matt Flynn (left) and ACC commissioner John Swofford (right) look on. Photo courtesy of Steve Franz/LSU Sports Information.

get a raise from Ole Miss, but he also got a severance package from Arkansas, even though he didn't get fired. Friends, that could only happen in Southern college football.

It was a year where, beginning on October 27, Tennessee and Coach Phillip Fulmer faced four elimination games in the SEC East race. The Vols won them all with two going to overtime and another coming by a single point as Tennessee reached the SEC championship game.

It was a year where South Florida, which began its football program just 11 years ago, started 6–0 and rose to become the No. 2–ranked team in the land. The ranking didn't last long as the Bulls proceeded to lose three straight games.

It was a year where Florida quarterback Tim Tebow changed all the rules. He became the first sophomore ever to win the Heisman Trophy with the greatest single season in the SEC's 75-year history.

It was a year where Bobby Petrino resigned as the head coach of the Atlanta Falcons on a Tuesday at 5:30 PM. By midnight he was in Fayetteville, Arkansas, calling the Hogs on national television as the new head coach at Arkansas.

It was a year where the rankings just didn't matter. Three times (October 13, November 23–24, and December 1) during the 2007 season, both No. 1 and No. 2 lost during the same weekend. And over the course of the season, 13 teams that were ranked in the top five lost to unranked opponents. Six of those upset victims were ranked No. 2 at the time.

In short, if 2007 wasn't the greatest year in the history of Southern college football, I will defer to whoever can show me a better one.

I couldn't think of a better way to begin this update of *Southern Fried Football* than with a detailed look back at a season we will be talking about with our children and our grandchildren.

Here is the other big reason I wanted to update the book: brothers and sisters, as the dearly departed Al Ciraldo, the voice of Georgia Tech, would say, a whole lot has happened since fall 2000, when we first published *Southern Fried Football*:

- Steve Spurrier, who won six SEC championships and a national championship in 12 seasons at Florida, left college football for a cup of coffee (and about $10 million) in the NFL. He came back in 2005 as the head coach at South Carolina.
- Florida State's Bobby Bowden has become college football's all-time winner among Division I-A coaches surpassing his hero, Alabama's Paul "Bear" Bryant. As the 2008 season begins, Bowden, 78, has 373 victories. But close behind is Joe Paterno, Penn State's ageless wonder at 81, who has 372 career victories.
- The terrorist attacks on September 11, 2001, put college football on hold as we mourned our collective loss. But ultimately the game served as part of the healing process. The first game after the Twin Towers came down in New York was played in Starkville, Mississippi, between Mississippi State and South Carolina.

- Georgia hired Mark Richt (in December 2000) as head coach, and the Bulldogs have enjoyed their greatest run of success since the glory days of Vince Dooley.
- The ACC has expanded, adding Boston College, Miami, and Virginia Tech. The league now has a conference championship game.
- Nick Saban won a national championship at LSU in 2003, left college football for two years to coach the Miami Dolphins, and has returned to the college game as the head coach at Alabama.
- Mississippi State hired the first African American head coach in SEC history. And in 2007 Sylvester Croom, who played for Bear Bryant at Alabama, took the Bulldogs to a bowl game and was the SEC Coach of the Year.
- Auburn went 13–0 in 2004 and did not get a sniff at the national championship, a fact that still leaves Southerners seething. If Auburn had been given a chance, the SEC could be entering the 2008 season having won four of the last five national championships.
- We lost some of the game's greatest men, including Erk Russell, John Vaught, and George Morris. That's because God always needs some good players and coaches.

All of that and much, much more has been included in this updated version of *Southern Fried Football*. When you start turning the pages I'm sure you'll be amazed at how much has happened in the past eight years. I know I was.

On January 4, 2007, Nick Saban became the new head coach at Alabama. Photo courtesy of the University of Alabama/Paul W. Bryant Museum.

But for now, please take a walk with me as we remember 2007, the greatest season ever for Southern Fried Football.

December 21, 2006: Nick Saban, the head coach of the Miami Dolphins said these words at a press conference: "I guess I have to say it. I'm not going to be the Alabama coach."

January 4, 2007: Two weeks later at a wild press conference in Tuscaloosa, where he was greeted like a conquering hero, Saban was introduced as Alabama's new head coach, replacing Mike Shula. Saban received an eight-year contract worth $32 million.

January 8, 2007: In Glendale, Arizona, No. 2 Florida dominated No. 1 Ohio State, 41–14, for the BCS national championship.

Quarterback Chris Leak was the MVP in his final game as a Gator.

Urban Meyer won the national championship in only his second season as the Florida head coach.

January 29, 2007: Veteran coach Bobby Ross, who led Georgia Tech to the 1990 UPI national championship, announced his retirement at Army.

April 16, 2007: The world was shocked when a deranged gunman murdered 32 people on the Virginia Tech campus. Hokies coach Frank Beamer canceled the final week of spring practice and the school's spring game. He vowed that on its September 1 return, Virginia Tech football would be part of the healing process.

April 21, 2007: On a brilliant Saturday afternoon in Tuscaloosa, Nick Saban received the first real referendum on his hiring as Alabama's head coach as a crowd of more than 92,138 turned out to watch the A-Day spring game at Bryant-Denny Stadium. Admission was free, and officials had to close the gates once the stadium was full. It was the largest recorded crowd ever for a spring game.

April 28, 2007: LSU quarterback JaMarcus Russell became the No. 1 overall pick in the 2007 NFL draft. LSU had four players taken in the first round. The SEC and ACC had 17 of the top 31 picks in the draft. Eleven of those players were from the SEC. Six were from the ACC.

May 17, 2007: Mike V, LSU's Bengal Tigers mascot, died at age 17.

August 12, 2007: The University of Miami announced that after the 2007 season it would be leaving the Orange Bowl where the Hurricanes had played their home games since 1937. Miami signed a 25-year lease to play home games at Dolphin Stadium, just north of Miami.

September 1, 2007: Appalachian State, which had won back-to-back national championships in NCAA Division I-AA, went to Michigan and knocked off the Wolverines 34–32 in one of the biggest upsets in college football history.

With his father, Hall of Fame coach Vince Dooley, sitting in the stadium, Derek Dooley began his career as the head coach at Louisiana Tech with a 28–7 win over Central Arkansas.

September 22, 2007: In Baton Rouge, LSU was clinging to a 14–7 lead in a game against South Carolina. The Tigers lined up for a 39-yard field goal in the second quarter. LSU quarterback Matt Flynn took the snap and flipped the ball over his shoulder to kicker Colt David, who ran untouched into the end zone. South Carolina never recovered, and LSU won, 28–16. After the play, the smile on Steve Spurrier's face said it all. The head ball coach wished he had thought of that.

In Tuscaloosa Matt Stafford threw a 25-yard touchdown pass on Georgia's first play in overtime to beat Alabama, 26–23.

September 29, 2007: Auburn's Wes Byrum kicked a 43-yard field goal as time expired, and the Tigers upset Florida, 20–17. Byrum, a freshman from Fort Lauderdale, actually had to kick the winning

Applachian State's Dexter Jackson scores on a 68-yard touchdown pass against Michigan. The Mountaineers stunned the college football world by beating the Wolverines 34–32 on September 1, 2007. Photo courtesy of Appalachian State University/Sports Information.

field goal twice. Florida coach Urban Meyer called timeout just a split-second before the first kick, which was good but did not count.

Alabama and Florida State set an all-time attendance record at Jacksonville Municipal Stadium as 85,412 turned out to watch the Seminoles win, 21–14.

October 6, 2007: In what some billed as the biggest regular-season game in LSU history, an overflow crowd of 92,910 inside Tiger Stadium and at least 50,000 outside in the parking lots, watched as the Tigers rallied from a 17–7 halftime deficit to beat Florida, 28–24. LSU drove 60 yards in 14 plays to score the winning touchdown with only 1:09 left. With 7:49 remaining in the third quarter, word came that Southern California had been upset by Stanford, meaning that LSU became No. 1 in both major polls on Sunday. Five times during the course of the game LSU coach Les Miles gambled on fourth down and made it.

October 13, 2007: Kentucky defeated No. 1 LSU 43–37 in triple overtime at Commonwealth Stadium in Lexington. Kentucky rallied from a 27–13 deficit to send the game into overtime. With LSU trailing by six in the third extra period, LSU faced a fourth down and two yards to go to keep the drive alive. LSU running back Charles Scott was stopped after a one-yard gain by Kentucky reserve linebacker Braxton Kelly. It was labeled as the biggest win in Kentucky's history. Kentucky fans stormed the field, and the school was fined $50,000 by the SEC.

October 14, 2007: After a 64–12 win over Central Florida, South Florida was ranked No. 2 in the nation. It was an amazing accomplishment for USF, located in Tampa, which began its football program from scratch in 1997. The joy, however, lasted only four days.

October 18, 2007: South Florida traveled to Rutgers for a Thursday night game and lost, 30–27.

October 20, 2007: Rather than play for the winning field goal, LSU's Matt Flynn threw a 22-yard touchdown pass to Demetrius Byrd with only one second left as the Tigers beat Auburn, 30–24, in Baton Rouge. The victory kept LSU's national championship hopes alive.

October 27, 2007: Looking for something extra to motivate his team, Georgia coach Mark Richt came up with a plan for the annual rivalry game with Florida in Jacksonville. After Georgia's Knowshon Moreno scored the first touchdown of the game, the entire Bulldogs team left the bench and stormed into the end zone. Georgia was penalized for unsportsmanlike conduct, but the message was sent. After losing 15 of its last 17 games to Florida, Georgia decided that October 27 would be different and dominated the Gators, 42–30. On Monday Richt apologized to SEC Commissioner Mike Slive for the action.

South Carolina came back from a 21–0 half-time deficit to take a 24–21 lead on Tennessee with 1:24 left in Knoxville. Tennessee's Daniel Lincoln kicked a 48-yard field goal to tie the game with only five seconds left in regulation. The Volunteers won in overtime, 27–24.

November 3, 2007: With 92,138 fans inside Bryant-Denny Stadium and another 30,000 in Alabama's Quad watching on television, LSU rallied with two touchdowns in the final three minutes to beat Alabama, 41–34. It was Nick Saban's first meeting with his old team.

November 10, 2007: For the first time in history, Georgia took the field in black jerseys for its game with Auburn. The Georgia team warmed up in the traditional red jerseys and then changed right before the game's start. With the Sanford Stadium crowd energized by the move, Georgia went on to dominate Auburn, 45–20.

Georgia takes the field for the first time ever in black jerseys for its game against Auburn on November 10, 2007. Photo courtesy of the University of Georgia/Sports Information.

The 2007 season was the last for Miami at the famed Orange Bowl, where the Hurricanes had played their home games since 1937. Photo courtesy of the University of Miami/Sports Information.

With dozens of former players on hand for Miami's last game in the Orange Bowl, the Hurricanes were dominated by Virginia, 48–0.

November 17, 2007: Tennessee trailed Vanderbilt 24–9 going into the fourth quarter, knowing that a loss would knock the Volunteers out of the SEC East race. The Volunteers rallied and took a 25–24 lead on Daniel Lincoln's 33-yard field goal with 2:46 left. Vanderbilt's 49-yard field-goal attempt with 33 seconds left grazed the upright, and Tennessee survived yet again.

November 23, 2007: In one of the greatest individual performances in SEC history, Arkansas running back Darren McFadden ran for 206 yards, including three touchdowns, and passed for another score as the Razorbacks stunned No. 1 LSU, 50–48, in triple overtime in Baton Rouge. Arkansas stopped a two-point conversion attempt in the third overtime to end LSU's 19-game home winning streak. Media reports on the game were unanimous in saying that the loss had ended LSU's hopes of playing for the national championship.

November 24, 2007: Ed Orgeron was fired after only three seasons as the head coach at Ole Miss. He had a record of 10–25. Auburn defeated Alabama 17–10 at Jordan-Hare Stadium for its sixth straight win over the Crimson Tide.

Tennessee stopped a two-point conversion in the fourth overtime to beat Kentucky 52–50 and advanced to the SEC championship game. The Volunteers finished in a tie with Georgia for the SEC East title at 6–2, but Tennessee earned the trip to Atlanta because it beat the Bulldogs, 35–14, back on October 6 in Knoxville.

November 26, 2007: After a year of turmoil, Houston Nutt resigned as the head coach at Arkansas. Hours later he agreed to become the new head coach at Ole Miss.

Just two days after its sixth straight loss to Georgia, Georgia Tech fired coach Chan Gailey. Gailey never had a losing season in six years at Georgia Tech, and his team had played in the ACC championship game the year before. But Gailey was 0–6 against Georgia.

December 1, 2007: Just two hours before the SEC championship game, LSU coach Les Miles called a press conference at the Georgia Dome in Atlanta to deny reports that he had reached an agreement with Michigan to become the Wolverines' next head coach. That was the bizarre beginning to what would turn out to be one of the more incredible days in the history of college football.

LSU beat Tennessee, 21–14, for the SEC championship. Later that night No. 1 Missouri lost to Oklahoma in the Big 12 championship game, and No. 2 West Virginia, a 28-point favorite, lost at home to Pittsburgh.

December 2, 2007: After all the numbers were crunched, LSU, whose national-championship hopes were apparently over when the Tigers lost to Arkansas on November 23, had jumped from No. 7 to No. 2 in the BCS standings to play No. 1 Ohio State in the January 7, 2008, national championship game in New Orleans.

December 7, 2007: Paul Johnson, who led Navy to five straight bowl games, was introduced as the new head coach at Georgia Tech.

December 8, 2007: Quarterback Tim Tebow of Florida became the first sophomore in history to win the Heisman Trophy. He became Florida's third Heisman winner along with Steve Spurrier (1966) and Danny Wuerffel (1996). Arkansas running back Darren McFadden finished as the runner-up for the second straight year.

December 10, 2007: Florida State announced that offensive coordinator Jimbo Fisher signed an agreement making him the Seminoles head coach when Bobby Bowden retires. If Fisher is not the head coach by the 2011 season, the school must pay him $2.5 million.

George Morris, one of the greatest players of the Bobby Dodd era at Georgia Tech, died suddenly. The Hall of Fame linebacker was 76.

December 11, 2007: Atlanta Falcons coach Bobby Petrino suddenly resigned. At 11:30 PM that same evening, Petrino was introduced as the new head coach at Arkansas.

December 14, 2007: Appalachian State beat Delaware 49–21 to become the first school in history to win three straight Division I-AA national championships.

December 15, 2007: Tennessee offensive coordinator David Cutcliffe, who posted five winning seasons in six years at Ole Miss, was introduced as the new head coach at Duke.

December 18, 2007: Florida State announced that as many as 25 of its players had been suspended due to an academic-cheating scandal. For some the suspensions carried over into the first three games of the 2008 season.

December 31, 2007: Freshman quarterback Kodi Burns scored a touchdown in overtime to lead Auburn to a 23–20 win in the Chick-fil-A Bowl. Burns scored the touchdown out of the new spread offense that was installed just a couple of weeks before the game by Tony Franklin, Auburn's new offensive coordinator.

Frank Broyles, who came to Arkansas in 1958 as head football coach, retired as the school's athletics director, ending a 50-year relationship with the school.

January 1, 2008: Georgia made the case that it should have gotten a shot at the BCS championship as the Bulldogs dominated Hawaii, 41–10, in the Sugar Bowl in New Orleans. Hawaii was the only undefeated team in Division I-A before the game. Georgia finished its season at 11–2.

In other bowl games that day, Tennessee beat Wisconsin, 21–17, in the Outback Bowl; Arkansas lost to Missouri, 38–7, in the Cotton Bowl; Florida lost to Michigan, 41–35, in the Capital One Bowl; and Virginia lost to Texas Tech, 31–28, in the Gator Bowl.

January 7, 2008: LSU fell behind 10–0 in the BCS championship game and then stormed back to beat Ohio State, 38–24, for the national title. Senior quarterback Matt Flynn threw four touchdown passes and was named the game's most outstanding offensive player.

January 8, 2008: Just hours after LSU claimed the national championship, University of Georgia president Michael Adams announced he would lead an effort to create an eight-team playoff to determine college football's national championship.

January 10, 2008: LSU defensive tackle Glenn Dorsey capped off a great career as he received the Outland Trophy as the nation's best interior lineman. Dorsey, the SEC Defensive Player of the Year in 2007, also won the Lombardi Award (outstanding lineman) and the Bronko Nagurski Trophy (outstanding defensive player).

January 18, 2008: Kentucky announced that offensive coordinator Joker Phillips will become the school's head coach when current head coach Rich Brooks, 66, retires.

January 26, 2008: College football fans everywhere recognized the 25th anniversary of Alabama legend Paul "Bear" Bryant's death.

February 15, 2008: Joey Jones, who played for Bear Bryant's final three teams at Alabama, was introduced as the first-ever head coach at South Alabama. The school will field its first football team in 2009.

April 30, 2008: At the BCS meetings in Hollywood, Florida, a plan for a four-team college football playoff—presented by SEC commissioner Mike Slive—does not receive support. The BCS decides to stick with its current format for the next six years.

May 1, 2008: LSU's Billy Cannon, the 1959 Heisman Trophy winner, and Florida State defensive tackle Ron Simmons are named to the College Football Hall of Fame.

May 2, 2008: LSU quarterback Ryan Perrilloux, who was the MVP of the 2007 SEC Championship Game, is kicked off the team by coach Les Miles.

PROLOGUE

It's Always Been More Than a Game

"In the East, college football is a cultural exercise...
On the West Coast, it is a tourist attraction...
In the Midwest, it is cannibalism...
But in the South it is religion...
And Saturday is the holy day.
　　　　　　　　—Marino Casem, Southern University

"College football is not a matter of life and death...
It's much more important than that."
　　　　　　—sign behind the desk of a Southern football coach

Save the unshakable belief that the Civil War was, in fact, the War of Northern Aggression, nothing is more ingrained in the Southern psyche than the love of college football—not as just a game, not as a mere diversion, but as a way of life.

Think about it. What other institution makes an otherwise normal, intelligent person choose to bark like a dog, wear red bib overalls, or paint his face and other assorted body parts with orange tiger paws?

What other activity makes seemingly sane people rise at the crack of dawn on Saturday, drive for six hours, sit in the hot sun for three hours, then drive six more hours home in order to make it to church on Sunday morning?

At what other event will you see the president of the Junior League, dressed in her very finest, hurl a string of obscenities that would make a sailor blush?

"The folks up North and other places around the country play college football and they enjoy it," said former Auburn coach Pat Dye, a member of the College Football Hall of Fame. "And that's fine. But down here we don't play college football. We live it. And we live it every day."

Only college football brings out such behavior. For more than 100 years, the people of the South have planned weddings, births, and, yes, even funerals, around these very special fall Saturdays.

Clemson's Gary Cooper celebrates with fans during a 1987 game against Georgia Tech. Photo courtesy of the *Atlanta Journal-Constitution*/Frank Nemeier.

"Every spring I would get calls from people wanting to double-check our schedule for the fall so that they don't plan anything when we have a home game," said Sue Hall, the former secretary to Florida State coach Bobby Bowden. "One woman said she had to change the date of her wedding because none of her bridesmaids were going to show up. They were all going to be here."

In the South, even the birth of a child has to work around football season. Deborah Ford, the wife of Clemson coach Danny Ford, was expecting to give birth on a Saturday when the Tigers had a home football game. The head coach corrected the doctor and explained why the baby would be born on Friday. Labor was induced and the baby was born Friday night.

"I just figured it was part of being a coach's wife," she said.

To you unbelievers who may see all this as merely an excessive exercise in Southern pride, we issue the following challenge: visit Athens, Georgia; Tuscaloosa, Alabama; Knoxville, Tennessee; Gainesville, Florida; or any of the other sleepy college towns that are magically energized, enlarged, and transformed each fall. If you can get a ticket—and that's a big *if*—don't watch the action on the field. Study the faces of the people in the seats.

This is what you'll see: while the people in South Bend, Indiana; Ann Arbor, Michigan; and Columbus, Ohio, dearly love the game of college football; in the South, love just ain't good enough. In our part of the world, when the subject is college football, the operative word is *passion*.

This passion, which grips the South not just in the fall but all year long, is the central character in *Southern Fried Football*.

Now if you've read this far and still believe college football is just a game to the people of the South, then pull up a chair, brother. You're about to get an education.

When Alabama and Tennessee meet on the third Saturday in October...

When Florida and Florida State battle for supremacy in the Sunshine State...

When Georgia and Florida meet in Jacksonville for "The World's Largest Outdoor Cocktail Party"...

When Alabama and Auburn square off in the Iron Bowl, the mother of all rivalries that divides families across an entire state...

On these special Saturdays, it's not about whose state or whose school has the better football team. Hell, no. The stakes are much higher than that.

A Georgia fan put it best many years ago prior to a big game between Clemson and his beloved Bulldogs.

"It's simple," he said. "It's our way of life against theirs."

The 2008 season will mark the 129th year that college football, in some form, has been a part of the Southern landscape. So now is a pretty good time to reflect on how far the game has come from its humble beginnings and to examine the special relationship college football still has with the people of the South.

From the very first games, where fans arrived by horse and buggy and passed the hat to pay the teams' expenses, college football has evolved into a multibillion-dollar enterprise. Where once the small but curious crowds stood along the sidelines to watch, today Southern college football is played before crowds of 100,000 or more in pastoral stadiums while millions more watch via worldwide television.

The players, once adventurous college boys just looking for a way to work off some excess energy, are now carefully trained and aggressively recruited to play the game. Some of these young men become Southern icons before they are old enough to shave.

Coaches, who once took money from their own pockets to pay expenses for the team, now command multimillion-dollar salaries. It is no coincidence that the first $2 million coach in college football was Steve Spurrier of Florida. In January 2007 Alabama shocked the college football world by signing Nick Saban to an eight-year contract worth $32 million.

For several generations, football coaches in the South have been treated with the respect and deference of a head of state, but only if they win, of course.

If a Southern football coach makes a habit of losing, he will awake one Sunday morning to find a moving van parked in front of his home, as Tennessee's Bill Battle did in 1976. Southern college football fans are a lot of things. Subtle, they ain't.

Southern Fried Football is not a dry, dusty recitation of facts and trivia, but a sentimental journey filled with special people, places, and moments, all of which have been frozen in time.

People like:

College professors Charles Herty of Georgia and George Petrie of Auburn, who learned the game of football when they were classmates at Johns Hopkins. In 1892 Herty and Petrie decided to field teams at their respective schools and play a game. More than 2,000 fans showed up for the first game ever between Auburn and Georgia in Atlanta's Piedmont Park. In 2008 at

Professors George Petrie of Auburn (above) and Charles Herty of Georgia organized the first game between the two schools in 1892. Photo courtesy of Auburn SID.

Georgia Tech coach John Heisman (far right) with three unidentified players in 1919. Photo courtesy of the Atlanta Journal-Constitution.

Auburn, the schools will meet for the 112th time. Over 87,000 will attend in person, while millions more will watch on television.

John Heisman, the legendary coach for whom college football's most famous award is named. Heisman came to the South from Ohio in 1895 and built winning programs at Clemson, Auburn, and Georgia Tech.

His favorite saying was, "Better to have died as a small boy than to fumble this football."

He coached Georgia Tech's infamous 222–0 win over Cumberland College in 1916. At halftime, with his team up 126–0, he told his players: "Be careful of that team from Cumberland. There's no telling what they have up their sleeves."

Dan McGugin, the most successful coach in Vanderbilt history. In 1910 McGugin took his team to Yale. The Civil War, which had ended only 45 years earlier, was still fresh in the minds of all Southerners. In his pregame speech McGugin reminded his players that many of their grandfathers were buried in Northern cemeteries and that the grandfathers of the Yale players across the way had put them there. Vanderbilt went out and tied Yale 0–0 in what was considered a huge upset.

McGugin, however, forgot to mention one thing in his speech: his own grandfather had served under Union General William T. Sherman during his infamous and destructive March to the Sea across Georgia.

Places like:

The Grove, a pastoral, tree-lined area on the University of Mississippi campus where fans gather to tailgate prior to the games in Oxford, Mississippi.

Two hours before kickoff, the Ole Miss team walks single-file through a human corridor of cheering fans in the Grove. This Walk of Champions is an awe-inspiring moment.

"If you ain't ready to play after walking through the Grove," said former coach Billy Brewer, "you're probably dead."

Toomer's Corner in Auburn, Alabama, where students gather to celebrate a big football victory by filling the trees with toilet paper. Toomer's Drugs, the store for which the corner is named, serves the best homemade lemonade on the planet.

LSU's Tiger Stadium. There is nothing louder or more intimidating than a Saturday night game in Baton Rouge. On October 8, 1988, when LSU scored to beat Auburn in the closing seconds, the explosion of sound was so great that it registered on the LSU Geology Department's seismograph.

Vanderbilt coach Dan McGugin. Photo courtesy of Vanderbilt SID.

The Esso Club in Clemson, South Carolina. A former gas station, the Esso Club has turned into a Southern institution where fans from all walks of life gather to enjoy a cold one before watching their beloved Clemson Tigers.

Moments like:

Halloween night, 1959, when LSU's Billy Cannon ran his way to immortality by returning a punt 89 yards for a touchdown as the Tigers upset Ole Miss, 7–3. Almost 50 years later, Cannon's Halloween run remains one of the defining moments in college football history.

December 2, 1989, when Alabama played at Auburn's Jordan-Hare Stadium for the first time. Since 1893 all but a handful of Alabama-Auburn games had been played in Birmingham, considered to be a Crimson Tide stronghold. Legendary coach Bear Bryant and his successor, Ray Perkins, swore that Alabama would never stoop so low as to take its team to Auburn. But after years of bitter negotiations, the day finally arrived.

Prior to the game, over 20,000 Auburn fans lined Donahue Drive, the road between the school's athletic dormitory and the stadium, for the traditional Tiger Walk. As the players walked through the waves of cheers, grown men cried.

"After years of bondage, our people were finally delivered to the Promised Land," said David Housel, the former Auburn athletics director.

Auburn won the game, upsetting No. 2 Alabama, 30–20.

November 18, 1961, when the football rivalry between Georgia Tech and Alabama turned ugly. During a 10–0 win by Alabama in Birmingham, Georgia Tech's Chick Granning suffered a broken nose, a broken jaw, and five lost teeth after receiving an elbow to the face from Darwin Holt of the Crimson Tide. The incident touched off a war of words between the major newspapers in the two states. The following year when the two teams met in Atlanta, Tech fans threw so many things at coach Bear Bryant that he had to wear a helmet onto the field.

When a liquor bottle bounced at his feet, Bryant picked it up and said, "I thought Tech people drank a better brand of whiskey than this."

So how did we get here? Why, after all these years and after all the changes that have taken place in the South, does the game still pull so strongly on our heartstrings?

Sociologists say college football has thrived in the South because the game pushes all the hot buttons of its people:

Regional pride: The South was left behind in the economic expansion after World War II, but football was always a way for the agrarian South to prove its worth against the industrialized North. Southerners knew that many Northerners looked down on them as uneducated hicks. Football was one area where the South could be superior.

Vince Dooley, the head coach at Georgia from 1964 to 1988, remembers the emotional reaction from Southerners when his team won at Michigan in 1965. When the Georgia team returned to Athens, several thousand people greeted the Bulldogs at the local airport.

"I didn't just hear from Georgia people, but from people all over the South," said Dooley, who has a master's degree in history from Auburn. "To go up there and invade the North and come back as a winner was the greatest thing for a lot of people. It was as if we had had a chance to go to Gettysburg again."

On January 1, 1981, undefeated Georgia went to the Sugar Bowl in

Georgia, coached by Vince Dooley, posted a huge upset over Michigan in 1965. Photo courtesy of the *Atlanta Journal-Constitution*.

New Orleans and won its first national championship by beating the ultimate symbol of supposed Northern superiority—the University of Notre Dame. The celebration began in the Super Dome and carried on into the streets of New Orleans. It was one of the most emotional occurrences people in the region had ever seen.

For Georgia, winning the national championship was sweet, but beating Notre Dame for the honor made the experience even sweeter.

"The celebration of that day was about some feelings that dated all the way back to 1865," said Jim Minter, a former editor of the *Atlanta Constitution*.

Race: Perhaps the biggest indicator of how strongly Southerners feel about college football is that eventually their love for the sport has proven stronger than the long-term racial prejudices held by some.

Most of the major Southern schools did not recruit African American students to play football until the late 1960s and early '70s. Some Southern schools would not play teams that had African American players. While the first African Americans played in the South as early as the mid-1960s, the defining moment for the integration of Southern college football came on September 12, 1970, in Birmingham, Alabama.

Alabama coach Bear Bryant huddles with players. Photo courtesy of Alabama SID.

Alabama coach Paul "Bear" Bryant, who had won three national championships in the '60s with all-white teams, saw his Crimson Tide embarrassed by the University of Southern California, 42–21, at Legion Field. The Trojans were led by African American fullback Sam "Bam" Cunningham, who ripped through Alabama's defense and scored two touchdowns in the victory.

That day it became clear to Bryant that signing African American players at the University of Alabama was no longer an issue of conscience; it was a matter of winning.

Alabama went on to fully integrate its team and became college football's dominant program in the 1970s with a record of 103–16–1, eight SEC titles, and three national titles.

Once Bryant had opened the door, the other Southern schools quickly began bringing African American athletes to their campuses, paving the way for greater racial understanding.

In 1962 one of the flashpoints of racial tensions in the United States occurred on the campus at Ole Miss, where James Meredith became the first African American man to enroll. Thirteen years later Ben Williams, an African American defensive tackle on the Ole Miss football team, was voted the school's Colonel Rebel, the highest honor that can be bestowed on male students attending the school.

Politics: More than one Southern politician has found that the best way to anger his or her constituents is to be less than supportive of college football. To this end, some have gone to extremes.

In 1934 Louisiana governor Huey Long heard that sales for an LSU football game in Baton Rouge were lagging because the circus was coming to town the same night. In an effort to boost sales for the game, Long contacted Barnum and Bailey officials and informed them of an obscure law that stated animals couldn't be washed on Saturdays in Baton Rouge. The show was canceled, and ticket sales for the LSU game soared.

Long also threatened a railroad company with financial ruin if it didn't give LSU students discounted tickets so they could attend road games.

Sometimes the line between college football and politics becomes a bit fuzzy. As icons of Southern culture, college football players and coaches already enjoy the respect and adoration of many Southerners and thus can easily parlay their success into political careers.

In 1955 Fob James of Auburn led the SEC in rushing. He later served two terms as Alabama's governor (1979–83 and 1995–99).

When Vince Dooley, who was James's roommate at Auburn, retired as head football coach at Georgia in 1988, he contemplated running for governor. In any other region of the country such an idea would have been laughable. Given the status accorded college football coaches in the South, the transition to governor seemed entirely logical.

Today, when there is more competition for the entertainment dollar than in any other time in our history, the South embraces and supports college football.

For the 27th straight year, the SEC led all major conferences in total attendance for college football as the league drew 6,687,342 fans to its 89 games. SEC schools averaged 75,139 fans per game, which was also number one in the nation. SEC stadiums were filled to 97.69 percent of capacity for the 2007 season. Six of the nation's top 10 schools in total attendance were from the SEC: Tennessee (4), Auburn (5), Georgia (6), LSU (7), Alabama (8), and Florida (9). Tennessee averaged 103,918 fans per game.

College football is still gaining popularity more than 100 years after it began in the South, which comes as no surprise to Bill

Bill Curry (left) with former Georgia Tech coach Bobby Dodd in 1983. Photo courtesy of the *Atlanta Journal-Constitution/* Charles Pugh.

Curry. Curry played at Georgia Tech in the 1960s and was also the head coach at Georgia Tech, Alabama, and Kentucky. Curry's father grew up in the shadow of Georgia's Sanford Stadium. As a young boy he would spend Saturdays with his grandmother in Athens, Georgia, and watch fans heading to and from the game.

"I really didn't understand what was going on in that stadium, but I knew that when those people came back, they were either very happy or very sad," said Curry. "I figured it must be pretty important."

That's how Curry began his love affair with a game that is as much a part of Southern living as pecan pie and Wednesday night prayer meetings. And like that old-time religion, once college football gets into a Southerner's blood, he cannot be cured. He's hooked forever.

"In the South, college football isn't just a game," Curry said. "It's who we are."

For Southerners, traveling to that first college football game is the initial step on a journey that will last a lifetime. This book is a celebration of that journey.

CHAPTER 1

A CHRONOLOGY OF SOUTHERN FRIED FOOTBALL

The Major Events That Shaped the Landscape of Southern College Football

1880: The first college football game in the South was played in Lexington, Kentucky, between Centre College and Kentucky University (now Transylvania University).

1881: The University of Kentucky, then known as Kentucky State College, beat Kentucky University 7¼–1 in the school's first football game. After the three-game season, football did not return to Kentucky until 1891.

1888: On October 18 the University of North Carolina and Wake Forest played a game in Raleigh, North Carolina, the first-ever college football game in the state. Wake Forest won, 6–4.

On November 27 Trinity College (which later became Duke) played its first game, beating North Carolina 16–0.

Virginia also played its first football game that year, beating Pantops Academy 20–0.

1890: In January, after one of its players suffered a broken collarbone, North Carolina's faculty voted to discontinue football at the school. The ban lasted for only one season.

1891: On November 21 Tennessee played its first football game, beating Sewanee 24–0.

1892: On February 20 Georgia and Auburn played before 2,000 fans at Atlanta's Piedmont Park, starting the first college football rivalry in the Deep South. The game was organized by professors Charles Herty of Georgia and George Petrie of Auburn, who had learned about football while they were classmates at Johns Hopkins University. Auburn won 10–0.

Georgia Tech played its first game on November 5 against Mercer in Macon, Georgia, and lost 12–6.

On November 11 Alabama played its first football game at a baseball park in Birmingham, beating a group of players from Birmingham High School 56–0.

On Thanksgiving Day a team of Mississippi A&M (now Mississippi State) faculty members challenged a group of students to a game of football, the first on that campus. The faculty won 4–0.

1893: LSU played its first football game, a 34–0 loss to Tulane.

On February 22 Alabama and Auburn played the first game in their storied rivalry. Auburn won the game 32–22 on George Washington's birthday. Auburn, eager to win the first game against Alabama, hired F.M. Balliet to coach the Tigers for that one afternoon.

On November 11 the University of Mississippi (Ole Miss) played its first football game, a 56–0 win over Southwest Baptist University of Jackson, Tennessee.

North Carolina A&M (now North Carolina State) played its first game against Tennessee in Raleigh, winning 12–6.

1894: On December 22 representatives from seven Southern schools met in Atlanta to form the first college football conference, the Southeastern Intercollegiate Athletic Association (SIAA). The league eventually grew to include as many as 30 schools.

Auburn beat Georgia Tech 94–0 but then scored only 12 points in its other three games to finish 1–3.

1895: John Heisman was hired as Auburn's football coach and led the school to a 2–1 record, including a 48–0 win over Alabama.

Glenn "Pop" Warner began his coaching career at Georgia. He stayed only two seasons but went on to record 319 career victories as the coach of various college football teams.

1896: On October 28 Clemson played its first football game, beating Furman 14–6 in Greenville, South Carolina.

At Mississippi A&M (now Mississippi State), members of the student body raised $300 to hire J.B. Hildebrand, the school's first full-time coach. However, a yellow fever epidemic and the outbreak of the Spanish-American War soon halted the school's attempts to create a winning football program.

1897: On October 30 Georgia player Richard Vonalbade Gammon died from injuries he sustained in a game against Virginia. The Georgia state legislature passed a bill making it illegal to play football at state institutions, but Gammon's mother, Rosalind, who knew her son's love of football, wrote a letter to Governor W.Y. Atkinson begging him not to sign the bill. The bill was not signed, and football continued in the state.

1898: Because of the Spanish-American War, Tennessee did not field a team in this year.

1899: A team representing the University of the South, which is located in Sewanee, Tennessee, pulled off one of the greatest feats in the history of college football. Beginning on November 9, 1899, Sewanee won five games in six days, all against national powers (Texas, Texas A&M, Tulane, LSU, and Mississippi), all on the road, and by a combined score of 91–0. Sewanee went on to finish 12–0 and was declared the Southern football champion.

On December 8 John Heisman left Auburn to become the head coach at Clemson.

1900: Kentucky defeated Louisville YMCA 12–6 without running a single offensive play. The Wildcats kicked on first down on every possession and scored on a pair of YMCA fumbles in the end zone.

Georgia's Richard Vonalbade Gammon died from football injuries in 1897. Photo courtesy of the *Atlanta Journal-Constitution.*

1901: Four years after the school's first attempt, Mississippi State made a second attempt to field a football team. On October 28 the school won the first game in its history, a 17–0 victory over Mississippi.

On October 5, in a game that was shortened to 30 minutes, Clemson beat Guilford 122–0. Clemson was coached by John Heisman, whose 1916 team at Georgia Tech beat Cumberland 222–0.

1903: On November 26 John Heisman was hired as Georgia Tech's first full-time head coach. Heisman remained at Georgia Tech until 1919, posting a record of 102–29–7. He might have stayed longer, but in a divorce settlement he agreed to live in a different city from his ex-wife. She chose Atlanta, and Heisman returned to Pennsylvania, his alma mater.

Coach John Heisman, who built programs at Clemson, Auburn, and Georgia Tech. Photo courtesy of the *Atlanta Journal-Constitution.*

Vanderbilt hired Dan McGugin as its head coach. He went on to build one of the South's greatest college football dynasties. In 30 years at Vanderbilt, McGugin posted a record of 197–55–19.

1907: From November 4 to 9, Clemson played—and lost—three games in a week's time. The Tigers lost to Auburn (12–0) on November 4 (12–0), to Georgia (8–0) in Augusta on November 7, and to Davidson (10–6) on November 9.

On Christmas Day in Havana, Cuba, LSU beat the University of Havana 56–0 in front of 10,000 fans.

Alabama and Auburn played to a 6–6 tie in Birmingham. Because of various disagreements between the two schools, they did not meet again until 1948.

Some Southern college teams, frustrated with Vanderbilt's dominance under coach Dan McGugin, began bringing in paid professionals, or "ringers," to play for their teams.

Auburn's Mike Donahue took one year off from coaching the football team to concentrate on being the school's athletics director.

1908: Clemson's hopes for a winning season were dashed when several football players were expelled along with 300 other students for stealing a Civil War cannon from the Pendleton town square and bringing it back to Clemson. The Tigers went 1–6 that season.

1909: The University of Kentucky adopted "Wildcats" as its official team name.

1912: On January 1, in the first and only game the team has played outside the United States, Mississippi A&M (Mississippi State) defeated Club Atlético de Cuba 12–0 in Havana.

1913: Georgia Tech students gathered to build the original west stands at Grant Field, which seated about 5,000 people. Today it is known as Bobby Dodd Stadium, and it remains the oldest on-campus Division I-A stadium in the country.

With a record of 8–0, Auburn won its first SIAA championship.

1915: Vanderbilt's "point-a-minute" team averaged 51 points per game, scoring 514 points in 510 minutes. The Commodores gave up only 38 points, 35 of those in a 35–10 loss to Virginia, Vanderbilt's only defeat of the season.

1916: On October 7 Georgia Tech defeated Cumberland 222–0 in the most lopsided game ever played in the history of college football. At halftime Georgia Tech led 126–0 and coach John Heisman told his players, "but you just can't tell what those Cumberland players have up their sleeves."

Kentucky dedicated its playing field as Stoll Field.

1917: Georgia Tech went 9–0 and won the first of its four national championships. The Yellow Jackets outscored their opponents 491–17 but declined a trip to the Rose Bowl so that many of their players could enlist and fight in World War I.

1918: Vanderbilt did not field a team because of World War I.

North Carolina did not field a team in 1917 or 1918 because of the war.

1920: William Alexander succeeded John Heisman as head coach at Georgia Tech. In 25 years at Tech, Alexander posted a record of 134-95-15. He was the first coach to take teams to the Sugar, Cotton, Orange, and Rose bowls.

Representatives from the larger schools in the SIAA met in Gainesville, Florida, and formed the Southern Conference.

Mississippi State students renamed the school's football field Scott Field in honor of track star and Olympian Don Scott, a football letterman for the Bulldogs in 1915 and 1916.

1921: On September 24 Tennessee played its first game at Shields-Watkins Field, which would later become Neyland Stadium. The capacity at the field was 3,200. Tennessee beat Emory & Henry 27–0.

1922: A record crowd of 24,300 turned out for a game between Auburn and Georgia Tech in Atlanta. The gate of $45,000 was the largest ever for a college football game in the South.

After winning 99 games in 18 seasons, Mike Donahue left Auburn to become the head coach at LSU, where he was only 23–19–3 in five seasons.

1926: In the biggest win of Curley Byrd's career as head coach, Maryland upset heavily favored Yale 15–0 in New Haven, Connecticut.

After Tennessee had lost 17 of its first 21 games against Vanderbilt, school officials hired then Captain Robert R. Neyland as the school's head football coach. Neyland's teams went on to beat Vanderbilt in 16 of the next 19 games.

1927: After a riot broke out at the end of the 1926 Ole Miss–Mississippi State football game, Ole Miss honor society Sigma Iota recommended that the two schools ease tensions by playing for a trophy, a golden football that later became known as the Golden Egg.

On November 12 North Carolina opened Kenan Stadium with a 27–0 win over Davidson.

1929: On January 1 Georgia Tech beat California 8–7 in the Rose Bowl to go undefeated and win its second national title. The most memorable moment of the game was when California's Roy Riegels picked up a fumble and ran toward his own goal line. He was eventually tackled by his own teammates.

On October 12 Georgia defeated mighty Yale 15–0 in the inaugural game at Sanford Stadium. The price of a ticket was $3.

1930: On March 6 Wallace Wade agreed to leave Alabama and become head coach at Duke. Wade remained at Alabama for the 1930 season, leading the Crimson Tide to a 10–0 record, a win in the Rose Bowl, and the national championship.

On July 15 Frank Thomas, a former Notre Dame player and the running backs coach at Georgia, was named the new head coach at Alabama.

1932: On October 15, in one of the greatest punting duels ever, Tennessee defeated Alabama 7–3 in Birmingham. Alabama's Johnny Cain averaged 48 yards on 19 kicks, and Tennessee's Beattie Feathers averaged 43 yards on 21 kicks.

Mississippi A&M was officially renamed Mississippi State.

1933: At a meeting on February 13, 13 charter members formed the Southeastern Conference. Alabama won the conference's first championship with a 5–0–1 record.

1934: Alabama went 10–0 and beat Stanford 29–13 in the Rose Bowl to share the national championship with Minnesota. Two ends on that Crimson Tide team—Don Hutson and Paul "Bear" Bryant—were destined for the Hall of Fame.

Suffering from poor health, coach Dan McGugin retired after 30 seasons as head coach at Vanderbilt. Over the course of those years, he won 197 games and had only one losing season.

1935: Tackle Frank "Bruiser" Kinard of Ole Miss defined the term *Iron Man* when he played 708 out of 720 possible minutes during the 1935 season.

1936: Dan McGugin, who presided over the most successful period in Vanderbilt football history, died at age 56.

Ole Miss adopted "Rebels" as the official name of the school's athletic teams.

1937: In the first bowl game played outside the continental United States, Auburn and Villanova played to a 7–7 tie in the Bacardi Bowl in Havana, Cuba. The game was the climax to Cuba's National Sports Festival and was almost canceled when dictator Fulgencio Batista, who had just assumed power, did not find his picture in the game program. A quick trip to the printer solved the problem, and the game went on.

1938: Duke had posted a 9–0 regular season without giving up a point. The Blue Devils were

Paul "Bear" Bryant was an end on Alabama's 1934 Rose Bowl team. Photo courtesy of the *Atlanta Journal-Constitution.*

40 seconds from perfection when they gave up a touchdown to Southern California in the waning moments of the Rose Bowl and lost 7–3. That team, the school's most famous, became known as the "Iron Dukes."

1939: Georgia named Wally Butts, "the Little Round Man" from Milledgeville, Georgia, its head coach. In 22 seasons Butts won 140 games and four SEC titles.

Tennessee posted a 10–0 regular season, during which it did not give up a single point. Without starting players Bob Suffridge and George Cafego, the Volunteers lost to Southern California 14–0 in the Rose Bowl.

On November 30 Auburn played its first game in the school's on-campus stadium against Florida. Seating capacity for what would become Jordan-Hare Stadium was 7,500.

1940: After being unable to win a conference game in eight seasons, Sewanee withdrew from the SEC.

On January 1, in Clemson's first bowl appearance, the Tigers beat Boston College 6–3 in the Cotton Bowl.

On January 10 Jess Neely resigned as Clemson's coach and accepted the head-coaching position at Rice. The next day, Frank Howard was named Clemson's head football coach, a position he held for 30 years.

1941: On January 1 Mississippi State won its first bowl game, a 14–7 win over Georgetown in the Orange Bowl. That fall, Mississippi State won its first and only SEC title.

On November 15 Grambling's Eddie Robinson, who would later become the winningest coach in the history of NCAA football, won his first game, a 37–6 victory over Tillotson College. Robinson went on to win 408 games in 57 seasons at Grambling.

Tennessee coach Robert Neyland was recalled to active duty when World War II began. John Barnhill took over the program until Neyland returned for the 1946 season.

1942: Because of the bombing of Pearl Harbor on December 7, 1941, large crowds were banned from gathering on the West Coast. As a result, the January 1 Rose Bowl was moved from Pasadena, California, to Durham, North Carolina, where Duke hosted Oregon State. Oregon State won the game 20–16 before 56,000 fans.

Georgia won its first SEC championship, led by the dream backfield of Frank Sinkwich and Charley Trippi.

On September 19 Clemson's Memorial Stadium opened with a seating capacity of 20,000.

In 1941 Tennessee coach Robert Neyland returned to military duty, where he would serve for five years. Photo courtesy of the *Atlanta Journal-Constitution*.

1943: At the height of World War II, a number of schools around the South shut down their football programs.

1944: With many players still fighting in the war, some schools fielded teams with freshmen and "4-Fs," players who were not physically able to serve in battle. Alabama fielded such a team, nicknamed the "War Babies" by coach Frank Thomas. That team, led by future Hall of Fame quarterback Harry Gilmer, went 5–2–2 and lost to Duke 29–26 in the Sugar Bowl.

1945: After 14 seasons as an assistant to head coach William Alexander, Bobby Dodd accepted the head-coaching position at Georgia Tech. Only the third head coach in Georgia Tech history, Dodd remained for 22 seasons and posted a record of 165–64–8.

Maryland hired Paul "Bear" Bryant as head coach. It was Bryant's first job as a head coach, and he put together a team of players from his Navy preflight squads and went 6–2–1.

1946: Georgia went 11–0 and won its second SEC title under Wally Butts.

After one year at Maryland, Bear Bryant left for Kentucky, where he coached for eight seasons.

After 16 years and 115 victories, poor health forced Frank Thomas to resign as Alabama's head coach. He was replaced by Harold "Red" Drew.

John Vaught (left) takes over for Red Drew at Ole Miss in 1947. Photo courtesy of the Atlanta Journal-Constitution.

1947: On January 1 Georgia played North Carolina in the Sugar Bowl. The game featured a matchup between two of the era's best players: Georgia's Charley Trippi and North Carolina's Charlie "Choo Choo" Justice. Trippi led the Bulldogs to a 20–10 win over North Carolina and Justice in New Orleans.

Florida State, which had been a women's college until the 1940s, fielded its first football team. The Seminoles went 0–5 that season.

On January 14 Ole Miss hired John Vaught as its head coach. Vaught's team won an SEC championship in his very first season. Over the next 24 years Vaught led the Rebels to 180 wins, six SEC titles, and three national championships.

On December 6 Kentucky played in the first and only Great Lakes Bowl, defeating Villanova 24–14 before 14,908 spectators at Cleveland Municipal Stadium.

Maryland hired Jim Tatum as its head coach.

George Petrie, the professor who brought football to Auburn in 1892, died.

1948: On December 4 Alabama and Auburn played each other for the first time since 1907. Alabama won the game 55–0 in Birmingham. Bear Bryant, Kentucky's head coach and the future head coach at Alabama, attended the game.

1949: Broadcaster Lindsey Nelson, with the support of Tennessee coach Robert Neyland, formed the Volunteer Radio Network.

1950: On September 30 Maryland dedicated Byrd Stadium with a 35–21 win over its archrival, Navy.

In a classic game played in the cold and snow, Tennessee defeated Kentucky's eventual SEC champion Kentucky 7–0 in Knoxville. It was the only loss all season for coach Bear Bryant's team.

1951: After an awful three-year record of 3–22–4 under coach Earl Brown, Auburn fired him and hired Auburn alumnus Ralph "Shug" Jordan as its head football coach. Jordan stayed for 25 years and became the school's all-time winningest coach.

Alabama met Tennessee in Birmingham to play the first televised game in the Deep South.

On January 1 Kentucky capped off its 1950 SEC championship season by beating No. 1 Oklahoma 13–7 in the Sugar Bowl, snapping the Sooners' 31-game winning streak. Also on January 1, No. 4 Tennessee upset No. 3 Texas 20–14 in the Cotton Bowl, setting the stage for the Volunteers' 10–0 regular season and national championship win that fall.

An internal study at Virginia recommended that the school should drop football and discontinue all athletics scholarships. This recommendation came in the middle of an 8–1 football season, and no action was taken.

The Southern Conference banned teams from playing in bowl games and limited squads to just 40 players for conference games.

1952: On January 1 Maryland completed its first undefeated season with a 28–13 upset of No. 1 Tennessee in the Sugar Bowl. That fall, however, Ole Miss upset No. 3 Maryland, a 20-point favorite, 21–14 in Oxford to break the Terps' 22-game winning streak.

Georgia Tech went 12–0 to win its third national title and its first under coach Bobby Dodd.

General Robert Neyland, Tennessee's legendary coach, was forced to retire due to poor health and left with a career record of 173–31–12. Neyland stepped down after the last regular-season game with Vanderbilt and was unable to coach in the Cotton Bowl. Harvey Robinson was named Tennessee's head coach.

Clemson and Maryland were declared ineligible for the 1952 Southern Conference championship after both schools went against the wishes of the conference and accepted bowl bids in 1951.

Brothers Dick and Ed Modzelewski helped Maryland upset Tennessee in the 1952 Sugar Bowl. Photo courtesy of the *Atlanta Journal-Constitution.*

Mississippi State quarterback Jackie Parker set an SEC scoring record for a single season with 120 points.

1953: Bear Bryant left for Texas A&M after growing tired of dueling with Adolph Rupp, Kentucky's dictatorial basketball coach. Bryant realized his status in Kentucky when, during an athletics award ceremony, alumni gave him a cigarette lighter and Rupp a new Cadillac. Bryant was replaced by Blanton Collier.

Upset by limitations on their football programs, seven of the larger schools in the Southern Conference met in Greensboro, North Carolina, to form the Atlantic Coast Conference.

On December 1 Maryland (10–0) finished No. 1 in the final Associated Press poll and was declared the national champion. A month later the Terps lost to Oklahoma in the Orange Bowl.

1954: On January 1, at the Cotton Bowl, Alabama's Tommy Lewis made a play that lives on in college football infamy. Rice led 7–6 in the second quarter when Owls running back Dickie Moegle broke free and ran up the Alabama sideline for an apparent touchdown. But before he could score on the run, Alabama's Lewis, who was on the sideline, jumped into the field of play and tackled Moegle. The officials awarded Moegle a 95-yard touchdown run, and Rice won the game 28–6. Lewis became such a national celebrity that Ed Sullivan called him from New York and asked him to appear on his show.

On February 1 Darrell Royal, who would later go on to fame as the head coach at Texas, was named head coach at Mississippi State. At 30, he was the youngest head coach in the SEC. He spent two years in Starkville and left with a record of 12–8.

1955: After a disagreement with Maryland officials concerning the funding of the football program, Jim Tatum left College Park to become the head coach at North Carolina, his alma mater.

Bowden Wyatt, a former star player at Tennessee, became the Vols' head coach.

On October 15 Auburn beat Georgia Tech 14–12 in Atlanta, its first win over the Yellow Jackets in 15 seasons.

1956: Tennessee went 10–0 before losing 13–7 to Baylor in the Sugar Bowl. Vols halfback Johnny Majors finished second to Notre Dame's Paul Hornung for the Heisman Trophy.

On January 1 Ole Miss rallied from a 13–0 deficit to beat TCU 14–13 in the Cotton Bowl. It was the Rebels' first major bowl win.

On November 10 in Atlanta, No. 3 Tennessee beat No. 2 Georgia Tech 6–0 in what many consider one of the classic games in Southern football history.

Tennessee coach Bowden Wyatt celebrates with his players after the Vols beat Georgia Tech in 1956. Photo courtesy of the Atlanta Journal-Constitution.

1957: Auburn won the AP national championship with a 10–0 record and a defense that posted six shutouts and allowed only 28 total points. The Tigers closed out that successful season with a 40–0 win over Alabama on November 30. As a result of this loss, a delegation of Alabama movers and shakers traveled to Texas A&M. Three days later, on December 3, Paul "Bear" Bryant was officially named the new head football coach of the Crimson Tide. When asked why he left Texas A&M when he had seven years left on his contract, Bryant simply said: "Mama called."

On October 19 Queen Elizabeth and Prince Phillip attended the Maryland–North Carolina football game at College Park.

On November 23, North Carolina State's Dick Christy had the best individual game in ACC history. In a game against South Carolina, Christy scored all of North Carolina State's points with four touchdowns, two extra points, and a 46-yard field goal with no time remaining. The 29–26 win over South Carolina gave North Carolina State its first ACC championship.

1958: LSU, led by running back Billy Cannon and a defensive unit known as the "Chinese Bandits," posted the school's first undefeated season in 50 years and won the national championship.

Only a 7–7 tie with Georgia Tech kept Auburn (9–0–1) from recording its second straight undefeated season.

LSU coach Paul Dietzel (right) accepts the 1958 national championship trophy. Photo courtesy of the *Atlanta Journal-Constitution.*

1959: LSU's Billy Cannon wrapped up the Heisman Trophy on a gloomy Halloween night in Baton Rouge. Cannon electrified the crowd with an 89-yard punt return to beat Ole Miss 7–3. In the final Associated Press poll of 1959, four SEC teams—Ole Miss (2), LSU (3), Georgia (5), and Alabama (10)—were ranked in the Top 10.

The 1959 Ole Miss team went on to avenge its only loss to LSU by beating the Tigers 21–0 in the Sugar Bowl. That Ole Miss team was later named the SEC Team of the Decade.

On September 26 Auburn lost to Tennessee 3–0, snapping the Tigers' string of 24 straight games without a loss.

North Carolina coach Jim Tatum died suddenly of Rocky Mountain Spotted Fever.

1960: Led by quarterback Jake Gibbs, Ole Miss went 10–0–1 and was declared the national champion by the Football Writers Association of America.

1961: In his fourth year at Alabama, Bear Bryant won his first of six national championships and his first of 13 SEC titles for the Crimson Tide.

On November 22 Georgia Tech's Chick Granning lost five teeth and suffered a broken jaw from an elbow to the face by Alabama's Darwin Holt. The incident touched off a war of words between the newspapers in Atlanta and Birmingham.

1962: On March 28 General Robert R. Neyland, the most successful coach in Tennessee history, died in Knoxville.

1963: *The Saturday Evening Post* published an article claiming that Alabama coach Bear Bryant and former Georgia coach Wally Butts conspired to fix the 1962 Georgia-Alabama game, which Alabama won 35–0. Both coaches later sued the magazine and won substantial judgments.

Georgia Tech's Billy Lothridge finished second to Navy's Roger Staubach in the Heisman Trophy voting.

On October 12, Florida upset No. 3 Alabama 10–6 in Tuscaloosa. It was one of the biggest wins in the Ray Graves era at Florida. Alabama would not lose another game at home until 1982.

On November 22 North Carolina State beat Wake Forest to earn a share of the ACC title. The game was overshadowed by the assassination of President John F. Kennedy in Dallas.

On November 30 Georgia Tech played its final game as a member of the SEC, a 14–3 win over Georgia.

On December 4 Vince Dooley, a 31-year-old assistant at Auburn, was named the head coach at Georgia.

Doug Dickey, 31, a top assistant at Arkansas, was hired as the head coach at Tennessee.

1964: On June 1 Georgia Tech officially withdrew from the SEC and became an Independent.

On October 17 Arkansas upset Texas 14–13 thanks to Ken Hatfield's 81-yard punt return for a touchdown. The Razorbacks won a share of the national championship, and Hatfield went on to become head coach at Arkansas and Clemson.

On November 14 Alabama beat Georgia Tech 24–7 in the last game the two old rivals would play until 1979.

On November 21 the University of Florida played at Florida State for the first time in college football history. Florida State won the game 16–7. After earning six straight wins over the Seminoles, Florida wore the words "Go for Seven" across the fronts of their jerseys.

1965: On September 18, using the now legendary "flea-flicker" play from Kirby Moore to Pat Hodgson to Bob Taylor, Georgia upset defending national champion Alabama 18–17 in Athens. Alabama still won its second straight national title.

Alabama quarterback Joe Namath signed the then-largest pro contract ever ($400,000) to play with the New York Jets.

Frank Broyles led Arkansas to a national championship in 1964. Photo courtesy of the *Atlanta Journal-Constitution.*

Florida quarterback Steve Spurrier. Photo courtesy of AP/Wide World Images.

On October 18, two days after a 7–7 tie with Alabama, three Tennessee assistant coaches—Bill Majors, Bob Jones, and Charles Rash—were killed in an automobile-train accident.

Kentucky's Nat Northington became the first African American football player to sign with an SEC school. In 1967 he would become the first African American to play in an SEC game.

On November 13 North Carolina State played its last game in Riddick Stadium, beating Florida State 3–0.

1966: On January 1 LSU upset Arkansas 14–7 in the Cotton Bowl, snapping the Razorbacks' 22-game winning streak.

Florida quarterback Steve Spurrier won the Heisman Trophy. Spurrier was the first winner from a Southern school since LSU's Billy Cannon won the trophy in 1959.

Georgia won its first SEC championship since 1959 and its first for third-year coach Vince Dooley.

On June 1 Tulane withdrew from the SEC.

1967: On January 1, after a 9–1 regular season, Bobby Dodd ended his legendary coaching career at Georgia Tech with a 27–12 loss to Florida in the Orange Bowl. The Florida team was led by quarterback Steve Spurrier.

On October 7, led by quarterback Jim Donnan and the "White Shoes" defense, North Carolina State went on the road and upset No. 2 Houston 16–6.

1968: Tennessee became the first team in the South to install artificial turf in its football stadium. On September 14 Georgia and Tennessee played to a 17–17 tie in the first game on the new surface. Georgia went on to win the SEC championship.

Lester McClain and Albert Davis became the first African Americans to play for Tennessee.

1969: On October 5 Alabama defeated Mississippi 33–32 at Birmingham's Legion Field in one of the great quarterback duels in Southern college football history. Archie Manning of Ole Miss completed 33 of 52 passes for 436 yards and had 540 yards of total offense. Alabama's Scott Hunter completed 22 of 29 passes for 300 yards.

On December 6, with President Richard Nixon looking on, No. 1 Texas beat No. 2 Arkansas 15–14 in Fayetteville, Arkansas. After the game Nixon went to the Texas locker room and proclaimed the Longhorns the national champions.

On December 10, Frank Howard resigned as Clemson's head football coach after 30 seasons.

Florida A&M coach Jake Gaither won the final game of his career when the Rattlers defeated Grambling 23–19 in the Orange Blossom Classic. At the time, Gaither (203–36–4) had the best winning percentage (84 percent) in all of college football.

1970: On January 6 Archie Manning of Ole Miss received the Walter Camp Award as the nation's best college football player.

In June Brian Piccolo, the 1964 ACC Player of the Year at Wake Forest and running back with the Chicago Bears, died of cancer.

On September 12, in Alabama's season opener against Southern California in Birmingham, the Trojans' Sam Cunningham ran for 135 yards and two touchdowns. That game convinced Alabama's Bear Bryant that the time had come to begin recruiting African American players.

Eddie McAshan, the first African American quarterback at Georgia Tech. Photo courtesy of the *Atlanta Journal-Constitution.*

After retiring in 1970, John Vaught returned as the coach at Ole Miss midway through the 1973 season. Photo courtesy of the Atlanta Journal-Constitution.

Quarterback Eddie McAshan became the first African American to play football at Georgia Tech. A year later, Georgia signed its first African American player, running back Horace King from Athens.

Doug Dickey suddenly left Tennessee to become head coach at Florida, his alma mater. Dickey was replaced by Bill Battle, a 28-year-old assistant coach and a former player at Alabama.

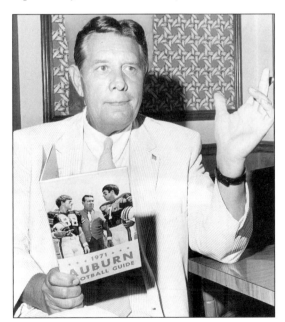

With Terry Beasley (No. 88) and Pat Sullivan (No. 7), Auburn coach Shug Jordan went 9–2 in 1971. Photo courtesy of the Atlanta Journal-Constitution.

1971: On January 13 John Vaught retired after 24 seasons as the head coach at Ole Miss.

Alabama's Bear Bryant and his coaching staff spent the summer with Darrell Royal of Texas, learning the wishbone offense. By the end of the 1970s, Alabama had won eight SEC titles and three national titles and had posted a 103–16–1 record.

On November 13, Auburn quarterback Pat Sullivan wrapped up the Heisman Trophy with a memorable performance in a 35–20 win over Georgia in Athens.

On November 24, 34-year-old Lou Holtz was named head coach at North Carolina State.

South Carolina dropped out of the ACC and became an Independent.

On December 11 Ben Williams and James Reed became the first African American players to sign with Ole Miss.

On December 31, in a battle between coaching brothers, Vince Dooley of Georgia beat Bill Dooley of North Carolina 7–3 in the Gator Bowl.

1972: On December 2, in the final minutes of the Auburn-Alabama game, Auburn's Bill Newton blocked two Alabama punts, and both were picked up and returned for touchdowns by David Langer. Auburn won 17–16, and the phrase "Punt, Bama, Punt!" was forever etched in SEC lore.

Tennessee's Condredge Holloway became the first African American quarterback in SEC history.

Virginia Tech's Don Strock led the nation in passing with 3,170 yards.

1973: On September 23, after a 17–13 loss to Memphis State left Ole Miss with a 1–2 record, coach Billy Kinard and athletics director Bruiser Kinard were fired. The next day, John Vaught came out of retirement to coach the rest of the 1973 season. Ole Miss won five of its final eight games. On December 21 Vaught announced his second retirement as coach.

1974: On January 1 No. 3 Notre Dame gambled and threw out of its own end zone, preserving a 24–23 upset of No. 1 Alabama in the Sugar Bowl. Alabama (11–1) was still declared 1973 national champion by United Press International.

On September 14 Alabama coach Bear Bryant returned to Maryland for the first time since 1945, when he was the Terps' head coach. His Crimson Tide won the game 21–16 before 54,412 fans, the largest crowd ever to see a game at Byrd Stadium in College Park.

On September 28 Georgia Tech played at Clemson for the first time. All previous games between the two schools had been at Grant Field in Atlanta.

1975: On January 1 Alabama was 11–0 for the second straight year when it met Notre Dame, this time in the Orange Bowl. Notre Dame's players, determined to send coach Ara Parseghian out a winner in his last game, beat the Crimson Tide 13–11.

At a hastily called press conference on April 9, Shug Jordan announced that the 1975 season would be his last as Auburn's head coach. Jordan retired after 25 seasons with 176 wins. Assistant Doug Barfield took over as head coach.

1976: Led by quarterback Ray Goff, Georgia won its third SEC title for coach Vince Dooley. The Bulldogs then lost to undefeated, top-ranked Pittsburgh and running back Tony Dorsett in the Sugar Bowl.

Bobby Bowden was hired as head coach at Florida State.

Tennessee coach Bill Battle resigned under pressure and was replaced by Johnny Majors, the former Volunteers star, who had just coached Pittsburgh to the national title.

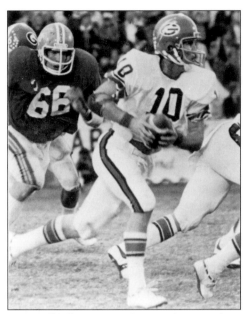

Ray Goff led Georgia to the SEC championship in 1976. Photo courtesy of the *Atlanta Journal-Constitution.*

Georgia Tech's Eddie Lee Ivery set an NCAA record with 356 yards rushing against Air Force in 1978. Photo courtesy of the *Atlanta Journal-Constitution.*

On November 6 in Atlanta, Georgia Tech upset No. 11 Notre Dame 23–14 without attempting a single pass.

1977: On January 1 the SEC began its agreement to send its champion to the Sugar Bowl.

On September 17 Clemson won at Georgia 7–6 in the Tigers' first victory in Athens since 1914.

On October 22 Prince Charles of Wales traveled to Athens, Georgia, to see his first American football game. It was not a good day for the home team, as Kentucky beat Georgia 33–0.

In one of the biggest upsets in school history, Ole Miss beat No. 3 Notre Dame 20–13 in Jackson. It would be Notre Dame's only loss all season, and the Irish went on to win the national championship.

1978: On January 2, Arkansas posted one of the biggest upsets in the history of the Orange Bowl. Although coach Lou Holtz had suspended his top two rushers, and Arkansas was given no chance to beat No. 2 Oklahoma, Arkansas dominated the Sooners and won 31–6.

In January Bill Dooley resigned at North Carolina and became head coach/athletics director at Virginia Tech. Dooley was replaced by Dick Crum of Miami (Ohio).

On November 11, Georgia Tech's Eddie Lee Ivery set an NCAA record by rushing for 356 yards against the Air Force Academy.

On December 4 Charley Pell resigned as Clemson's head coach to become the head coach at Florida.

On December 29, in Danny Ford's first game as Clemson's coach, the Tigers beat Ohio State 17–15 in the Gator Bowl. During that game, Ohio State coach Woody Hayes struck Clemson player Charlie Bauman. Soon after the incident Hayes was forced out as coach.

1979: On January 1 Alabama defeated Penn State 14–7 at the Sugar Bowl to win the national championship.

On February 12 Emory Bellard, the inventor of the wishbone offense, was named the head coach at Mississippi State. He remained there until January 15, 1986.

On October 20 former Alabama coach Harold "Red" Drew died at age 84.

1980: On January 1 Alabama defeated Arkansas 24–9 in the Sugar Bowl to win the 1979 national championship, its third of the decade.

South Carolina running back George Rogers won the Heisman Trophy, the first ever for the school.

In July former Auburn coach Shug Jordan died.

On November 1 Mississippi State posted the biggest upset in school history, a 6–3 win over No. 1 Alabama in Jackson, Mississippi.

On November 8 1–7 Georgia Tech stunned the football world by tying No. 1 Notre Dame 3–3 in Atlanta. On the same day, No. 2 Georgia rallied from behind in the final minutes to beat Florida 26–21 on a miracle 93-yard touchdown pass from Buck Belue to Lindsay Scott. Georgia was ranked No. 1 in the next polls and stayed there. The Bulldogs, led by freshman tailback Herschel Walker, finished the regular season 11–0 and won their first SEC title since 1976.

On December 1 Doug Barfield resigned as Auburn's head coach with a record of 29–25–1. Auburn persued Georgia's Vince Dooley, an Auburn grad, but Dooley declined the job offer.

Coach Vince Dooley with Georgia's 1980 national championship trophy. Photo courtesy of the *Atlanta Journal-Constitution.*

1981: On January 1, with U.S. President and Georgia native Jimmy Carter looking on, Georgia defeated Notre Dame 17–10 in the Sugar Bowl for the school's first consensus national championship.

On January 2 Pat Dye, a former All-American player at Georgia and an assistant coach at Alabama, was named head coach at Auburn.

On September 19 Auburn played its first regular-season night game against Wake Forest.

On November 7 in Chapel Hill, Clemson defeated North Carolina 10–8 in the first battle between two top 10 teams in ACC history. Clemson would go on to post an 11–0 season and win the ACC title.

On November 28 Alabama defeated Auburn 28–17 to give coach Paul "Bear" Bryant his 315th career win, which broke the Division I record held by Amos Alonzo Stagg.

1982: On January 1 Clemson beat Nebraska 22–15 in the Orange Bowl to win its first national championship.

On October 16 Ole Miss renamed its stadium Vaught-Hemingway Stadium in honor of former coach John Vaught.

For the first few weeks of Tennessee's season, Knoxville also hosted the World's Fair.

Alabama's Bear Bryant died just 28 days after coaching his final game. Photo courtesy of the *Atlanta Journal-Constitution.*

Alabama started the 1982 season with a 7–1 record before losing its final three games. On December 15 Bear Bryant announced that he would retire after the Liberty Bowl, and on December 29 Bryant won his 323rd and final game as a coach, a 21–15 win over Illinois.

Georgia's Herschel Walker won the Heisman Trophy. He was only the second Bulldogs player to be so honored.

1983: On January 26, just 42 days after he had announced his retirement as head coach, Alabama's Bear Bryant died at age 69. Ray Perkins, a former Crimson Tide player, became Alabama's new head coach.

Georgia Tech, an Independent since 1964, joined the ACC.

Georgia's Herschel Walker gave up his final year of eligibility and signed with the USFL's New Jersey Generals.

On November 12 Auburn beat Georgia 13–7 in Athens to clinch its first SEC championship since 1957 and its first of four under coach Pat Dye.

1984: On January 2 Al Del Greco kicked a 19-yard field goal with seconds remaining to lead Auburn to a 9–7 victory over Michigan in the Sugar Bowl. The Tigers finished 11–1 with a final No. 3 ranking.

Florida finished first in the SEC but was stripped of the championship after being found guilty by the NCAA of rules violations.

After 14 years with an artificial surface, Ole Miss's Vaught-Hemingway Stadium switched to natural grass.

1985: On October 5 Grambling coach Eddie Robinson became the winningest coach in NCAA history when his team defeated Prairie View 27–7. Robinson's 324 wins moved him ahead of Alabama's Bear Bryant on the NCAA's all-time list for victories.

Auburn's Bo Jackson won the Heisman Trophy, the first for the school since Pat Sullivan won it in 1971.

1986: On September 27 Ole Miss retired the No. 18 jersey of quarterback Archie Manning. It remains the only number the school has ever taken out of competition.

On December 31 Ray Perkins resigned as Alabama's head coach to become the head coach of the NFL's Tampa Bay Buccaneers.

1987: On January 3 Bobby Ross was hired as Georgia Tech's eighth head coach. Ross, who won three ACC championships at Maryland, would remain at Tech for five seasons.

On January 4 Bill Curry, a former player and the former head coach at Georgia Tech, was named the head coach at Alabama.

Tulane's Mack Brown replaced Dick Crum as the head coach at North Carolina.

1988: On October 8 Ole Miss upset Alabama 22–12 in Tuscaloosa on Alabama's homecoming. It was the Rebels' first win ever over the Crimson Tide in Alabama, and it spoiled the dedication of the Bear Bryant Museum. Later, a disgruntled Alabama fan threw a brick through coach Bill Curry's office window.

That same day LSU's Tommy Hodson threw an 11-yard touchdown pass to Eddie Fuller with 1:41 remaining to beat Auburn 7–6. The explosion of sound was so loud that it registered as a small earthquake on the LSU Geology Department's seismograph.

1989: On January 1, in Vince Dooley's last game as coach, Georgia defeated Michigan State 34–27 at the Gator Bowl. Dooley's final record in 25 seasons was 201 wins, six SEC titles, one national title, and 20 bowl appearances. The next day at a press conference in Jacksonville, Dooley was replaced by Ray Goff, a former Bulldogs quarterback.

On December 2 second-ranked Alabama played at Auburn's Jordan-Hare Stadium for the first time in history. A crowd of 85,319—the largest football crowd ever in the state of Alabama—watched as Auburn upset Alabama 30–20.

Duke won the ACC championship under coach Steve Spurrier, who would leave on December 31 to become the head coach at Florida, his alma mater.

1990: Despite having led Alabama to a 10–2 record in 1989 and having been named SEC Coach of the Year, Bill Curry could not win the hearts and minds of most of the Alabama fan base. After the school offered him a new contract limiting his power to run the football program, Curry resigned, and on January 8 he became the head coach at Kentucky.

On January 11 Gene Stallings, a former player for Bear Bryant at Texas A&M, was named the new head coach at Alabama.

On January 18 Danny Ford resigned after 11 seasons as Clemson's head coach. Three days later Ken Hatfield became head coach.

Steve Spurrier led Florida to its first SEC championship in 1991. Photo courtesy of the Atlanta Journal-Constitution.

On November 3 Scott Sisson kicked a 37-yard field goal with seven seconds left as Georgia Tech upset No. 1 Virginia 41–38 in Charlottesville. Georgia Tech then beat Nebraska in the Citrus Bowl to finish 11–0–1 and win the UPI national championship.

On December 9 Jackie Sherrill, a former Alabama player and the former head coach at Pittsburgh and Texas A&M, became the 30th head coach in the history of Mississippi State.

1991: On May 6 Ole Miss football player Roy Lee "Chucky" Mullins, who had been paralyzed from the neck down after a collision in a 1989 game against Vanderbilt, died in a Memphis hospital.

On July 1 South Carolina and Arkansas joined the SEC, and Florida State became a member of the ACC.

On November 16 Florida beat Kentucky 35–26 to win the school's first official SEC title.

1992: Miami's Gino Torretta won the Heisman Trophy.

Alabama defeated Florida 28–21 in the first SEC championship game played at Legion Field in Birmingham.

On Thanksgiving Day, just moments after a 17–0 loss to Alabama, Pat Dye resigned as Auburn's football coach.

Tennessee coach Johnny Majors missed four games due to heart surgery. Assistant coach Phillip Fulmer went 4–0 as the interim head coach. When Majors resigned at the end of the season, Fulmer became Tennessee's head coach.

1993: On January 1 No. 2 Alabama defeated No. 1 Miami 34–13 in New Orleans to win the school's 12th national championship.

In December Florida State quarterback Charlie Ward won the Heisman Trophy while Tennessee quarterback Heath Shuler finished second.

Auburn, under first-year coach Terry Bowden, went 11–0. The Tigers could not play in a bowl game because of NCAA penalties handed down for recruiting violations.

1994: On January 1 Florida State defeated Nebraska 18–16 in the Orange Bowl for the school's first national championship.

Georgia coach Vince Dooley, who won 201 games, six SEC championships, and one national championship in 25 seasons, was inducted into the College Football Hall of Fame.

On September 3, after a 70-year hiatus, Kentucky and Louisville resumed their football rivalry.

1995: Grambling's Eddie Robinson became the first coach in college football history to win 400 games.

Tennessee's Neyland Stadium returned to natural grass after 27 years of using artificial turf.

Kentucky's Moe Williams posted 429 all-purpose yards in a 35–30 win at South Carolina. The total is the highest in SEC history and the second highest in NCAA history.

On November 2 in Charlottesville, Virginia, No. 2 Florida State was upset by Virginia 33–28. Before the loss Florida State was 30–0 in ACC games since it joined the league in 1992.

1996: Florida won its fourth straight SEC championship, one short of the record held by Alabama.

Tennessee's Neyland Stadium expanded to 102,854 and became the nation's second-largest on-campus football stadium.

Charley Conerly, one of the greatest quarterbacks in Ole Miss history, died on February 13 after a lengthy illness.

Frank Howard, Clemson's legendary coach from 1940 to 1969, died at his home in Clemson.

Florida quarterback Danny Wuerffel won the Heisman Trophy.

1997: On January 2 Florida defeated Florida State 52–20 in the Sugar Bowl for the school's first national championship.

Grambling's Eddie Robinson coached his final season.

Tennessee quarterback Peyton Manning, who would leave college football as the SEC's all-time total offense leader (11,020 yards), finished second to Michigan's Charles Woodson for the Heisman Trophy. He was the fourth Tennessee player to finish second for the award.

On December 5, after a 10–1 regular season, Mack Brown resigned from North Carolina to become the head coach at Texas. Brown was replaced as head coach by defensive coordinator Carl Torbush.

1998: In Knoxville, before 107,653 fans, the largest crowd to ever see a football game in the South, Tennessee defeated Florida 20–17 in overtime. It was Tennessee's first win over Florida since 1992.

In April Tennessee's Peyton Manning was the No. 1 pick in the NFL draft by the Indianapolis Colts.

On October 23, midway through the season, Terry Bowden resigned as Auburn's coach and was replaced by Bill Oliver.

On November 28 Tommy Tuberville left Ole Miss to become Auburn's new head coach.

1999: On January 4 Tennessee and Florida State played in the Fiesta Bowl for the national championship. Tennessee won 23–16 in Tempe, Arizona, for its first national championship since 1951.

On October 23 Florida State's Bobby Bowden became only the fifth Division I-A coach in college football history to win 300 games. Bowden beat his son, Tommy, the head coach at Clemson, 17–14, for win number 300.

On December 7 Georgia running back Herschel Walker, Alabama lineman John Hannah, Arkansas wide receiver Chuck Dicus, and former Kentucky coach Jerry Claiborne were inducted into the College Football Hall of Fame.

Tennessee's Peyton Manning, son of Archie Manning.
Photo courtesy of Tennessee SID.

Former North Carolina State and Notre Dame coach Lou Holtz, hired to rebuild the troubled program at South Carolina, went 0–11 in his first season.

Alabama won its first SEC championship since 1992.

Florida State went 11–0 and won its eighth straight ACC championship.

2000: On January 4 No. 1 Florida State defeated No. 2 Virginia Tech 43–29 for coach Bobby Bowden's second national championship. The 1999 season was also Bowden's first undefeated season (12–0).

Florida State, ranked No. 1 in preseason, became the first team to stay on top of the Associated Press poll wire-to-wire since the preseason poll began in 1950.

Eli Manning, the son of Ole Miss great Archie Manning, followed in his father's footsteps and signed with the Rebels.

On October 31, just three days after losing 40–38 to Central Florida, Alabama announced that Mike DuBose would be relieved of his coaching duties at the season's end. After winning the SEC championship the season before, Alabama finished 3–8 in 2000.

On December 2 Florida beat Auburn 28–6 in the SEC championship game in Atlanta, giving the Gators their sixth conference title under Steve Spurrier.

On December 9 Chris Weinke, the 28-year-old quarterback from Florida State, won the Heisman Trophy.

On December 26 Mark Richt, the offensive coordinator at Florida State, was named head coach at Georgia, replacing Jim Donnan.

Despite beating Florida State 27–24 during the regular season, Miami finished No. 3 in the final BCS standings behind the Seminoles and was left out of the national championship game. The Hurricanes beat Florida 37–20 in the Sugar Bowl and finished 11–1.

Mark Richt, who was hired as Georgia's head coach on December 26, 2000, has won 72 games and two SEC championships (2002, 2005) in seven seasons on the job. Photo courtesy of the University of Georgia/Sports Information.

Lou Holtz, who won a national championship at Notre Dame in 1988, led South Carolina to two straight New Year's Day victories. Photo courtesy of the University of South Carolina/Sports Information.

2001: On January 1, just one year after an 0–11 season, South Carolina beat Ohio State, 24–7, in the Outback Bowl to finish 8–4.

On January 4 Oklahoma beat Florida State 13–2 in the Orange Bowl for the 2000 BCS national championship.

On February 3 Larry Coker was named the head coach at Miami, replacing Butch Davis, who left for the Cleveland Browns.

On September 15 the entire college football schedule was postponed because of the 9/11 terrorist attacks.

On Thursday, September 20, in Starkville, Mississippi State and South Carolina played the first game since the 9/11 attacks.

On December 1, in a game delayed by the attacks of 9/11, Tennessee went to Florida and stunned the Gators 34–32.

On December 8 Matt Mauck came off the bench for injured quarterback Rohan Davey to lead LSU to a 31–20 win over Tennessee in the SEC championship game at the Georgia Dome in Atlanta. The loss cost the Volunteers a trip to the BCS championship game at the Rose Bowl.

Ralph Friedgen, in his first year as head coach at Maryland, won the ACC championship and went to the Orange Bowl. Friedgen won 31 games in his first three seasons at his alma mater.

On December 9 Georgia Tech's George O'Leary was named the new head coach at Notre Dame. Just five days later O'Leary resigned after several inaccuracies were found on his résumé.

2002: On January 1 Florida State beat Virginia Tech 30–17 in the Gator Bowl, giving coach Bobby Bowden his 323rd career win. That tied Bowden with his idol, Alabama's Bear Bryant, for all-time wins for a Division I-A coach.

On January 3 Miami knocked off Nebraska 37–14 in the Rose Bowl and gave the Hurricanes the 2001 BCS national championship in Larry Coker's first year as head coach.

On January 5 Steve Spurrier shocked the college football world by announcing his resignation from Florida after 12 seasons, 122 victories, and six SEC championships. Later in the month, Ron Zook was hired as Florida's new head coach.

On February 1 the Alabama football program was slapped with a five-year probation by the NCAA for recruiting violations. The Crimson Tide was banned from postseason play for two years and lost 21 scholarships over three years.

On March 12 Roy Kramer announced his retirement as SEC commissioner, and on July 2 Mike Slive was hired as the new SEC commissioner.

On December 5 Dennis Franchione resigned from Alabama after just two seasons to become the head coach at Texas A&M.

On December 7 Georgia beat Arkansas 30–3 in Atlanta to win its first SEC championship since 1982.

2003: On January 3 Miami lost the 2002 BCS national championship to Ohio State, 31–24, in double overtime at the Fiesta Bowl. The loss denied Miami its second straight national title and snapped the Hurricanes' 34-game winning streak.

On May 3 Alabama coach Mike Price was fired before he had coached a single game for the Crimson Tide. Price was let go after it was revealed that he had behaved improperly at a topless bar.

Mike Slive, a former judge and attorney, was named the SEC's seventh commissioner on July 2, 2002. Photo courtesy of the Southeastern Conference.

On May 9 Mike Shula, a former Alabama quarterback and son of NFL coaching legend Don Shula, was hired as the new coach of the Crimson Tide.

On October 18 Mississippi State coach Jackie Sherrill announced that he would retire at the end of the 2003 season.

On October 25 Florida State beat Wake Forest 48–24 to give coach Bobby Bowden his 339th career win. That moved him ahead of Penn State's Joe Paterno to become Division I-A football's all-time winningest coach.

On November 20, just two days before Auburn's big game with Alabama, university president William Walker flew to Kentucky and had a secret meeting with Louisville coach Bobby Petrino about replacing current coach Tommy Tuberville. After the meeting was reported in the media, Walker apologized to Tuberville, who remained as coach.

Former Alabama player Sylvester Croom became the first African American head coach in the history of the SEC. Photo courtesy of Mississippi State University/Sports Information.

On December 1 Sylvester Croom became the first African American head football coach in SEC history when he took over at Mississippi State.

On December 6 LSU defeated Georgia 34–13 to win its second SEC championship in three years. Running back Justin Vincent became the first freshman named the game's MVP with 201 yards rushing.

On December 11 Ole Miss quarterback Eli Manning won the Maxwell Award as college football's best player. His brother, Peyton, won the award in 1997.

2004: On January 4 LSU beat Oklahoma 21–14 in the Sugar Bowl to win the 2003 BCS national championship.

Southern California won the AP national title after beating Michigan in the Rose Bowl.

On June 30 Vince Dooley retired as the athletics director at Georgia, ending a 41-year relationship with the school.

On July 2, after a tumultuous expansion process the year before, Miami and Virginia Tech left the Big East and officially joined the ACC.

Due to Hurricane Frances, Florida State's game with Miami, scheduled for Monday, September 6, was moved to Friday, September 10. The day before the game, FSU coach Bobby Bowden attended the funeral of his grandson, Bowden Madden, who was killed with his father on September 5 in an automobile accident.

On October 25, after a loss to Mississippi State just two days before, Florida announced that head coach Ron Zook would be relieved of his duties at the season's end.

On October 30 Florida State lost to Maryland (20–17), Miami lost to North Carolina (31–28), and Florida lost to Georgia (31–24). It marked the first time since October 14, 1978, that all three Florida schools lost on the same day.

On November 20, at Clemson's Death Valley, players from South Carolina and Clemson engaged in a 10-minute brawl at the end of their annual game. As a result, both teams were banned from postseason play. On the Monday after the fight, South Carolina coach Lou Holtz announced his retirement.

Also on November 20, Florida State dedicated its field to Bowden.

On November 23 Steve Spurrier returned to college football after a three-year absence when he was named the new head coach at South Carolina.

On December 4 Auburn beat Tennessee in the SEC championship game to finish the regular season at 12–0. Despite being unbeaten, the Tigers did not get a shot at the BCS national championship. Southern California and Oklahoma also finished undefeated and played for the title. Auburn beat Virginia Tech in the Sugar Bowl to finish 13–0.

Also on December 4, Urban Meyer was named the new head coach at Florida.

On December 16 Southern California assistant Ed Orgeron was named the new head coach at Ole Miss.

Steve Spurrier was introduced as the new head coach at South Carolina on November 23, 2004. Photo courtesy of the University of South Carolina/Sports Information.

2005: On July 2 Boston College officially joined the ACC to create a 12-team league.

Hurricane Katrina caused catastrophic damage to Louisiana and Mississippi. As a result, LSU's opening game with North Texas on September 3 was canceled. Its second game with Arizona State, scheduled for Baton Rouge, was moved to Tempe, Arizona, and played on September 10. Because of concerns about another hurricane, this one named Rita, LSU's third game with Tennessee was moved to Monday, September 26.

Because of the widespread hurricane damage to New Orleans, Tulane's team was displaced for the entire season and had to play 11 road games.

On October 22 Miami's home game with Georgia Tech and South Florida's home game with West Virginia were postponed due to Hurricane Wilma.

On November 12, in Steve Spurrier's first meeting with his former school, South Carolina knocked off Florida 30–22 in Columbia.

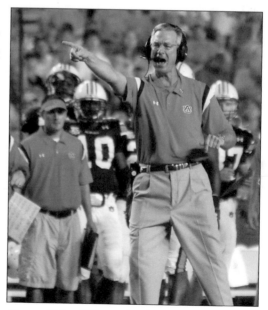

Tommy Tuberville's 2004 Auburn team went 13–0 but did not get a chance to play for the national championship. Photo courtesy of Auburn University/Sports Information.

On November 19 Vanderbilt beat Tennessee 28–24 to snap a 22-game losing streak to the Volunteers. Tennessee went on to finish 5–6 to end a string of 16 straight bowl appearances.

On December 3 Georgia beat LSU 34–14 for the SEC championship, the second in four seasons for the Bulldogs. Quarterback D.J. Shockley was the game's MVP.

Also on December 3, Florida State beat Virginia Tech 27–22 in the first ACC championship game played at Jacksonville's Municipal Stadium.

2006: On January 2 the Sugar Bowl moved to the Georgia Dome in Atlanta because of the damage Hurricane Katrina caused to the Louisiana Superdome. West Virginia upset Georgia, the SEC champion, 38–35.

On February 3 legendary coach John Vaught, who won 190 games and six SEC championships in 24 seasons at Ole Miss, died at age 96.

On April 17 Tom Mickle, the former ACC associate commissioner who originally drew up the BCS format on the back of a cocktail napkin, passed away after a battle with cancer.

On September 8 Erk Russell, the legendary defensive coordinator at Georgia who built a Division I-AA powerhouse at Georgia Southern, died at age 80.

On September 16 Clemson upset Florida State 27–20, giving the Tigers their first win in Tallahassee since 1989. It was the third win in four games for Clemson coach Tommy Bowden over his father, Florida State's Bobby Bowden.

On October 14 Miami and Florida International had a bench-clearing brawl at the Orange Bowl that led to the suspension of 31 players and a ton of bad press for Miami and the ACC.

On November 7 Miami's difficult on-field season turned tragic off the field when defensive lineman Bryan Pata was shot and killed outside of his apartment.

On November 8 Butch Davis, the former Miami coach, was named head football coach at North Carolina.

On November 9 Rutgers upset undefeated and No. 3–ranked Louisville, 28–25, knocking the Cardinals out of a shot for the national championship.

On November 11 Wake Forest stunned Florida State 30–0, handing coach Bobby Bowden his first-ever shutout at Doak Campbell Stadium.

Also on November 11, South Carolina coach Steve Spurrier made his first return visit to The Swamp, which he made famous in his 12 seasons as Florida's head coach. Florida blocked a field goal on the last play of game to win 17–16.

On November 18 Auburn beat Alabama 22–15, giving the Tigers their fifth straight win over the Crimson Tide. Nine days later Mike Shula was fired as head coach.

On November 24 Miami coach Larry Coker was fired. Coker was 53–9 with a national championship in his first five seasons. He was 7–6 in his last season.

On December 2 Florida beat Arkansas 38–28 to win its first SEC championship since 2000. After Southern California was upset by UCLA earlier in the day, Florida advanced to the BCS championship game against Ohio State in Glendale, Arizona.

On December 2 Wake Forest beat Georgia Tech 9–6 to win its second ACC championship (the other was in 1970). Jim Grobe was named the AP National Coach of the Year.

On December 5 Emmitt Smith (Florida), Bobby Bowden (Florida State), Charlie Ward (Florida State), and Chip Kell (Tennessee) were inducted into the College Football Hall of Fame.

On December 8 Tom O'Brien left Boston College to become the new coach at North Carolina State.

CHAPTER 2

SOUTHERN FRIED FOOTBALL FROM A TO Z

AUBIE THE TIGER: Auburn's award-winning mascot who began as a cartoon character drawn by artist Phil Neel of the *Birmingham Post-Herald* for a 1959 game program. Since 1979, a student dressed as a Tiger has filled the role.

ARTIFICIAL TURF: Tennessee was the first school in the South to use an artificial playing surface when it installed one made by the 3-M Company for the 1968 season. The first game played on the new field in Knoxville was a 17–17 tie with Georgia on September 14. After Tennessee's success with the artificial surface, many more Southern schools had them installed. Eventually coaches concluded they were the cause of more injuries, and opposing schools with grass fields began to make it an issue in recruiting. In the '90s schools began returning to natural grass fields. Tennessee finally replaced its artificial turf with natural grass in 1994.

BEER BARRELL: Painted orange and blue and filled with beer, it once went to the winner of the annual Tennessee-Kentucky game. The tradition was discontinued in 1999 after a Kentucky football player was killed in an alcohol-related automobile accident.

BOURBON BARRELL: Presented to the winner of the Kentucky-Indiana football game. The series began in 1893 but is not played every year. The schools met every year from 1987 to 2005 before taking a break in the series. They have met 36 times.

CHARLIE BAUMAN: A Clemson player struck by Ohio State coach Woody Hayes in the final minutes of the Buckeyes' 17–15 loss to the Tigers in the 1978 Gator Bowl. Hayes was forced to resign as a result of the incident.

BACARDI BOWL: Played on January 1, 1937, in Havana, Cuba, between Auburn and Villanova. The first and only bowl game played outside the United States was a flop, as only 9,000 paid to see it. It ended in a 7–7 tie.

BIG THURSDAY: From 1896 to 1959, Clemson and South Carolina played their traditional rivalry on the third Thursday of October during the State Fair in Columbia, South Carolina. Clemson fans eventually grew tired of playing such an important game on the road every year, so in 1960, at the insistence of coach Frank Howard, the Tigers' home games were moved back to campus. Clemson won the last Big Thursday game 27–0.

BETWEEN THE HEDGES: A reference to the English privet hedge that surrounds the field at Georgia's Sanford Stadium. The hedges were only a foot tall when the stadium was dedicated in 1929. Legendary sportswriter Grantland Rice is believed to have been the first to say that Georgia had an advantage any time it played "Between the Hedges." In late 1995 the original hedges were removed in order to make way for the women's soccer competition during the 1996 Summer Olympics. New hedges, which were grown from cuttings of the originals, were replanted that fall and today are stronger than ever.

CHECKERBOARD END ZONES: A series of orange and white blocks that comprise the end zones at Tennessee's Neyland Stadium. It was a trademark that began when Doug Dickey arrived as coach in 1964, and it was discontinued in 1968, when Tennessee installed artificial turf. The tradition was resumed in 1989 and remains one of the school's best-known trademarks.

CHIEF OSCEOLA: Since 1978 the Chief has been Florida State's official mascot. Before each game, Chief Osceola, an FSU student chosen for the honor, rides to the middle of the field on an Appaloosa horse named Renegade. In front of the opposing bench, Chief Osceola plants a flaming spear into the turf of Doak Campbell Stadium, signifying that the battle is about to begin.

CHINESE BANDITS: The nickname for one of the defensive units on LSU's 1958 national championship team. Coach Paul Dietzel named the unit after a line from the *Terry and the Pirates* comic strip that referred to the Chinese Bandits as "the most vicious people in the world." The unit became so famous that it was featured in *Life* magazine with the players wearing Chinese masks.

COWBELLS: Favorite noise-making device among Mississippi State fans. Although the SEC banned the use of them during conference games in 1974, determined fans still manage to sneak them into games both at home and on the road.

Mississippi State's famed cowbells. Photo courtesy of Mississippi State SID.

DEATH VALLEY: Nickname for Clemson's Memorial Stadium. The name was given to the stadium by a former coach at Presbyterian College, Lonnie McMillian, whose teams always struggled there.

ESSO CLUB: Located just across the street from the Clemson campus, this converted gas station serves as a popular gathering place for fans before and after Tigers games. It is one of the most popular locations in Clemson to sing, dance, and have a cold one.

GATOR GROWL: Takes place each year on the Friday night before the Homecoming game at Florida. It is an entertainment extravaganza that draws more than 72,000 students and alumni.

GOLDEN EGG: After a near riot at the 1926 Mississippi–Mississippi State game, an Ole Miss honor society proposed that the two teams play for a trophy each year. That trophy, a gold-plated football on a pedestal, became known as the Golden Egg.

"GOOD OLD SONG": Sung to the tune of "Auld Lang Syne," it has served as Virginia's unofficial alma mater since 1893.

H-BOYS: Name given to the Ole Miss backfield of Junie Hovious and Merle Hapes, who became two of the biggest names in college football from 1939 to 1941.

CONDREDGE HOLLOWAY: The first African American quarterback in SEC history when he lined up for Tennessee in 1972. Holloway turned down an $85,000 signing bonus to play baseball for the Montreal Expos. After leaving Tennessee, Holloway went on to play 13 seasons in the Canadian Football League. Today he is an assistant athletics director at Tennessee.

HOUNDSTOOTH HAT: The preferred headwear for Paul "Bear" Bryant, Alabama's legendary coach from 1958 to 1982.

HOWARD'S ROCK: Located at the top of a grassy hill on the east end of Clemson's Memorial Stadium. Former coach Frank Howard originally received the rock from a friend who picked it up in Death Valley, California. Howard placed the rock on a pedestal on September 24, 1966, prior to a game with Virginia. Clemson's players touched the rock and ran down the hill for good luck. Clemson won the game 40–35, and running down the hill after touching Howard's Rock has been a tradition ever since.

ICE BOWL: The nickname for the January 1, 1947, Cotton Bowl between LSU and Arkansas. LSU was led by quarterback Y.A. Tittle. Arkansas

Bear Bryant and his houndstooth hat. Photo courtesy of the *Atlanta Journal-Constitution.*

was led by future Hall of Fame player Clyde Scott. Dallas was pelted with ice, sleet, and snow that day. Fans had to build fires in the stands so they could stay and watch. LSU dominated the game, 15 first downs to 1, but could not score. The game ended in a 0–0 tie.

IRON BOWL: Nickname for the annual rivalry between Auburn and Alabama. Fans came up with the name because Birmingham, which hosted the game annually from 1948 until 1989, is known as the Iron City.

IRON DUKES: Duke University's most famous team, which went through the 1938 regular season without giving up a point. The Blue Devils almost enjoyed complete perfection that season, but Southern California scored a touchdown with 40 seconds left in the Rose Bowl and won 7–3.

KOOL KOYOTES: The 1967 North Carolina State team is best known for its "White Shoes" defense. But that same year the North Carolina State students charged with buying the school's live wolf mascot were duped into buying a coyote by a dishonest animal dealer. *Sports Illustrated* did an article on the incident, and the nickname stuck.

MIKE THE TIGER: The real, honest-to-goodness Bengal tiger that prowls in his cage on the sideline during LSU's games in Baton Rouge. Before the game Mike's cage is parked near the opponents' dressing room so that the players must walk past his imposing presence as they go to and from the field. The tradition began in 1935. Mike V, who began his reign in April 1990, died on May 18, 2007. Mike VI made his debut on October 6, 2007, at the Florida-LSU game.

1A and 1B: The numbering system used by Bear Bryant to identify twins Harry and Larry Jones, who played at Kentucky from 1950 to 1952. Harry wore 1A and Larry wore 1B. Harry led the Wildcats in all-purpose yardage in 1951, while Larry led them in kickoff returns in 1952.

"PUNT, BAMA, PUNT": Perhaps the most famous game of the storied series between Alabama and Auburn was played on December 2, 1972. Trailing 16–0 going into the fourth quarter, Auburn got a field goal from Gardner Jett to make it 16–3. Then the incredible happened. Auburn's Bill Newton blocked an Alabama punt, and David Langer returned it 25 yards for a touchdown. Three minutes later, Newton blocked another punt, and again Langer returned it for a touchdown, this time from 20 yards out, to give Auburn the victory. The phrase was soon found on bumper stickers throughout the state.

RAMBLIN' WRECK: The nickname of the restored 1930 Model A Ford Sports Coupe that leads the Georgia Tech football team onto the field before the beginning of each home game. It is also the name of one of the most famous fight songs in college football history. (For the words, see the Georgia Tech section of chapter 6.)

"ROCKY TOP": It's not the official fight song at Tennessee, but it is the most popular. Released in 1967, it is played almost continuously during Tennessee's games by the Pride of the Southland Band. (For the words, see the Tennessee section of chapter 6.)

SMOKEY: This bluetick hound dog serves as Tennessee's mascot. First adopted in 1953, Smokey IX now roams the Tennessee sideline.

SOD CEMETERY: In Bobby Bowden's early days as coach at Florida State, he had to play the nation's toughest teams on the road in order to get his program established. When Florida State won one of those big road games, a manager gathered a piece of the opposing field, brought it back to Tallahassee, and buried it in the "Sod Cemetery" near the Florida State practice field. A brass plate bearing the game's final score is placed next to each burial site, signifying each of Florida State's "Sod Games."

TESTUDO: Name of Maryland's diamondback turtle, the school's official mascot. He made his first appearance on May 23, 1933.

TEXTILE BOWL: Another name for the annual game between Clemson and North Carolina State. Both North Carolina and South Carolina are noted for their textile manufacturing, and the universities have two of the best textile schools in the world.

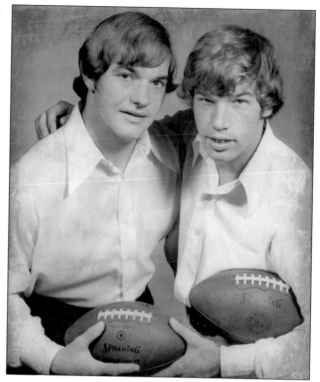

Auburn's Bill Newton (left) and David Langer were heroes against Alabama in 1972. Photo courtesy of the *Atlanta Journal-Constitution.*

THE AMAZIN'S: In 1972 Auburn was picked to finish seventh in the SEC after the departure of Heisman Trophy winner Pat Sullivan and receiver Terry Beasley. Auburn went 10–1, including a 17–16 win over Alabama. "The Amazin's" as they became known, finished fifth in the Associated Press poll.

THE AWARD-WINNING, FIGHTING CAVALIER INDOOR/OUTDOOR PRECISION MARCHING PEP BAND AND CHOWDER SOCIETY-REVUE, UNLIMITED: Nickname for the University of Virginia Pep Band.

THE GROVE: A 10-acre plot of land in the middle of the Ole Miss campus where fans traditionally go to enjoy tailgating prior to the game. Some consider it to be the best tailgating scene in all of college football.

THE IMMORTALS: Name for the 1898 Kentucky team that was unbeaten (7–0), untied, and unscored upon. Coached by W.R. Bass, the Immortals outscored the opposition 180–0.

THE RAG: Goes to the winner of the LSU-Tulane game.

THE SWAMP: The nickname given to Florida's Ben Hill Griffin Stadium when Steve Spurrier took over as head coach in 1990. Spurrier liked the name because he wanted opponents to believe that the Swamp was a place where "only Gators get out alive."

THE THIN RED LINE: Alabama's nickname in the early part of the century before it became the Crimson Tide.

THE THIRD SATURDAY IN OCTOBER: The traditional date for the Alabama-Tennessee game.

THE THIN THIRTY: When Blanton Collier left as Kentucky's football coach in 1962, the program was taken over by Charlie Bradshaw, a disciple of Paul "Bear" Bryant. Bradshaw pushed that first team so hard that more than 50 players quit. The remaining 30, who posted a record of 3–5–2, were given this nickname.

THE WRECK TECH PAJAMA PARADE: Before the 1896 game with Georgia Tech, Auburn students slipped out under the cover of night and greased the tracks where the Tech team would be arriving by train the next day. When Tech arrived, the train could not be stopped and skidded for an additional five miles. The Georgia Tech players had to walk back to Auburn and the next day lost the game 45–0. Auburn students never greased the tracks again, but each year before playing Georgia Tech, they would march in their pajamas to celebrate that historic event.

TIGERAMA: A large pep rally that takes place each year on the Friday night before Homecoming at Clemson. More than 35,000 come to Memorial Stadium each year for this combination of pep rally, beauty pageant, and fireworks display. In 2006 Clemson celebrated the 50th anniversary of Tigerama.

TIGER WALK: About two hours before each home game, Auburn's players walk from Sewell Hall, where most of the football players live, down Donahue Drive to Jordan-Hare Stadium. Fans form a human corridor on either side of the players and cheer them as they make their way to the stadium. Prior to the historic Alabama game on December 2, 1989, more than 20,000 people turned out for the Tiger Walk.

TOOMER'S CORNER: Located in the center of Auburn, where the university campus meets the town. At the intersection of College Street and Magnolia Avenue, fans have long gathered after games to celebrate. After big victories, students and fans cover the trees and other objects with toilet paper. Students also toilet-papered Toomer's corner in 1995 when rival Alabama was placed on NCAA probation.

UGA (pronounced "Ugh-gah"): This purebred English Bulldog is the University of Georgia's official mascot. Georgia began with UGA I in the fall of 1955, and today UGA VI reigns supreme over the Bulldogs' sideline. UGA V, who retired before the 1999 season, was the most recognized of all UGAs, appearing on the cover of *Sports Illustrated* on April 28, 1997, as college football's best mascot. Later that year he appeared in the movie *Midnight in the Garden of Good and Evil*, directed by Clint Eastwood.

VOLUNTEER NAVY: In 1962 Tennessee radio broadcaster George Mooney found a way to beat the notorious Knoxville traffic around Neyland Stadium. He took his small boat down the Tennessee

River and docked it near the stadium. It caught on, and today more than 200 boats make the trek prior to a Tennessee home game.

WAHOOS: "Cavaliers" is the official name of the University of Virginia's team. But in the 1890s Virginia's baseball players were called a "rowdy bunch of Wahoos" by fans from state rival Washington & Lee. The name stuck, and now Virginia fans proudly call themselves Wahoos.

WAR EAGLE!: Auburn's battle cry. Legend has it that among those in attendance at the first game between Auburn and Georgia in Atlanta in 1892 was a former Civil War soldier who had become a member of the Auburn faculty. With the man was an eagle he had raised from a baby after the war. After Auburn scored the first touchdown, the eagle broke free and began to soar above the field. Seeing the figure above, the Auburn crowd shouted "War Eagle!" and a tradition was born.

UGA, Georgia's mascot. Photo courtesy of Dan Evans/University of Georgia.

WORLD'S LARGEST OUTDOOR COCKTAIL PARTY: Nickname for the annual Georgia-Florida game played in Jacksonville, Florida. In 2006 officials from both schools asked that the name no longer be used after incidents involving alcohol resulted in the death of two Florida students.

WRONG WAY RIEGELS: Georgia Tech won the 1929 Rose Bowl and the national championship thanks to one of the most famous gaffes in college football history. In the second quarter, Georgia Tech fumbled on its own 36-yard line, and Roy Riegels, the captain of the California football team, picked up the ball and began running the wrong way. Teammates tried to turn him around, but he would not listen and was finally tackled near the goal line. When California tried to punt, Tech blocked the kick for a safety, earning the winning points in an 8–7 Georgia Tech victory.

XEN C. SCOTT: In 1919 Alabama hired Scott, a Cleveland sportswriter, as its head football coach. Scott, a tiny man (5'6", 135 pounds) who had played at Cleveland's Western Reserve, coached Alabama for four seasons, winning 29 games.

ZIPP NEWMAN: Former sports editor of the *Birmingham News* who is generally given credit for creating Alabama's nickname, "The Crimson Tide," in 1919.

CHAPTER 3

THE PLAYERS

I f Southerners view college football as a vicarious battle, then it stands to reason that the players are their gladiators, their Saturday afternoon heroes. And nowhere have college football players performed more heroically or been held in higher esteem than in the South.

Still, a lot of their history is not known. Did you know, for example, that of the 73 Heisman Trophies awarded by New York's Downtown Athletic Club since 1935, 13 have gone to players from the South? These men range from Georgia's Frank Sinkwich, who accepted the trophy wearing his Marine Corps uniform in 1942, to Florida's Danny Wuerffel, the son of a Presbyterian minister, who won in 1996. Wuerffel was coached by Steve Spurrier, also the son of a minister, who had won the award 30 years before. Four years later Chris Weinke, a 28-year-old former professional baseball player, won the Heisman at Florida State. And in 2007 Florida quarterback Tim Tebow became the first sophomore in history to win college football's highest award.

What may be more compelling, and what is not widely known, is how many Southern players have finished second in the voting for the Heisman Trophy. Georgia's Charley Trippi finished second to Army's great Glenn Davis in 1946. North Carolina's Charlie "Choo Choo" Justice finished second in the Heisman voting twice, in 1948 (to Doak Walker, SMU) and in 1949 (to Leon Hart, Notre Dame). A total of 15 Southern players have finished second in the Heisman Trophy voting.

There is even a father-son-brother team of near-Heisman winners. Ole Miss quarterback Archie Manning finished third in 1970 when Jim Plunkett won. Manning's son Peyton finished second to Michigan's Charles Woodson in 1997. Another Manning son, Eli, finished third in 2003 when Jason White of Oklahoma won.

These, of course, were the glamour boys of Southern college football. Their names were always in the headlines. But the South has produced more than its share of bruisers—the rough and tough men who gave the Southern game its rugged flavor.

Men like:

- Auburn's Zeke Smith, who was so good that as a junior in 1958 that a professional team from Canada offered him a contract, something that was unheard of during that time. Smith turned down the money and came back to Auburn.

- Frank "Bruiser" Kinard of Ole Miss, the ultimate iron man. During the 1936 season, Kinard was on the field for 708 out of the 720 minutes his team played.
- Tennessee defensive tackle Doug Atkins, who never won a major award but was still named the SEC's Player of the Quarter Century (1950–75). Atkins became a member of both the College Football and Pro Football Halls of Fame.

These are the heroes whose efforts are frozen in time and will forever remain in the hearts and the minds of those who love the great Southern game. Many are gone. Most of those who remain have seen their once-powerful bodies submit to the inevitable changes of time.

But as long as someone remembers what these special men did on those wonderful Saturdays long, long ago, they will remain forever young.

These are their stories.

In 1942 Heisman Trophy winner Frank Sinkwich led the Georgia Bulldogs to the Rose Bowl. Photo courtesy of the *Atlanta Journal-Constitution.*

THE HEISMAN WINNERS

Since 1935 the Downtown Athletic Club in New York has annually presented the Heisman Trophy to college football's most outstanding player. Thirteen Heisman Trophies have gone to players from the South.

FRANK SINKWICH, GEORGIA, 1942

To this day two images of Sinkwich, the South's first Heisman winner, are seared into the collective unconscious of college football fans.

The first is that of Sinkwich, his jaw broken by an errant knee during a pileup against South Carolina, running and passing with a protective mask that covered half his face. The 1941 photograph went nationwide, and fans everywhere started buzzing about "Flatfoot Frankie," Georgia's triple-threat halfback. Despite that injured jaw, Sinkwich put on one of the greatest performances in bowl history in the 1942 Orange Bowl when he ran for 139 yards and passed for 243 yards and three touchdowns. That total offense record of 382 yards still stands.

As a senior Sinkwich led Georgia to an 11–1 record, an SEC championship, and a berth in the Rose Bowl, where the Bulldogs beat UCLA. But before he went to Pasadena, Sinkwich picked up the Heisman Trophy wearing his Marine Corps uniform. After the Rose Bowl Sinkwich entered military service.

Sinkwich played several years of professional football and coached briefly at Tampa before becoming a wholesale beer distributor. He was inducted into the College Football Hall of Fame in 1954 and died on October 22, 1990.

BILLY CANNON, LSU, 1959

At 6'1", 210 pounds, Cannon possessed a deadly combination of speed and power. He led LSU to an undefeated season and a national championship in 1958, but Cannon's career, and perhaps his life, has been defined by a few seconds on Halloween night, 1959.

LSU, undefeated and ranked No. 3, trailed Ole Miss, also undefeated and ranked No. 1, 3–0 on a foggy Baton Rouge Saturday night. With about 10 minutes left in the game, Cannon dropped back to receive a punt. He took the ball on a bounce at his 11-yard line.

The old films show that eight Mississippi players got at least one hand on Cannon, but he was able to elude them all, including Rebel All-American Jake Gibbs, who was the punter and the last man to miss. Cannon scored on the 89-yard run, and LSU won the game 7–3.

LSU's Billy Cannon, the 1959 Heisman Trophy winner. Photo courtesy of the Atlanta Journal-Constitution.

While many people know of Cannon's run, few remember that Ole Miss almost came back to win the game. The Rebels drove down to the 1-yard line where Cannon and Warren Rabb tackled the ball carrier and stopped the drive with 18 seconds left.

Cannon went on to play 11 years of professional football before enrolling in a Tennessee dental school. He spent over two years in prison for his part in a counterfeiting scheme. Today he is the resident dentist at the Louisiana State Penitentiary. He was named to the College Football Hall of Fame on May 1, 2008.

Florida quarterback Steve Spurrier won the Heisman Trophy in 1966. Photo courtesy of Florida SID.

STEVE SPURRIER, FLORIDA, 1966

Whatever Spurrier may have lacked in physical ability, he more than made up for in confidence. This son of an East Tennessee minister had total belief in his ability to lead football teams to victory. It is a trait that would serve him well throughout his life.

That confidence was never more evident than on October 29, 1966, when Spurrier made the play that launched him to the Heisman Trophy.

Florida was undefeated and ranked No. 6 going into a big game with Auburn. Thanks to the work of Norm Carlson, Florida's sports information director, the press box was full of national writers that Saturday wanting to see Spurrier.

Spurrier had already played a brilliant game, throwing for 259 yards and punting for a 47-yard average. But with the score tied at 27–27, Florida faced a fourth and long at the Auburn 25-yard line.

Florida called timeout and coach Ray Graves pondered his options. The 40-yard field goal was out of the range of Florida's regular kicker. Going for the first down against the Auburn defense was a long shot. Spurrier then jogged over to Graves and said, "Coach, let me give it a shot."

The request didn't register with Graves, who was deep in thought. Spurrier asked again, this time more forcefully. Graves then looked at him and yelled, "Go kick it, Orr!" calling Spurrier by his middle name.

Spurrier made the field goal, Florida won 30–27, and the Heisman voters gave him a lopsided victory over Purdue's Bob Griese.

Spurrier went on to play 10 years in the NFL before entering coaching. He was head coach at Duke for three seasons before returning to Florida in 1990. Spurrier won six SEC championships in 12 seasons at Florida. After two seasons with the Washington Redskins of the NFL, Spurrier returned to college football as the head coach at South Carolina in 2005.

Spurrier was inducted into the College Football Hall of Fame in 1986.

PAT SULLIVAN, AUBURN, 1971

Like Steve Spurrier, Auburn's Pat Sullivan locked up the Heisman Trophy with one of the greatest performances of his career.

It came on November 13, 1971, when undefeated and sixth-ranked Auburn played at undefeated and seventh-ranked Georgia. Sanford Stadium was overflowing as the winner would still be in the race with Alabama for the SEC championship.

The fans also came to see if Sullivan could do something to overtake Cornell's Ed Marinaro in the Heisman Trophy race. The handsome running back, who later became an actor, was perceived to have the edge over the low-key Southern boy from Birmingham, Alabama.

But Sullivan defied the oddsmakers, throwing for an impressive 248 yards and four touchdowns. One of his completions, a 27-yarder to wide receiver Dick Schmaltz, came when he was falling to the ground and simply threw the ball side-armed up the field. Auburn went on to win the game 35–20.

"What I remember most is that time after time we had him, but he always found a way to make the play," said former Georgia coach Vince Dooley. "He was a super player having a super day. We tried everything we could to stop him, but nothing worked. That day he was the best quarterback I had ever seen."

Pat Sullivan. Photo courtesy of the *Atlanta Journal-Constitution.*

Sullivan edged Marinaro by only 152 points in the Heisman voting.

Sullivan played briefly in the NFL and returned to Auburn in 1986 as an assistant coach. He was named head coach at Texas Christian in 1992. After leaving TCU, Sullivan returned to Birmingham and entered private business. He joined the staff at Alabama–Birmingham in 1998. In 2007 he was named the head coach at Samford, located in his hometown of Birmingham.

Sullivan was inducted into the College Football Hall of Fame in 1991.

South Carolina running back George Rogers won the 1980 Heisman Trophy. Photo courtesy of South Carolina SID.

GEORGE ROGERS, SOUTH CAROLINA, 1980

Few players have overcome more obstacles on the way to greatness than George Rogers. Born into poverty in tiny Duluth, Georgia, Rogers was only six years old when his parents divorced and the hard times came.

Rogers had two brothers, two sisters, and a mother with no money. His father had gone to prison for killing a woman with whom he was involved.

"What I remember most is that we moved about eight times, just to stay ahead of the bills," said Rogers. "Kids would taunt me because of my old clothes. You don't forget things like that."

Football would be his way out. Rogers first played in junior high, but in order to get the $2 fee for team insurance, he lied about his age and joined a labor pool, working at $1.80 an hour. In high school Rogers moved from his Atlanta housing project to live with an aunt who would only allow him to play football if he did his schoolwork and helped around the house.

The structure and discipline worked. Rogers enrolled at Duluth High School, where he was named the Georgia Class AA Player of the Year in his final two seasons.

At South Carolina Rogers had three straight seasons of over 1,000 yards, and in 1980 he led the nation with 1,781 yards rushing. He had 21 consecutive games of 100 yards or more.

"He was the most complete back I ever coached," said former South Carolina coach Jim Carlen. "He could run around people or over people. And once he got ahead of them, he could outrun them."

Rogers was the No. 1 pick in the 1981 NFL draft by New Orleans and finished his pro career with the Washington Redskins in 1987. He was inducted into the College Football Hall of Fame in 1997.

HERSCHEL WALKER, GEORGIA, 1982

While most of the Southern Heisman winners forged their legends as seniors, Georgia's Herschel Walker became a star in his very first college game.

Georgia trailed Tennessee 15–2 in the 1980 opener for both teams, which was played on a steamy Saturday night in Knoxville, Tennessee. Walker, a true freshman, had come to Georgia after one of the most publicized recruiting battles ever. But Coach Vince Dooley was hesitant to throw such a young player into this kind of fire. Assistant coach Mike Cavan, who had recruited Walker out of Wrightsville, Georgia, pleaded with Dooley to give the kid a chance.

"I just told Coach Dooley that I didn't see any way we were going to win the game if we didn't give the ball to Herschel," Cavan said.

Trailing by 13 points with time running out in the third quarter, Georgia finally decided to give the ball to Herschel.

Walker scored his first college touchdown by running over Tennessee safety Bill Bates for 16 yards. Then early in the fourth quarter Walker scored again from nine yards out, which gave the Bulldogs a 16–15 victory.

Herschel Walker won the Heisman Trophy in 1982. Photo courtesy of the *Atlanta Journal-Constitution.*

That game launched Walker's storybook career and carried Georgia to a 12–0 season and the 1980 national championship.

Over the next three years Georgia just kept giving the ball to Walker, who rushed for 5,097 yards, an NCAA record for total yards in three seasons. The Bulldogs went 33–3 with three SEC championships with Walker in their backfield.

Walker finished third in the Heisman voting in 1980 and second to Marcus Allen in 1981. In 1982 he won the award, finishing ahead of Stanford's John Elway.

Walker left Georgia after his junior season to sign with the New Jersey Generals of the now-defunct United States Football League.

He was inducted into the College Football Hall of Fame in 1999.

Auburn's Bo Jackson won the Heisman Trophy in 1985. Photo courtesy of *the Atlanta Journal-Constitution.*

VINCENT "BO" JACKSON, AUBURN, 1985

There were times during his brilliant career (1982–85) that the athletic talents of Vincent "Bo" Jackson simply defied description.

The 6'1", 222-pound running back had the speed and power to either run around or run over defenders. As a baseball player he left Auburn with a career average of .335 and 28 homers. If he had wanted to, he could have been a world-class track star.

As it was, Jackson ran for 4,303 yards in four seasons and led Auburn to an SEC championship in 1983.

"If you're lucky, you get to coach one like him in a lifetime, and I was lucky," said Pat Dye, his coach at Auburn.

But it should be noted that Jackson's nickname was not one given to him with affection. His nickname was originally "Boar," as in "wild," which is what he was as a youngster. Even Jackson's mother predicted that he would eventually land in jail if he didn't change his wild ways.

Jackson did change when he arrived at Auburn after a brilliant, multisport high school career. In 1982 Jackson was taken in the second round of the amateur baseball draft by the New York Yankees but deferred his dream of the major leagues to play football for Auburn.

After rushing for 1,213 yards and leading the Tigers to an SEC championship as a sophomore in 1983, Jackson was a leading candidate for the Heisman in 1984. Unfortunately, a shoulder injury all but knocked him out for the season.

Jackson played the 1985 season with a vengeance, rushing for 1,786 yards and 17 touchdowns. Jackson won the Heisman Trophy over Iowa quarterback Chuck Long by a mere 45 points, the narrowest margin ever.

When he left Auburn the following spring, Jackson was the SEC's first three-sport letterman (football, baseball, and track) in 30 years.

Jackson went on to become an All-Pro in the NFL and an All-Star in baseball. A hip injury in 1991 shortened his professional career, but Jackson will always be remembered as one of the greatest athletes to ever put on a college uniform.

Vinny Testaverde, Miami, 1986

Some say a dream delayed is a dream denied, but not Vinny Testaverde.

Since Testaverde's birth in November 1963, his father, Al, dreamed that his son would win the Heisman Trophy. Testaverde was but a few days old when Big Al placed a football in his crib.

But Testaverde, a powerful 6'5", 220-pound quarterback, would face roadblocks between him and his dream at every turn.

After a brilliant high school career in Elmont, New York, his grades were not sufficient to enter a big-time college. Testaverde improved his grades and further honed his skills with a year at Virginia's Fork Union Military Academy.

In 1982, Testaverde's first year at the University of Miami, he played behind Jim Kelly, who went on to an All-Pro career in the NFL.

In 1983 Testaverde lost the battle for the quarterback job to Bernie Kosar, who led the Hurricanes to a national championship. Testaverde redshirted that season and backed up Kosar in 1984.

Miami's Vinny Testaverde. Photo courtesy of Miami SID.

Testaverde finally got his chance in 1985 when Kosar left school early for the NFL. Then came another obstacle as he lost his very first start to Florida, 35–23.

It turned out to be the only regular-season loss Testaverde experienced as Miami's quarterback. The Hurricanes went 10–1 that season before losing to Tennessee in the Sugar Bowl. Testaverde finished fifth in the Heisman Trophy voting.

The next season Testaverde led the Heisman race from wire to wire, beating Temple's Paul Palmer by 1,541 points. Miami had an undefeated regular season but was stopped short of the national championship by Penn State in the Fiesta Bowl.

Testaverde finished his college career with 6,058 yards passing and 48 touchdowns. He was the No. 1 overall pick in the 1987 NFL draft by Tampa Bay.

Gino Torretta, Heisman Trophy winner. Photo courtesy of Miami SID.

GINO TORRETTA, MIAMI, 1992

The list of great quarterbacks from the University of Miami reads like a Who's Who of college football: Jim Kelly, Vinny Testaverde, Bernie Kosar, Steve Walsh, and Craig Erickson. But Gino Torretta won more games (26) and passed for more yards (7,690) than any of them.

Slow of foot with suspect arm strength, Torretta was the least physically gifted of the bunch. Despite these shortcomings, as a high school junior Torretta promised his mother that he would someday win the Heisman Trophy.

A native of tiny Pinole, California, where his father, Al, ran a tavern, Torretta defied the critics at every turn. Al Torretta had taught his son that he could do anything he put his mind to. As a result, Torretta's statistics were not always impressive, but invariably, when the game was on the line, he found a way to help his team win.

He led the Hurricanes to a national championship in 1991 but barely scratched in the Heisman Trophy voting.

But in 1992 Torretta was brilliant, particularly in the big games. In a 19–16 win over Florida State, in what was billed as "The Game of the Century," Torretta made every big completion down the stretch to allow the Hurricanes to hold on to victory.

When asked about the difference in the tightly fought game, an exhausted Bobby Bowden, the Florida State coach, gave a one-word answer: "Torretta."

When Torretta beat out Marshall Faulk of San Diego State for the 1992 Heisman Trophy, the Antler's Tavern in Pinole was packed and in a jovial mood.

The only person missing was Al Torretta, who died in 1988.

CHARLIE WARD, FLORIDA STATE, 1993

The whole room disagreed with him, but Wayne McDuffie was adamant. He was convinced that this skinny kid from Thomasville, Georgia, could play quarterback for Florida State. The rest of the coaching staff, including head coach Bobby Bowden, disagreed.

McDuffie jumped on his chair and said the meeting would not end until they all agreed to sign this kid. The coaches finally relented, if for no other reason than to calm McDuffie down.

McDuffie was proven right when, in 1993, Charlie Ward won the Heisman Trophy and led the Seminoles to their first national championship.

Ward's journey to greatness, however, was not an easy one. He sat out a year of college football to work on his academics. When he arrived at Florida State, there were already so many good quarterbacks that he had to take a redshirt year. One year he got on the field but only as a punter, and another year he was a little-used backup.

As a junior in 1992 Ward finally earned the starting quarterback job but struggled early, throwing eight interceptions in his first two games. Against Clemson Ward's four interceptions were the major reason the Seminoles were trailing 20–17 with only a few minutes left. But Ward led FSU on a 77-yard drive and won the game with a nine-yard touchdown pass.

"After that I knew that there was no way to rattle this guy," said Bowden. "It never occurred to Charlie to quit. All he cared about was winning."

Quarterback Charlie Ward led Florida State to the 1993 national championship. Photo courtesy of the *Atlanta Journal-Constitution*/Jonathan Newton.

But it was three weeks later against Georgia Tech when the legend of Charlie Ward truly began. Florida State trailed 21–7 in the second half when assistant coach Brad Scott convinced Bowden to put Ward into a no-huddle, fast-break offense they had worked on during the week.

It turned out to be the perfect outlet for Ward's skills. Florida State came back to win 29–24 and stuck with the offense for the rest of the season.

As a senior Ward was brilliant, completing almost 70 percent of his passes and throwing only four interceptions all season. Florida State went 11–1 and earned a berth against Nebraska in the Orange Bowl for the national championship.

Before that game Ward picked up the Heisman Trophy, beating Tennessee's Heath Shuler by the second-largest margin in the award's history.

Ward put the fitting cap on his college career in the Orange Bowl. With his team trailing 16–15, Ward led his team down the field in the closing seconds and set up a field goal that gave the Seminoles an 18–16 victory and the national championship.

Ward, also a starter on the Florida State basketball team, was a first-round pick of the New York Knicks and played in the 1999 NBA Finals. He played in the NBA until 2005.

Ward ended his college football career with a 23–2 record, 2,647 yards passing, and 22 touchdowns. Said Bowden: "It was a great ride for all of us. We just appreciated the fact that Charlie let us go along."

In December 2006 Ward was inducted into the College Football Hall of Fame.

Danny Wuerffel won the Heisman Trophy and led Florida to a national title in 1996. Photo courtesy of the *Atlanta Journal-Constitution.*

DANNY WUERFFEL, FLORIDA, 1996

The highest praise for Wuerffel once came from his coach, Steve Spurrier.

"Danny is a better person than he is a quarterback," said Spurrier. "And Danny is a great, great quarterback."

Spurrier often argued that despite an unconventional throwing style that looked more like a man tossing a shot put than a football, Wuerffel should be considered the greatest quarterback in college football history.

The numbers certainly back up that claim. When he left Florida after the 1996 season, Wuerffel was the most efficient quarterback in NCAA history with a career rating of 163.6. He led the Gators to four straight SEC championships (1993–96) and a national championship as a senior in 1996. He was 32–3–1 as a starting quarterback with a record of 27–1 in the rugged Southeastern Conference.

Invariably the discussion of Danny Wuerffel always turned away from his numbers to his character, which was off the charts.

The son of a Presbyterian minister (Spurrier, coincidently, was also the son of a minister), Wuerffel played four years of college football at the highest level and was never affected by the hype or the glamour. During his college career he held Bible study classes on Tuesdays, hosted the Fellowship of Christian Athletes meeting on Wednesdays, and graduated with a 3.75 grade point average. Wuerffel is the only Heisman Trophy winner in history to also win the Draddy Award, which each year goes to college football's top scholar-athlete.

"I enjoy football, but it has never been the most important thing in my life," Wuerffel said in a 1996 interview.

Running Spurrier's sophisticated passing system to near perfection, Wuerffel became only the second quarterback in NCAA history (BYU's Ty Detmer is the other) to throw more than 100 touchdown passes. In the big games, Wuerffel was at his best. In 19 games against top 25 teams, he threw for 5,683 yards and 56 touchdowns.

After a short career in professional football, Wuerffel joined Desire Street Ministries, an organization that serves the needs of underprivileged children in New Orleans. Today Wuerffel is the organization's executive director.

CHRIS WEINKE, FLORIDA STATA, 2000

Weinke took an unconventional route to his college football career, but it ended with a national championship in 1999 and the Heisman Trophy in 2000.

In 1990, as a high school senior in his native Minnesota, Weinke was one of the nation's most highly recruited quarterbacks. He signed with Florida State, but then professional baseball came calling, and Weinke took a $350,000 bonus from the Toronto Blue Jays.

Florida State coach Bobby Bowden wrote Weinke and told him that if he ever wanted to come back to college football, a scholarship was waiting for him at Florida State.

"I never thought I'd hear from him again," Bowden said.

Six years later Weinke's baseball career stalled, and he reached out to Bowden. The rest is college football history.

In 1998 Weinke's career got off to an inauspicious start. In only his second start he threw six interceptions in a 24–7 loss to North Carolina State. But from that point on Weinke was a star. The Seminoles reached the national championship game against Tennessee, but Weinke did not play because of a serious neck surgery.

In 1999 Weinke led the Seminoles to a 12–0 season. They beat Virginia Tech in the Sugar Bowl to give Bowden his second national championship.

In 2000 Weinke led the nation with 4,167 yards passing while throwing 33 touchdowns and only 11 inter-

Chris Weinke, a former professional baseball player, was 28 years old when he won the Heisman Trophy in 2000. He led Florida State to the 1999 national championship. Photo courtesy of Florida State University/Sports Information.

ceptions. At the age of 28, he edged Oklahoma quarterback Josh Heupel by only 76 votes to win the Heisman Trophy.

Weinke's college career ended with a 13–2 loss to Oklahoma in the Orange Bowl, which gave the Sooners the national championship. Weinke finished his career with a record of 32–3 as Florida State's starting quarterback.

In 2007 Tim Tebow became the youngest player ever to win the Heisman Trophy. Photo courtesy of the University of Florida.

Tim Tebow, Florida, 2007

There were a number of reasons the experts didn't think Tebow could win the Heisman Trophy.

First of all he was a sophomore, and in the 73-year history of the trophy, no second-year player had ever gone home with the award.

Tebow played in the same conference with running back Darren McFadden of Arkansas, who finished second to Ohio State quarterback Josh Smith in 2006. If anybody from the SEC was going to win the Heisman in 2007, most thought it would be McFadden.

But when all the votes had been counted on December 8, 2007, there was no denying that Tebow had earned the Heisman after putting together one of the greatest individual seasons in college football history.

The numbers were simply staggering. In 2007 Tebow became the first player in Division I-A history to run for 20 touchdowns and throw for 20 touchdowns in a single season. Tebow finished the regular season with 3,286 yards passing and 32 touchdowns. He also ran for 895 yards and 23 touchdowns.

His 55 total touchdowns in a season broke the SEC season record of 46 set by another Florida quarterback, 1996 Heisman Trophy winner Danny Wuerffel. His 55 touchdowns were also more than 94 of the 119 Division I-A teams scored during the 2007 season.

Tebow's 23 rushing touchdowns were more than any running back in SEC history—more than Georgia's 1982 Heisman Trophy winner Herschel Walker, and more than Auburn's 1985 Heisman Trophy winner Bo Jackson.

Tebow put together one magnificent performance after another in 2007, but none was quite as impressive as his November 10 game at South Carolina. Tebow accounted for seven touchdowns against the Gamecocks, completing 22 of 32 passes for 304 yards and two touchdowns, while running for 120 yards and five touchdowns.

The performance left coach Urban Meyer grasping for some new adjectives.

"He is simply the most competitive person I have ever been around," Meyer said. "He was magnificent."

Tebow was home-schooled by missionary parents who ran an orphanage in the Philippines. He is in heavy demand as a public speaker to deliver his sincere message of faith.

After he signed to play at the University of Florida in 2006, Tebow became an immediate folk hero because of his endearing personality and his exceptional talent.

As a freshman in 2006 he was the backup to Chris Leak as the Gators won the national championship. Then, in his first season as a starter, he put together a season that college football will never forget.

"I am fortunate, fortunate in a lot of things," Tebow said on the night he received the Heisman. "God truly blessed me and this just adds on. It's an honor. I'm so happy to be here."

Tebow enters the 2008 season trying to become only the second man ever to repeat as the Heisman Trophy winner. Ohio State's Archie Griffin won the award in 1974 and 1975.

CLOSE BUT NO TROPHY:
THE SOUTH'S HEISMAN RUNNERS-UP

TENNESSEE'S FABULOUS FOUR

Tennessee has made a lot of college football history over the past 100 years, but here's a distinction the Volunteers do not necessarily enjoy: Tennessee is the only school to have four players finish second for the Heisman Trophy and not have a winner. Only one other school, Southern California, has had four Heisman runners-up, but the Trojans have also had several winners. Here is a look at the four men from Tennessee who came so close to college football's biggest award.

In 1951 tailback Hank Lauricella led Tennessee to a 10–0 regular season, an SEC championship, and the school's first consensus national championship. Despite an impressive season, Lauricella could not overcome the Eastern voting bloc in the Heisman race. Princeton's Dick Kazmaier, who led the Tigers to a 22-game winning streak, won the Heisman in a lopsided vote, 1,777 points to 424.

In 1956 tailback Johnny Majors led the Volunteers to a 10–0 regular season and an SEC championship. No player in the country could equal Majors's playing versatility. But Majors's talent was no match for the good looks and star power of Notre Dame's Paul Hornung, who won the Heisman despite playing on a 2–8 team.

In 1993 quarterback Heath Shuler led Tennessee to a 9–1–1 regular season while throwing for 25 touchdowns. Shuler was a big, powerful man from the hills of western North Carolina who could beat teams with his arm and with his feet. But nobody was going to beat out Florida State quarterback Charlie Ward, who won the Heisman and led the Seminoles to the national championship.

Tennessee's first three Heisman second-place finishes may have been disappointing to fans, but when Peyton Manning finished second to Michigan defensive back Charles Woodson in 1997, it was a bitter pill to swallow for everyone in Big Orange Country.

Charlie Justice. Photo courtesy of the *Atlanta Journal-Constitution.*

No player in school history was more revered than Manning, the son of former Ole Miss quarterback Archie Manning. When Peyton passed up millions from the NFL to return for his senior season, Tennessee fans were convinced that the Heisman was his to lose. Despite leading Tennessee to an 11–1 regular-season record and the SEC championship, Manning finished second to Woodson, who had several big performances in key nationally televised games.

It's been more than 10 years, but still many Tennessee fans have not gotten over it.

YOU CALL THIS JUSTICE?

While Tennessee holds the distinction of four Heisman runners-up, North Carolina's Charlie Justice was the first player in college football history to finish second in the Heisman Trophy race two times. In 1948 Justice, the all-purpose halfback, finished second to SMU's Doak Walker. In 1949 he was second to Notre Dame's Hall of Fame end, Leon Hart. Justice finished his career with 4,883 yards of total offense. As a punter he had a 42.6-yard career average. Justice died on October 17, 2003.

ANOTHER CHARLEY COMES CLOSE

Georgia has had two Heisman Trophy winners (Frank Sinkwich, 1942; Herschel Walker, 1982), but Charley Trippi is still considered to be the best all-around athlete to play football for the Bulldogs. An all-purpose halfback like North Carolina's Justice, Trippi played in the same backfield with Sinkwich on Georgia's Rose Bowl team of 1942. He spent the 1943 and 1944 seasons in the air force. He played the last five games of 1945 and led Georgia to an SEC championship in 1946. Trippi finished second to Army's Glenn Davis for the Heisman Trophy. He is in both the College Football and the Pro Football Halls of Fame.

Charley Trippi, All-American. Photo courtesy of the *Atlanta Journal-Constitution.*

STILL NO HEISMAN AT GEORGIA TECH

John Heisman enjoyed his greatest success as a coach during his 16 years (1904–19) at Georgia Tech. It is one of college football's greatest ironies that the school so associated with the famous coach has never won a Heisman Trophy. The closest Georgia Tech has come to the prize was 1963 when Billy Lothridge finished second to Navy's Roger Staubach. Lothridge did it all for Georgia Tech that season. Not only was he a great quarterback who could run and throw, but Lothridge was also the team's punter, place-kicker, and kickoff man. In 1963 Lothridge threw for 1,017 yards. He averaged 41.0 yards punting and made 12 of 17 field goals. He was responsible for 13 touchdowns. Lothridge finished eighth in the Heisman voting in 1962. Florida coach Ray Graves called him "the greatest quarterback we've ever faced."

Georgia Tech All-American quarterback Billy Lothridge with center Bill Curry, 1963. Photo courtesy of the *Atlanta Journal-Constitution.*

In 1999 Georgia Tech quarterback Joe Hamilton became the ACC's all-time total offense leader. But it wasn't quite enough to catch fullback Ron Dayne of Wisconsin, who won the Heisman Trophy and gave the Yellow Jackets their second runner-up.

Georgia Tech quarterback Joe Hamilton, seen here with offensive coordinator Ralph Friedgen (right), finished second to Ron Dayne for the Heisman Trophy in 1999. Photo courtesy of the Georgia Institute of Technology/Sports Information.

LSU quarterback Jerry Stovall finished second in competition for the Heisman Trophy in 1962. Photo courtesy of the *Atlanta Journal-Constitution.*

Casey Weldon. Photo courtesy of the *Atlanta Journal-Constitution.*

A Close Call for Stovall

In 1960 Jerry Stovall came to LSU with some big shoes to fill—those belonging to halfback Billy Cannon, the 1959 Heisman Trophy winner. He came close to matching most of Cannon's achievements. A rugged, two-way player, Stovall was a two-time All-American on offense, but among coaches he was considered one of the best defensive backs in the country. He proved that later as an All-Pro with the St. Louis Cardinals. In 1961 he led the Tigers to a 10–1 record and an SEC championship. In 1962 he finished second for the Heisman to Terry Baker of Oregon State in what was, to that date, the closest voting ever—707 points to 618.

A Tough Break for a Terp

Maryland was one of the dominant teams in early 1950s college football because coach Jim Tatum found the perfect quarterback for his split-T offense. In three years as the Terps' starter (1950–52), Jack Scarbath posted a record of 24–4–1, which included a 19-game winning streak. Scarbath's biggest victory came after the 1951 season when Maryland upset undefeated and No. 1–ranked Tennessee, which had already been declared the national champion, 28–13, in the Sugar Bowl. After that 10–0 season, Scarbath was a strong favorite for the Heisman going into 1952. But in the eighth game of the season Maryland's winning streak ended with a 21–14 loss at Mississippi. Maryland didn't go to a bowl that year, and the Heisman went to Billy Vessels of Oklahoma.

Mighty Casey Finishes Second to Howard

Casey Weldon grew up in Tallahassee, Florida, wanting nothing more than to play quarterback for the hometown Florida State Seminoles. In 1989 he finally got his wish, and in 1991 Weldon threw for 2,527 yards and 22 touchdowns. Weldon led Florida State to an 11–2 finish and a No. 3 ranking in the final Associated Press poll. Weldon won the Johnny Unitas Golden Arm Award, which goes to the nation's best quarterback. But in the Heisman voting he finished second to Michigan wide receiver Desmond Howard.

KING REX COMES UP SHORT

Florida fans will tell you that if any sophomore before Tim Tebow deserved to win the Heisman, it was the Gators' Rex Grossman in 2001.

The native of Bloomington, Indiana, whose father played for the Indiana Hoosiers, put up some incredible numbers in Steve Spurrier's offense. Grossman threw a school record 3,896 yards and 34 touchdowns on the season as Florida went 10–2 and beat Maryland in the Orange Bowl.

But Grossman finished second in the Heisman Trophy voting to quarterback Eric Crouch of Nebraska, who led the Cornhuskers to the BCS championship game against Miami. Crouch had 162 first-place votes and 770 points. Grossman had 137 first-place votes and 708 points.

"D-MAC" IS A HEISMAN BRIDESMAID—TWICE

As a sophomore at Arkansas in 2006, running back Darren McFadden proved that he could do just about anything on the football field.

He led the SEC in rushing with 1,647 yards, the fifth best season in SEC history. He threw the ball and ran the ball out of Arkansas' shotgun formation, which later became known as the "Wild Hog" formation. He led Arkansas to the SEC championship game where the Razorbacks lost to Florida, the eventual national champion. He won the Doak Walker Award as the nation's best running back and finished second to Ohio State quarterback Troy Smith for the Heisman Trophy.

As a junior in 2007 D-Mac was again the best running back in the SEC and proved it in November. He ran for a career-high 321 yards in a 48–36 win over South Carolina on November 3.

On November 23, the day after Thanksgiving, McFadden put together one of the greatest individual performances in SEC history against No. 1 LSU. McFadden ran for 206 yards and three touchdowns and passed for another score as the Razorbacks upset the Tigers, 50–48, in triple overtime.

McFadden became the second player in history to be the Heisman runner-up twice when he finished second to Tebow.

Rex Grossman was the Heisman Trophy runner-up in 2001. Photo courtesy of the University of Florida.

Arkansas running back Darren McFadden finished second for the Heisman Trophy in 2006 and 2007. Photo courtesy of the University of Arkansas/Sports Information.

Heisman Runners-Up

Year	Name	Position	School	Winner
1946	Charley Trippi	HB	Georgia	Glenn Davis, Army
1948	Charlie Justice	HB	North Carolina	Doak Walker, SMU
1949	Charlie Justice	HB	North Carolina	Leon Hart, Notre Dame
1951	Hank Lauricella	RB	Tennessee	Dick Kazmaier, Princeton
1952	Jack Scarbath	QB	Maryland	Billy Vessels, Oklahoma
1956	Johnny Majors	RB	Tennessee	Paul Hornung, Notre Dame
1962	Jerry Stovall	HB	LSU	Terry Baker, Oregon State
1963	Billy Lothridge	QB	Georgia Tech	Roger Staubach, Navy
1981	Herschel Walker	RB	Georgia	Marcus Allen, USC
1991	Casey Weldon	QB	Florida State	Desmond Howard, Michigan
1993	Heath Shuler	QB	Tennessee	Charlie Ward, Florida State
1997	Peyton Manning	QB	Tennessee	Charles Woodson, Michigan
1999	Joe Hamilton	QB	Georgia Tech	Ron Dayne, Wisconsin
2001	Rex Grossman	QB	Florida	Eric Crouch, Nebraska
2006	Darren McFadden	RB	Arkansas	Troy Smith, Ohio State
2007	Darren McFadden	RB	Arkansas	Tim Tebow, Florida

Third-Place Finishers for the Heisman

Year	Name	Position	School	Winner
1942	Clint Castleberry	RB	Georgia Tech	Frank Sinkwich, Georgia
1951	Babe Parilli	QB	Kentucky	Dick Kazmaier, Princeton
1958	Billy Cannon	HB	LSU	Pete Dawkins, Army
1960	Jake Gibbs	QB	Mississippi	Joe Bellino, Navy
1970	Archie Manning	QB	Mississippi	Jim Plunkett, Stanford
1980	Herschel Walker	RB	Georgia	George Rogers, South Carolina
1992	Garrison Hearst	RB	Georgia	Gino Torretta, Miami
1993	David Palmer	WR	Alabama	Charlie Ward, Florida State
1994	Steve McNair	QB	Alcorn State	Rashaan Salaam, Colorado
1995	Danny Wuerffel	QB	Florida	Eddie George, Ohio State
1999	Michael Vick	QB	Virginia Tech	Ron Dayne, Wisconsin
2001	Ken Dorsey	QB	Miami	Eric Crouch, Nebraska
2003	Eli Manning	QB	Mississippi	Jason White, Oklahoma

THE SOUTHERN FRIED FOOTBALL HALL OF FAME: 100 MORE PLAYERS WHO MADE A DIFFERENCE

1. Don Hutson, WR, Alabama: The first Heisman Trophy was awarded in 1935. Had it been given in 1934, it surely would have gone to Alabama's Hutson. In the 1935 Rose Bowl, Hutson caught six passes for 165 yards and touchdowns of 59 and 54 yards. Hutson went on to NFL glory with the Green Bay Packers and is a member of both the College and Pro Football Halls of Fame. Frank Thomas, his coach at Alabama, called Hutson "the best player I ever coached."

2. Archie Manning, QB, Mississippi: Manning finished fourth in the Heisman voting as a junior in 1969 and third behind Jim Plunkett of Stanford and Joe Theismann of Notre Dame in 1970. Manning still holds the SEC record for total offense in a single game with 540 yards against Alabama in 1969. Manning went on to a long career with the NFL's New Orleans Saints and Minnesota Vikings. Two of his sons, Cooper and Eli, played football at Ole Miss. Another son, Peyton, was an All-American quarterback at Tennessee, the runner-up for the Heisman Trophy in 1997, and the No. 1 pick in the 1998 NFL draft. In 2004 Eli Manning became the No. 1 draft choice for the San Diego Chargers and was immediately traded to the New York Giants, where he won the 2008 Super Bowl.

Ole Miss coach John Vaught with Archie Manning (left) and Glenn Cannon (right) prior to the 1968 Liberty Bowl. Photo courtesy of the Atlanta Journal-Constitution.

3. Doug Atkins, E, Tennessee: Atkins, a big, rugged defensive end, was an All-American in 1952 and a key player in Tennessee's national championship team of 1951. Atkins was selected as the SEC Player of the Quarter Century by the Football Writers Association of America. He went on to have a successful pro career with the Chicago Bears, who acquired him two years after the Cleveland Browns made him a first-round pick in the 1953 draft. Atkins is in both the College and Pro Football Halls of Fame.

4. "Bullet" Bill Dudley, HB, Virginia: Dudley was one of the most versatile players in the history of college football. In 1941, as a 19-year-old senior, Dudley was responsible for 206 of the 279 points scored by the Cavaliers. Dudley finished fifth in the Heisman balloting that season.

5. Babe Parilli, QB, Kentucky: Parilli finished fourth in the Heisman balloting in 1950, and third in 1951. In three seasons, Parilli threw for 50 touchdowns and led the Wildcats to the Orange, Sugar, and Cotton Bowls.

Charlie Conerly led Ole Miss to an SEC championship in 1947 and went on to star with the New York Giants. Photo courtesy of the *Atlanta Journal-Constitution.*

Clint Castleberry. Photo courtesy of the *Atlanta Journal-Constitution.*

6. Charley Conerly, QB, Mississippi: Finished fourth in the Heisman Trophy voting in 1947. Conerly led the Rebels to their first SEC championship and as a pro led the Giants to four NFL championship games, winning the title in 1956.

7. Lee Roy Jordan, LB, Alabama: Jordan may have been the best inside linebacker in the history of college football. A two-time All-American, Jordan recorded 31 tackles in a 17–0 win over Oklahoma in the 1963 Orange Bowl. He was Alabama's player of the decade in the 1960s. He went on to an All-Pro career with the Dallas Cowboys.

8. Jake Gibbs, QB, Mississippi: Gibbs was third in the Heisman voting in 1960 after leading Ole Miss to a 10–0–1 season and a national championship. After a distinguished college football career, Gibbs signed with the New York Yankees, where he played for seven full seasons.

9. Harry Gilmer, QB, Alabama: One of the most versatile players the South has ever produced. As a sophomore in 1945 Gilmer was an All-American and the SEC Player of the Year. He was voted the MVP in the Rose Bowl after leading the Crimson Tide to a 34–14 win over Southern California. In 1946 he led the Crimson Tide in passing, rushing, interceptions, punt returns, and kickoff returns.

10. Clint Castleberry, RB, Georgia Tech: As a freshman in 1942, Castleberry appeared destined for greatness after finishing third in the Heisman Trophy voting. But six weeks after playing in the 1943 Cotton Bowl, Castleberry enlisted in the service as a member of the Army Air Corps. On November 7, 1944, Castleberry's plane disappeared off the West African coast. He was never found.

11. Tucker Fredrickson, HB/DB, Auburn: Fredrickson finished sixth in the Heisman voting in 1964 but was the first player picked in the next NFL draft. Frederickson was both a great runner and defensive back. Auburn coach Shug Jordan called him the most complete player he had ever seen.

12. Tommy Casanova, WR/DB, LSU: Casanova did not fare well in the 1971 Heisman voting, but he should have. In an era of two-platoon football, Casanova played offense, defense, and returned punts. In 1970 Casanova returned two punts for touchdowns in a win over Ole Miss that gave LSU the SEC championship.

13. Bob Gain, T, Kentucky: Gain was a two-time All-American and a three-time All-SEC pick. In Gain's four years as a tackle (1947–50), Kentucky was 33–10–2 and won an SEC title under coach Paul "Bear" Bryant.

14. Dick Modzelewski, DL, Maryland: In 1952 he was Maryland's first winner of a major award when he claimed the Outland Trophy. A three-time All-American, he led a Maryland defense that gave up more than a touchdown only four times in 29 games.

15. Gene McEver, RB, Tennessee: McEver led the nation in scoring in 1929. Coach Robert Neyland, not known for idle praise, called McEver the best player he ever coached. McEver was elected to the College Football Hall of Fame in 1954.

16. Zeke Smith, OG/LB, Auburn: Smith won the Outland Trophy as a junior in 1958 and was an All-American in 1959. Smith, who played both offensive guard and linebacker, was so good that the Baltimore Colts drafted him after his junior season. He was also offered a $15,000 signing bonus from a CFL team. He turned both offers down to return to Auburn in 1959.

17. Vaughn Mancha, C, Alabama: Mancha started his first game as a freshman in 1944 and never gave up the spot over a brilliant four-year career. Mancha played in one Rose Bowl and two Sugar Bowls. He was a consensus All-American pick in 1945. He was elected to the College Football Hall of Fame in 1990.

18. Walter Payton, RB, Jackson State: After a brilliant career on the small college level, the native of Columbia, Mississippi, became the fourth overall pick in the 1975 NFL draft by the Chicago Bears. Peyton went on to became the NFL's all-time leading rusher with 16,726 yards in 13 seasons. Payton, who died in 1999 of a rare liver disease, is in both the College Football and Pro Football Halls of Fame.

19. Steve DeLong, MG, Tennessee: Tennessee's team struggled in 1964, but that didn't keep DeLong from becoming one of the nation's most dominant defensive players. DeLong was a two-time All-American and the number six pick in the first round of the 1965 NFL draft. In 1993 DeLong was inducted into the College Football Hall of Fame.

20. Art Weiner, E, North Carolina: A two-time All-American, Weiner was one of the greatest two-way ends in the history of college football. Weiner led the nation in receiving with 52 catches in 1949 and was seventh nationally the year before with 31 catches. A three-time All-Southern Conference player, Weiner was chosen in the second round of the 1950 NFL draft by the New York Bulldogs.

North Carolina Hall of Famers Charlie Justice (No. 22) and Art Weiner (No. 50) in 1949. Photo courtesy of the *Atlanta Journal-Constitution.*

Frank "Bruiser" Kinard of Ole Miss was an All-American in 1936 and 1937. Photo courtesy of the *Atlanta Journal-Constitution.*

21. Bill Stanfill, DE, Georgia: Stanfill was a quick and rangy defensive end that other teams simply could not block. Stanfill led the Bulldogs to an SEC championship in 1968 and later starred in the Super Bowl with the Miami Dolphins. Stanfill was inducted into the College Football Hall of Fame in 1998.

22. Frank "Bruiser" Kinard, Mississippi: Kinard was a two-time All-American in 1935–36. His name should have been Iron Man. During the 1936 season Kinard was on the field 708 out of 720 minutes his team played.

23. Jack Youngblood, DE, Florida: An All-American in 1970, Youngblood was named to the All-SEC Quarter Century Team for 1950–74. A first-round pick of the Los Angeles Rams in 1971, Youngblood was twice named the NFL's Defensive Player of the Year. He was inducted into the College Football Hall of Fame in 1992.

24. Bob Suffridge, G, Tennessee: Suffridge was Tennessee's first three-time All-American who played on the great teams of 1938, 1939, and 1940. The hometown boy from Knoxville, Tennessee, was elected to the College Football Hall of Fame in 1961.

25. Randy White, DT, Maryland: White forever changed the position of defensive lineman. White was big, but was considered one of the quickest linemen ever to play the game. He won every major award for linemen in 1974, including the Outland and Lombardi Trophies, and was a first-round pick of the Dallas Cowboys. He is in both the College Football and Pro Football Halls of Fame.

26. Terry Bradshaw, QB, Louisiana Tech: Bradshaw put up some impressive numbers during his four years at Louisiana Tech (1966–69), completing 52.5 percent of his passes for 7,149 yards and 42 touchdowns. Bradshaw was the first player taken in the 1970 NFL draft by the Pittsburgh Steelers. Bradshaw led the Steelers to four Super Bowl titles and was the MVP in Super Bowls XIII and XIV. He finished his career with 27,989 yards passing. Bradshaw retired after the 1983 season. He was inducted into the Pro Football Hall of Fame in 1989 and the College Football Hall of Fame in 1996.

27. Bruce Smith, DT, Virginia Tech: Smith was the first player from the state of Virginia to ever win the Outland Trophy. Smith was the most dominant lineman in college football for four seasons, accounting for 504 yards in losses. He was the first player taken in the 1985 NFL draft.

28. Mike McGee, G, Duke: The All-American guard won the Outland Trophy in 1959 despite playing on a 4–6 team. McGee was a second-round draft choice by the St. Louis Cardinals and finished third in the NFL Rookie of the Year balloting. After a playing career cut short by injury, McGee entered coaching and finally athletics administration. He retired as athletics director at South Carolina in 2005.

29. Fran Tarkenton, QB, Georgia: Tarkenton led the Bulldogs to an SEC championship in 1959 and went on to become a record-setting quarterback in the NFL with 47,003 yards passing. He played in three Super Bowls and nine Pro Bowls over an 18-year pro career. He was inducted into the Pro Football Hall of Fame in 1986 and the College Football Hall of Fame in 1987.

30. Jim Ritcher, C, North Carolina State: Ritcher is considered to be one of the best centers to ever play college football. A two-time All-American, Ritcher won the Outland Trophy in 1979 and spent 14 years of his 16-year professional career with the Buffalo Bills.

31. Tracy Rocker, DT, Auburn: In 1988 Rocker became the first player in SEC history to win both the Outland Trophy and the Lombardi Award. Rocker was a three-time All-SEC player and a two-time All-American.

Georgia coach Wally Butts with quarterback Fran Tarkenton in 1959. Photo courtesy of the *Atlanta Journal-Constitution.*

Tracy Rocker of Auburn. Photo courtesy of the *Atlanta Journal-Constitution.*

32. Johnny Mack Brown, HB, Alabama: Brown was All–Southern Conference in 1924 and 1925 but is best remembered for his performance in the 1926 Rose Bowl. Brown caught touchdown passes for 59 and 30 yards in the historic 20–19 win over heavily favored Washington, which gave the Crimson Tide a national championship. After playing in the Rose Bowl, Brown remained in California and eventually became a cowboy movie star.

33. Buck Buchanan, DT, Grambling: A rugged tackle who played for Coach Eddie Robinson from 1959 to 1962. Buchanan was the first player chosen in the 1963 American Football League draft by the Dallas Texans, who later became the Kansas City Chiefs. He played his entire 13-year pro career with the Chiefs and appeared in two Super Bowls. Buchanan was inducted into the Pro Football Hall of Fame in 1990 and the College Football Hall of Fame in 1996.

34. George Cafego, RB, Tennessee: Nicknamed "Bad News," Cafego was an All-American tailback for the Volunteers in 1938 and 1939. Coach Robert Neyland found Cafego playing sandlot baseball in his native West Virginia. He had not planned to go to college, but Neyland talked him into coming to Tennessee. Cafego, the number one pick in the 1940 NFL draft, was named to the College Football Hall of Fame in 1969.

35. Johnny Cain, FB, Alabama: Cain, the only sophomore starter on Alabama's 1930 national championship team, was a two-time All-America pick. Nicknamed "Hurry," Cain earned fame as a powerful left-footed punter. In a 1932 game with Tennessee, Cain averaged 48 yards on 19 kicks in a driving rain. The native of Montgomery, Alabama, was named to the College Football Hall of Fame in 1973.

36. Ted Hendricks, DE, Miami: A three-time All-American (1966, 1967, 1968), Hendricks defined the position of defensive end as a collegian and then perfected it with a brilliant NFL career. The second Miami player named to the College Football Hall of Fame (Jim Otto was the first), Hendricks finished fifth in the 1968 Heisman Trophy voting.

37. Jimmy Hitchcock, HB, Auburn: Known as the "Phantom from Union Springs," Hitchcock became Auburn's first All-America player in 1932 when he led the Tigers to a 9–0–1 record and the Southern Conference championship. Hitchcock was a triple threat as a runner, passer, and punter. In a 1932 game against Tulane, Hitchcock returned an intercepted pass 60 yards for a touchdown. Later in the game, he picked up an errant snap on a punt attempt and ran 63 yards for another score in a 19–7 win. Hitchcock was also an All-American in baseball and later played in the major leagues.

38. Beattie Feathers, HB, Tennessee: Feathers was a three-year starter (1931–33) at tailback for the Volunteers and was voted the SEC's Most Valuable Player in 1933. The native of Bristol, Virginia, was the second Tennessee player to be elected to the Hall of Fame when he was named in 1955. He went on to a career in coaching.

39. Russell Maryland, DT, Miami: In 1990 Maryland became the first player in Miami history to win the Outland Trophy, which goes to the nation's best interior lineman. He was the first player chosen in the 1991 NFL draft by the Dallas Cowboys.

40. Bobby Dodd, QB, Tennessee: One of only three players in the College Football Hall of Fame as both a player and a coach. Tennessee was 27–1–1 in Dodd's three years at quarterback (1928–30). The native of Kingsport, Tennessee, was named an All-America pick in 1930. He left Tennessee to become an assistant coach at Georgia Tech in 1931. He was head coach at Georgia Tech from 1945 to 1966.

41. Charlie Flowers, FB, Mississippi: Flowers was an All-American and captain of the 1959 Ole Miss team, which was named the SEC's Team of the Decade for the 1950s. Flowers led the SEC in rushing in 1957 and led the conference in rushing and scoring in 1959. Flowers finished fifth in the 1959 Heisman Trophy voting. The native of Marianna, Arkansas, was elected to the College Football Hall of Fame in 1997.

Miami defensive tackle Russell Maryland. Photo courtesy of the *Atlanta Journal-Constitution.*

42. Reggie White, DT, Tennessee: A big but fast tackle who could run around blockers or through them. White was an All-American in 1983 when he led the Vols to a 9–3 season. He went on to an All-Pro career with the Green Bay Packers.

43. Jackie Parker, QB, Mississippi State: In 1952 Parker led the nation in scoring and set an SEC record for points in a season with 120. It was an even greater accomplishment because Parker played on a 5–4 team. Parker, a junior college transfer, played two seasons at Mississippi State but is still considered the best quarterback in Mississippi State history. He is in the College Football Hall of Fame.

44. John Hannah, OG, Alabama: Considered by many to be the finest offensive lineman in the history of football, pro or college. A two-time All-America pick (1971–72), Hannah was named to Alabama's Team of the Century and was also on ESPN's All-Time College Football Team. Hannah went on to an All-Pro career with the New England Patriots and was elected to the Pro Football Hall of Fame. Hannah was inducted into the College Football Hall of Fame in 1999.

45. Walter Gilbert, C/LB, Auburn: Auburn has been playing football since 1892 and Gilbert remains its only three-time All-American (1934–36). In the era of one-platoon football, Gilbert was considered by many to be the best to play both center and linebacker. Gilbert's 1936 team went 7–2–2 and played in the school's first bowl game, the Bacardi Bowl in Havana, Cuba. Gilbert was elected to the College Football Hall of Fame in 1956.

46. Herman Hickman, G, Tennessee: In Hickman's three years at guard (1929–31), the Volunteers won 27 games and lost only one. He was an All-American in 1931 and was named to the All-Time SEC Team as chosen by the Football Writers Association of America. Hickman was named to the College Football Hall of Fame in 1959.

47. Bob McWhorter, HB, Georgia: McWhorter was an All–Southern Conference performer for four consecutive years (1910–13) and was the Bulldogs' first-ever All-American player. With McWhorter in the backfield, Georgia won 25 out of 34 games in four years, its first real sustained success. One of seven members of the McWhorter family to play at Georgia, Bob McWhorter was inducted into the College Football Hall of Fame in 1954.

48. Doug Williams, QB, Grambling: Threw for 8,411 yards and 93 touchdowns in a brilliant career (1974–77) for the Tigers of Eddie Robinson. He led Grambling to a 35–5 record in four seasons and finished fourth in the 1977 Heisman Trophy voting. Williams was picked in the first round of the 1978 NFL draft by Tampa Bay. He was later traded to the Washington Redskins and led his team to a 42–10 victory over Denver in Super Bowl XXII. Williams was named the Most Valuable Player in that game. In 1998 Williams replaced Robinson as the head coach at Grambling.

49. Barney Poole, E, Ole Miss: Poole was as one of the great ends in SEC history. Eligibility rules were relaxed during World War II, and as a result Poole played seven years of college football: three at Ole Miss, one at North Carolina, and three at Army. Poole finished his career at Ole Miss in 1947–48.

50. Fred Sington, T, Alabama: Notre Dame's Knute Rockne called Sington "the greatest lineman in the county." A member of Phi Beta Kappa as well as an All-American, Sington played from 1928 to 1930 and was a leader on the 1930 Alabama team that went undefeated and beat Washington State in the Rose Bowl. Sington, from Birmingham, was named to the College Football Hall of Fame in 1955.

51. George Morris, C/LB, Georgia Tech: One of the cornerstones on Georgia Tech's SEC championship team of 1951 and its undefeated and national championship team of 1952. A native of Vicksburg, Mississippi, Morris was an All-America selection in 1952, when he was the SEC's Most Valuable Player. Morris was later a second-round draft choice of the San Francisco 49ers. He was inducted into the College Football Hall of Fame in 1981 and died in December 2007.

52. Bill Hartman, QB, Georgia: Hartman capped off a brilliant college career (1934–37) by being named captain of Georgia's 1937 team. In that same year he was named All-SEC and All-America.

Hartman went on to a pro career with the Washington Redskins. After his retirement from pro football, Hartman returned to Georgia as an assistant coach. He later left full-time coaching to become very successful in the insurance business. Hartman remained at Georgia as a part-time coach of the Bulldogs kickers. Hartman was inducted into the College Football Hall of Fame in 1984. He died on March 16, 2006.

53. Bert Jones, QB, LSU: An All-American in 1972, Jones was a strong-armed leader with a knack for winning. Jones led the Tigers to an SEC championship as a sophomore and ended his career with a record of 26–6–1 and three bowl appearances. Jones is best remembered for a 17–16 win over Ole Miss in 1972 when he threw a touchdown pass to Brad Davis as time expired. Jones finished fourth in the Heisman Trophy voting in 1972 and was later the number one pick in the NFL draft by the Baltimore Colts.

54. Bob Johnson, C, Tennessee: Johnson was a two-time All-American in 1966–67 and a member of Tennessee's SEC championship team in 1967. Johnson was also an academic All-American in 1967 and was named to the all-time All-SEC football team.

55. Ron Simmons, NG, Florida State: Still considered the greatest defensive player in Florida State history. Ron was the Seminoles' first two-time consensus All-American (1979–80), leading them to a pair of Orange Bowl appearances. He posted 25 quarterback sacks in his career and was the first defensive Florida State player in history to have his jersey (No. 50) retired. He was named to the College Football Hall of Fame on May 1, 2008.

56. Condredge Holloway, QB, Tennessee: Holloway didn't break the color barrier at Tennessee. That honor went to wide receiver Lester McClain. But Holloway was the first African American man to play quarterback in the SEC. As a sophomore in 1972 Holloway led the Vols to a 10–2 record. After leaving Tennessee in 1974, Holloway went on to play professional football in Canada.

Georgia Tech All-American George Morris in 1952. Photo courtesy of the *Atlanta Journal-Constitution.*

Tennessee's Condredge Holloway, the first African American to play quarterback in the SEC (1972–74). Photo courtesy of the *Atlanta Journal-Constitution.*

Emmitt Smith, University of Florida. Photo courtesy of the *Atlanta Journal-Constitution*.

57. Emmitt Smith, RB, Florida: From the first day he walked onto the Florida campus Smith was a star. He was the National Freshman of the Year in 1987 and the SEC Player of the Year in 1989. Smith finished ninth in the Heisman voting as a freshman and seventh as a junior. He left Florida after only three seasons with 58 school records, including the career rushing mark of 3,928 yards. A first-round pick of the Dallas Cowboys, Smith was the first back in NFL history to rush for more than 1,400 yards in five consecutive seasons (1991–95). He was the NFL MVP in 1993 and the MVP of Super Bowl XXVIII. He was inducted into the College Football Hall of Fame in December 2006.

58. Gaynell "Gus" Tinsley, E, LSU: Tinsley was the first LSU player to be named All-America when he was tapped for the honor in 1935 and 1936. Playing both offense and defense, Tinsley led the Tigers to two SEC championships and two berths in the Sugar Bowl. After a pro career with the Chicago Cardinals, Tinsley returned to LSU as head coach from 1948 to 1954.

59. Ed Molinski, G, Tennessee: Another standout on the great Neyland teams of 1938–40, Molinski was an All-American in 1939 and 1940. Molinski was named to the College Football Hall of Fame in 1990.

60. Ozzie Newsome, WR, Alabama: Next to Don Hutson, the best receiver in Crimson Tide history. From 1974 to 1977 Newsome started 47 games for Alabama. He averaged 20.3 yards per catch and helped the Crimson Tide win three SEC championships. He went on to play 13 seasons for the NFL's Cleveland Browns. Newsome was named to the College Football Hall of Fame in 1994.

61. Clyde Scott, HB/DB, Arkansas: A star in both track and football, Scott had tremendous speed for his era (1946–48). He won a silver medal in the hurdles in the 1948 Olympics and then went on to have an All-America season in football even though the Razorbacks went 5–5. Scott, who played both halfback and defensive back, made great plays on both sides of the ball. In the 1947 Cotton Bowl, Scott preserved a 0–0 tie with LSU by tackling Tigers wide receiver Jeff Odom at the Arkansas one-yard line. His 1,463 yards rushing was a career mark for Arkansas at the time. Nicknamed "Smackover" after his hometown in Arkansas, Scott was inducted into the College Football Hall of Fame in 1971.

62. Bowden Wyatt, E, Tennessee: Along with Bobby Dodd and Amos Alonzo Stagg, Wyatt is one of only three men in the Hall of Fame as both a player and a coach. Wyatt was an end on the unde-feated Tennessee team of 1938. He later went on to become head coach at Wyoming, Arkansas, and Tennessee.

63. Banks McFadden, HB, Clemson: The most versatile athlete in Clemson history. In the same academic year (1938–39) McFadden was an All-American in both football and basketball. In 1939 he led Clemson to its first conference basketball championship and later that fall took the Tigers to their first bowl (1940 Cotton Bowl). McFadden is the only Clemson athlete in history to have both his foot-ball and his basketball jersey retired.

64. Pooley Hubert, QB, Alabama: Hubert was Alabama's second All-American player. He was a four-year letterman (1922–25) on teams that had a combined record of 31–6–2. He quarterbacked Alabama in the 1926 Rose Bowl where the Crimson Tide beat Washington 20–19. Hubert, from Meridian, Mississippi, was elected to the College Football Hall of Fame in 1964.

65. Jimmy Taylor, FB, LSU: Taylor rushed for 1,314 yards in two seasons as a starter at LSU and was considered one of the most complete players of his day. He was an All-American in 1957 despite playing on a team that finished 5–5. He shared the backfield with sophomore Billy Cannon and went on to have a brilliant pro career with the Green Bay Packers. He was inducted into the Pro Football Hall of Fame in 1976.

66. Lance Alworth, WR, Arkansas: Alworth might be the greatest athlete to put on a Razorbacks uniform. As a senior in 1961, Alworth led the team in rushing (516 yards), caught 18 passes for 320 yards, led the nation in punt returns (17.1 average), and handled kickoff returns. He also was the team's punter. In three years with Alworth in the lineup (1959–61), Arkansas either won or shared the Southwest Conference championship. If that wasn't enough, Alworth was on the SWC All-Academic Team and lettered in baseball. He set school records in the 100-yard dash (9.6) and 220-yard dash (21.4). He went on to have a brilliant pro career with the San Diego Chargers. Alworth was inducted into the College Football Hall of Fame in 1984.

67. Dale Van Sickel, E, Florida: Florida's first All-America player, Van Sickel was one of the nation's best pass receivers in 1928, when he played on college football's highest scoring team (336 points in nine games). After football, Van Sickel went on to become a successful stunt man in Hollywood for nearly five decades. He died as a result of his injuries in the late '60s.

68. Henry Goldthwaite "Diddy" Seibels, HB, Sewanee: Seibels was a four-year (1897–1900) star at Sewanee and the key player on the 1899 Iron Man team that went 12–0 and won five road games in six days, all by shutouts. A native of Montgomery, Alabama, Seibels came to Sewanee to play baseball but eventually became a three-sport star (baseball, football, and golf). During his last three seasons at Sewanee, the Tigers went 20–1–1. He died in 1967 at age 91 and was inducted into the College Football Hall of Fame in 1973.

69. Vernon "Catfish" Smith, E, Georgia: Smith had a solid college career (1929–31), but he is best remembered for an incredible performance in the 1929 game with Yale. Georgia used the game against Yale, one of the powers in that era, to dedicate Sanford Stadium. Few gave the Bulldogs a chance, but Smith scored all of Georgia's points in a 15–0 win. As a senior Smith was named an All-American. He was named to the College Football Hall of Fame in 1979.

70. Lou Michaels, T/K, Kentucky: A two-time All-America pick (1956–57) who lettered three years at Kentucky as a tackle, punter, and place-kicker, Michaels was voted SEC Lineman of the Year in both 1956 (Birmingham TD Club) and 1957 (Atlanta TD Club). He had a successful career as a kicker with the Baltimore Colts and was inducted into the College Football Hall of Fame in 1992.

71. Dixie Howell, QB, Alabama: Millard "Dixie" Howell, who played from 1932 to 1934, is best remembered for his great performance in the 1935 Rose Bowl victory over Stanford. Howell, from Hartford, Alabama, rushed for 111 yards, passed for 160 more, and punted six times for a 43.8 average. Howell was named to the College Football Hall of Fame in 1970. He was named to the Rose Bowl Hall of Fame in 1993.

72. E.G. "Doc" Fenton, RB/QB, LSU: Fenton is considered the first great football player in LSU history. He led the Tigers to a 10–0 season in 1908. The rangy Fenton scored 132 points in 10 games in the era when a touchdown counted for only five points.

73. Steve Kiner, LB, Tennessee: Kiner was known as one of the toughest linebackers to ever play in the SEC. He was an All-American in 1968 and 1969. He went on to play professional football with three different NFL teams. Kiner was inducted into the College Football Hall of Fame in 1999.

74. Ken Kavanaugh, E, LSU: An All-America pick in 1939, Kavanaugh was ahead of his time as a pass receiver. Kavanaugh, who also played baseball at LSU, led the nation in receiving with 30 catches for 467 yards and eight touchdowns. Kavanaugh finished seventh in the Heisman Trophy voting and had an outstanding pro career with the New York Giants.

75. Parker Hall, HB, Mississippi: One of the best two-way players in Ole Miss history. In 1938 Hall led the nation in scoring (73 points), in yards per rush (6.46), in touchdowns (22), and in all-purpose yards per game (129.1). On defense Hall led the nation with the most yards in pass interception returns (128) and was second in the nation with seven interceptions. Hall went on to be named NFL Rookie of the Year in 1939. He was inducted into the College Football Hall of Fame in 1991.

76. Joe Namath, QB, Alabama: A native of Beaver Falls, Pennsylvania, Namath led Alabama to a three-year (1962–64) record of 29–4. As a sophomore in 1962, Namath led the Crimson Tide to a 10–1 record and a 17–0 victory over Oklahoma in the Orange Bowl. In 1964 Namath led Alabama to

Alabama coach Bear Bryant with quarterback Joe Namath in 1964. Photo courtesy of the *Atlanta Journal-Constitution*/Billy Downs.

a 10–0 regular season and the national championship in the Associated Press poll, which was awarded before the bowls. After multiple knee injuries Namath was not expected to play in his final college game against Texas in the Orange Bowl. But with Alabama trailing 14–0, Namath hobbled onto the field and threw for 255 yards and a touchdown. Alabama lost 21–17, but Namath was named the game's Most Valuable Player.

77. Loyd Phillips, T, Arkansas: Phillips, still considered the best lineman in Arkansas history, was an All-American in 1965 and 1966. He won the Outland Trophy in 1966 and was named to the All–Southwest Conference team three times (1964–66). In Phillips's three years in the lineup, the Razorbacks were 11-0 in 1964 (national champions), 10–1 in 1965, and 8–2 in 1966. He had 304 career tackles.

78. D.D. Lewis, LB, Mississippi State: A two-time (1966–67) All-SEC and All-American linebacker for the Bulldogs, Lewis did not get a lot of recognition in college because he never played on a winning team. The Dallas Cowboys waited until the sixth round (the 159th pick overall) to take Lewis, who played in five Super Bowls during a 13-year pro career.

79. Nate Dougherty, G, Tennessee: Dougherty was a standout in the early part of the century (1906–1909) and played on the first two Tennessee teams (1907–08) to win seven games in a season. The native of Scott County, Virginia, was named All–Southern Conference in 1907–08. He was elected to the College Football Hall of Fame in 1967.

80. Wilber Marshall, LB, Florida: Marshall is considered by many to be the best linebacker to ever play for the Gators. Marshall was an All-American in 1982 and 1983 and a finalist for the Lombardi Award both seasons. He was college football's National Player of the Year in 1983. Marshall was the first-round draft choice of the Chicago Bears in 1984 and a starter on the Super Bowl championship team in 1985. He was named to the College Football Hall of Fame on May 1, 2008.

81. John Michels, G, Tennessee: Michels helped anchor the Tennessee line in 1950, 1951, and 1952, a stretch where the Volunteers went 29–4–1. The 1951 team was declared national champions after an undefeated regular season. Michels was named to the College Football Hall of Fame in 1996.

82. Jerry Rice, WR, Mississippi Valley: Perhaps the best wide receiver to ever play the game, college or pro, Rice left Mississippi Valley after the 1984 season with 4,693 receiving yards and 18 NCAA Division II records. He was brilliant as a senior with 1,845 yards receiving and 28 touchdowns, and he was the 16th overall pick of the San Francisco 49ers in the 1985 draft. He retired from the NFL after the 2004 season with 208 career touchdowns, more than any player in history.

83. Abe Mickal, HB, LSU: Mickal, a native of Syria, came to the United States as a small boy after the outbreak of World War I. He considered going to Notre Dame but chose LSU after Notre Dame coach Knute Rockne was killed in a plane crash in 1931. Mickal led the Tigers to a record of 23–4–5 from 1933 to 1935. Mickal, who was president of the LSU student body, went on to become a doctor. He was elected to the College Football Hall of Fame in 1967.

84. Bob Ward, G, Maryland: Some thought Ward was too small (165 pounds) to be a lineman, but he became an All-America middle guard in 1950 and an All-America offensive guard on the undefeated Maryland team of 1951. In Ward's four seasons in College Park the Terps had a record of 32–7–1. In 1951 he was the Southern Conference Player of the Year, and he was inducted into the College Football Hall of Fame in 1980.

85. Deion Sanders, DB, Florida State: The best defensive back to ever play at Florida State and one of only seven Seminole players to have his jersey (No. 2) retired. Sanders was the winner of the 1988 Jim Thorpe Award, which goes to the nation's best defensive back. Sanders also lettered in baseball and

Florida State's incomparable Deion Sanders. Photo courtesy of the *Atlanta Journal-Constitution.*

track for the Seminoles. Sanders left Florida State with 14 career interceptions. Sanders played on Super Bowl championship teams in San Francisco and Dallas. He also played in the World Series for the Atlanta Braves.

86. Pat Trammell, QB, Alabama: Trammell, who quarterbacked Bear Bryant's first national championship in 1961, is remembered for the way he lived and the way he died. In 1961 Trammell led the Crimson Tide to a 10–0 regular season and then closed out his career by scoring the only touchdown in a 10–3 win over Arkansas in the Sugar Bowl. Trammell later went to medical school and began his practice in Birmingham. In 1968 he was diagnosed with a brain tumor and died the following year at age 28.

87. Jake Scott, DB, Georgia: Scott was one of the best defensive backs and punt return specialists to ever play in the South. In 1968 Scott intercepted 10 passes, which tied an SEC record that stood until 1982. That same season Scott was Georgia's primary punt-return man, averaging 12.6 yards on 35 returns. Scott, who left Georgia after the 1968 season, went on to a successful pro career with the Miami Dolphins and the Washington Redskins. The four-time All-Pro was a member of the Dolphins undefeated Super Bowl champs of 1972.

88. George Mira, QB, Miami: A two-time All-American (1962, 1963), Mira was the first in a long line of great quarterbacks at Miami. Mira led the nation in total offense (2,318 yards) as a senior, despite playing on a 3–7 team. Mira finished fifth in the Heisman Trophy voting in 1962 and was a second-round draft choice of the San Francisco 49ers in 1964. He played with four different NFL teams as well as in the World Football League and the Canadian Football League before his retirement. His No. 10 jersey is one of only four that have been retired at Miami.

89. Cornelius Bennett, LB, Alabama: The winner of the 1986 Lombardi Award, Bennett was a three-time (1984–86) All-American for the Crimson Tide. Named the SEC Athlete of the Year in 1987, Bennett went on to a successful NFL career and played in four Super Bowls for the Buffalo Bills.

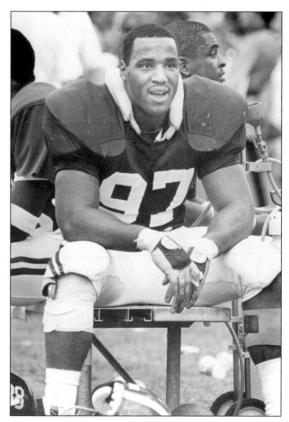

Alabama's Cornelius Bennett was a three-time All-American. Photo courtesy of the *Atlanta Journal-Constitution.*

90. Ray Beck, OG, Georgia Tech: One of the most dominating linemen in the history of Southern college football. Beck, who played from 1948 to 1951, played a major role in Georgia Tech's 11–0–1 season in 1951. As a senior he was an All-American and the SEC's Most Valuable Player. The native of Cedartown, Georgia, was inducted into the College Football Hall of Fame in 1997.

91. Fred Biletnikoff, WR, Florida State: Biletnikoff was Florida State's first consensus All-American in 1964 when he caught 57 passes. He went on to a successful pro career with the Oakland Raiders, playing in six Pro Bowls, and was named the MVP in Super Bowl XI. Biletnikoff was inducted into the Pro Football Hall of Fame in 1988 and the College Football Hall of Fame in 1991.

92. Don McCauley, RB, North Carolina: The Tar Heels have 24 backs to run for over 1,000 yards in a season. McCauley was the first and perhaps the best. He was the ACC Player of the Year as a junior and a senior and a consensus All-American in 1970. His 1,720 yards rushing in 1970 broke the NCAA record at the time, held by Southern California's O.J. Simpson. As a senior McCauley led the nation in all-purpose running. McCauley was a first-round pick by the Baltimore Colts in the 1971 NFL draft.

93. Jerry Butler, WR, Clemson: Butler was named first-team All-American in 1978, with 2,223 yards receiving. Along with quarterback Steve Fuller, he helped lead the Tigers to an 11–1 season. Butler went on to be a Buffalo Bills first-round draft choice and was the AFC Rookie of the Year in 1979.

94. Carl Hinkle, C, Vanderbilt: Hinkle was the strongest of the famed Vanderbilt Iron Men of 1937. Hinkle, who played all 60 minutes in seven of Vanderbilt's games that season, led the Commodores to a 7–2 record. He was the SEC's Most Valuable Player that season. Hinkle later attended West Point and became a highly decorated soldier in World War II. He was inducted into the College Football Hall of Fame in 1959.

95. Clarence "Ace" Parker, QB, Duke: From 1934 to 1936, Parker led coach Wallace Wade's Blue Devils to a combined record of 24–5. Parker was first-team All-America and All–Southern Conference that season. He played seven seasons of professional football with the Brooklyn Dodgers, Boston Yanks, and New York Yankees. A charter member of the Duke Athletic Hall of Fame, Parker was inducted into the College Football Hall of Fame in 1955.

96. Larry Morris, C/LB, Georgia Tech: A four-year starter (1951–54) during the most successful period in school history, Morris started as a true freshman on Georgia Tech's 11–0–1 team in 1951 and as a sophomore on the Yellow Jackets' 12–0 national championship team of 1952. A first-round draft choice of the Los Angeles Rams, Morris was the SEC Lineman of the Year in 1954. He was also named to the SEC Quarter-Century Team for 1950–74. Morris was inducted into the College Football Hall of Fame in 1992.

97. Ted Brown, RB, N.C. State: Brown wasn't big (5'11", 190 pounds), but he was able to punch through ACC defenses for three 1,000-yard seasons and 4,602 career rushing yards. A consensus

All-American as a senior in 1978, Brown was the NCAA's fourth all-time leading rusher at the end of his college career. Brown went on to play eight years with the Minnesota Vikings.

98. George McAfee, QB, Duke: McAfee quarterbacked the Blue Devils to a 24–4–1 record in three seasons (1937–39), which included an appearance in the 1939 Rose Bowl. McAfee's 1938 team, known as the Iron Dukes, went undefeated and unscored upon during the regular season before losing to Southern California 7–3 in the Rose Bowl. McAfee was a first-round draft choice of the Philadelphia Eagles, who immediately traded him to the Chicago Bears in 1940, where he played both offense and defense, posting 25 career interceptions. He is a member of both the Pro Football and College Football Halls of Fame.

99. Chuck Dicus, WR, Arkansas: A speedy wide receiver who was a generation ahead of his time, Dicus was a three-year All–Southwest Conference pick (1968–70) and an All-American in 1969

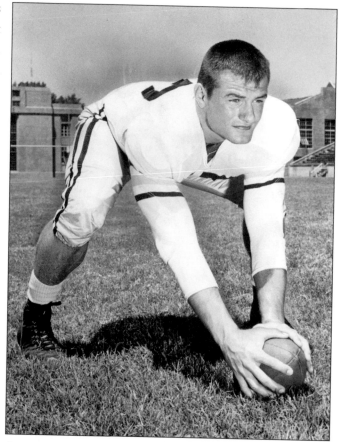

Larry Morris was an All-American linebacker in 1953. Photo courtesy of the *Atlanta Journal-Constitution.*

and 1970. Dicus, who had 118 career catches, had a reputation for playing well in big games. He led the Razorbacks to a 16–2 win over Georgia in the 1969 Sugar Bowl with 12 catches for 169 yards. In the famous No. 1-versus-No. 2 game against Texas in 1969, Dicus caught nine passes for 146 yards and had a touchdown pass called back. Dicus was inducted into the College Football Hall of Fame in 1999.

100. Ron Sellers, WR, Florida State: With all the great receivers that have played at Florida State, Sellers still remains the most prolific. From 1966 to 1968 Sellers caught 212 passes for 3,598 yards, an average of 119.9 yards per game. He had 70 catches for 1,228 yards as a junior and 86 receptions for 1,496 yards as a senior. Sellers was inducted into the College Football Hall of Fame in 1988.

50 HONORABLE MENTIONS

1. Bill Armstrong, DB, Wake Forest (1973–76)
2. Charles Alexander, RB, LSU (1975–78)
3. Bill Banker, HB, Tulane (1927–29)
4. Maxie Baughan, C/LB, Georgia Tech (1957–59)
5. Bobby Bryant, DB, South Carolina (1964–66)
6. Don Bosseler, FB, Miami (1953–56)
7. Hunter Carpenter, HB, North Carolina/Virginia Tech (1900–05)
8. Jack Cloud, FB, William & Mary (1946–49)
9. Josh Cody, T, Vanderbilt (1914–19)
10. Fred Crawford, T, Duke (1931–33)
11. Carroll Dale, WR, Virginia Tech (1956–59)
12. Jerry Dalrymple, E, Tulane (1929–31)
13. Bobby Davis, T, Georgia Tech (1944–47)
14. Al DeRogatis, C/T, Duke (1945–48)
15. Joe Delaney, RB, Northwestern State (Louisiana) (1977–80)
16. Bill Fincher, E/T, Georgia Tech (1916–20)
17. Buck Flowers, HB, Davidson/Georgia Tech (1916–20)
18. William Fuller, DT, North Carolina (1980–83)
19. Roman Gabriel, QB, North Carolina State (1959–61)
20. Bill George, QB, Wake Forest (1948–51)
21. Dan Hill, C, Duke (1936–38)
22. Sonny Jurgensen, QB, Duke (1954–56)
23. Gary "Big Hands" Johnson, DT, Grambling (1971–74)
24. Frank Juhan, C, Sewanee (1908–10)
25. Les Lautenschlaeger, QB, Tulane (1922–25)
26. Bob Matheson, LB, Duke (1964–66)
27 Jack McDowall, HB, N.C. State (1925–27)
28. Bob Pellegrini, C, Maryland (1953–55)
29. Henry Phillips, C, Sewanee (1900–05)
30. Eddie Price, FB, Tulane (1946–49)
31. Peter Pund, C, Georgia Tech (1926–28)
32. Buster Ramsey, G, William & Mary (1939–42)
33. Gary Reasons, LB, Northwestern State (1980–83)
34. Jack Reynolds, LB, Tennessee (1967–69)

35. Randy Rhino, DB, Georgia Tech (1972–74)
36. Wear Schoonover, E, Arkansas (1927–29)
37. Tom Scott, E, Virginia (1950–52)
38. Glenn Dorsey, DT, LSU (2004–07)
39. Monk Simons, RB, Tulane (1932–34)
40. Riley Smith, QB/FB, Alabama (1933–35)
41. Norm Snead, QB, Wake Forest (1958–60)
42. Bill Spears, QB, Vanderbilt (1925–27)
43. Ken Stabler, QB, Alabama (1965–67)
44. Joe Steffy, G, Tennessee (1944–47)
45. Everett Strupper, HB, Georgia Tech (1915–17)
46. Lynn Bomar, E, Vanderbilt (1921–24)
47. Eric Tipton, HB, Duke (1936–38)
48. Y.A. Tittle, QB, LSU (1944–47)
49. Don Whitmire, T, Alabama (1941–42)
50. Jim Youngblood, LB, Tennessee Tech (1969–72)

PLAYERS BY AWARDS

OUTLAND TROPHY

The Outland honors the best interior lineman in the nation and was first presented in 1946 by the Football Writers Association of America. The award is named for its benefactor, Dr. John H. Outland. The Southern winners are:

Bob Gain, Kentucky, 1950
Dick Modzelewski, Maryland, 1952
Bill Brooks, Arkansas, 1954
Zeke Smith, Auburn, 1958
Mike McGee, Duke, 1959
Steve DeLong, Tennessee, 1964
Loyd Phillips, Arkansas, 1966
Bill Stanfill, Georgia, 1968
Randy White, Maryland, 1974
Jim Ritcher, N.C. State, 1979

Zeke Smith with coach Shug Jordan. Photo courtesy of the *Atlanta Journal-Constitution.*

Bruce Smith, Virginia Tech, 1984
Tracy Rocker, Auburn, 1988
Russell Maryland, Miami, 1990
Chris Samuels, Alabama, 1999
John Henderson, Tennessee, 2000
Bryant McKinnie, Miami, 2001
Glenn Dorsey, LSU, 2007

MAXWELL AWARD

This award goes to the nation's outstanding football player and has been presented since 1937 by the Maxwell Memorial Football Club of Philadelphia. The award is named after Robert "Tiny" Maxwell, a Philadelphia native who played at the University of Chicago at the turn of the century. The Southern winners are:

Bill Dudley, Virginia, 1941
Charley Trippi, Georgia, 1946
Herschel Walker, Georgia, 1982
Vinny Testaverde, Miami, 1986
Gino Torretta, Miami, 1992
Charlie Ward, Florida State, 1993
Danny Wuerffel, Florida, 1996
Peyton Manning, Tennessee, 1997
Ken Dorsey, Miami, 2001
Eli Manning, Ole Miss, 2003
Tim Tebow, Florida, 2007

WALTER CAMP AWARD

The Walter Camp Award goes to the nation's outstanding football player and was first presented in 1967 by the Walter Camp Football Foundation. The award is based on balloting by major college coaches and sports information directors and is named after the legendary coach Walter Camp, one of the innovators of American football. The Southern winners are:

Pat Sullivan, Auburn, 1971
Herschel Walker, Georgia, 1982
Bo Jackson, Auburn, 1985
Vinny Testaverde, Miami, 1986
Gino Torretta, Miami, 1992

Charlie Ward, Florida State, 1993

Danny Wuerffel, Florida, 1996

Darren McFadden, Arkansas, 2007

LOMBARDI AWARD

The Lombardi Award is given to the outstanding lineman or linebacker of the year. The Lombardi Award is presented in the name of Vince Lombardi, the Green Bay Packers' Hall of Fame coach. Since 1970 the Rotary Club of Houston has presented the Lombardi Award. The Southern winners are:

Randy White, Maryland, 1974

Cornelius Bennett, Alabama, 1986

Tracy Rocker, Auburn, 1988

Marvin Jones, Florida State, 1992

Warren Sapp, Miami, 1994

Corey Moore, Virginia Tech, 1999

Jamal Reynolds, Florida State, 2000

Julius Peppers, North Carolina, 2001

David Pollack, Georgia, 2004

Glenn Dorsey, LSU, 2007

BUTKUS AWARD

The Butkus Award was first presented in 1985 by the Downtown Athletic Club of Orlando to the nation's best linebacker. The award is named after Dick Butkus, a two-time All-American from Illinois and a six-time All-Pro with the Chicago Bears. The Southern winners are:

Paul McGowan, Florida State, 1987

Derrick Thomas, Alabama, 1988

Marvin Jones, Florida State, 1992

Dan Morgan, Miami, 2000

E.J. Henderson, Maryland, 2002

Patrick Willis, Mississippi, 2006

JIM THORPE AWARD

The Jim Thorpe Award was first presented in 1986 to honor the nation's best defensive back by the Jim Thorpe Athletic Club of Oklahoma City. The award is named after Olympic champion Jim Thorpe, a two-time All-America halfback at Carlisle. The Southern winners are:

Bennie Blades, Miami, 1987

Deion Sanders, Florida State, 1988
Terrell Buckley, Florida State, 1991
Antonio Langham, Alabama, 1993
Lawrence Wright, Florida, 1996
Carlos Rogers, Auburn, 2004

DAVEY O'BRIEN AWARD

The Davey O'Brien award was first presented in 1977 to the outstanding player in the Southwest. Since 1981 the award has gone to the nation's best quarterback. It is presented by the Davey O'Brien Education and Charitable Trust of Fort Worth, Texas. It is named after the legendary quarterback from Texas Christian. The Southern winners are:

Vinny Testaverde, Miami, 1986
Gino Torretta, Miami, 1992
Charlie Ward, Florida State, 1993
Danny Wuerffel, Florida, 1995, 1996
Peyton Manning, Tennessee, 1997
Joe Hamilton, Georgia Tech, 1999
Chris Weinke, Florida State, 2000
Tim Tebow, Florida, 2007

LOU GROZA AWARD

Since 1992 this award has been presented to the nation's best place-kicker. The award is sponsored by the Palm Beach County Sports Authority in conjunction with the Orange Bowl committee. It is named after the NFL Hall of Fame place-kicker. The Southern winners are:

Joe Allison, Memphis, 1992
Judd Davis, Florida, 1993
Marc Primanti, N.C. State, 1996
Sebastian Janikowski, Florida State, 1998, 1999
Seth Marler, Tulane, 2001
Jonathan Nichols, Ole Miss, 2003
Art Carmody, Louisville, 2006

DOAK WALKER AWARD

Since 1990, this award has been presented to the nation's best running back. It is sponsored by the GTE/Southern Methodist Athletic Forum in Dallas, Texas. It is named after the three-time All-American from SMU. The Southern winners are:

Garrison Hearst, Georgia, 1992

Darren McFadden, Arkansas, 2006, 2007

BRONKO NAGURSKI TROPHY

Since 1993 this award has been presented by the Football Writers Association of America and the Charlotte (North Carolina) Touchdown Club. It goes to the nation's best defensive player and is named after the former All-American tackle and running back at Minnesota. The Southern winners are:

Warren Sapp, Miami, 1994

Champ Bailey, Georgia, 1998

Corey Moore, Virginia Tech, 1999

Dan Morgan, Miami, 2000

Elvis Dumervil, Louisville, 2005

Glenn Dorsey, LSU, 2007

FRED BILETNIKOFF AWARD

Since 1994 this award has gone to college football's best wide receiver. The award is presented each season by the Quarterback Club of Tallahassee and is named after the former Florida State All-American who went on to become an All-Pro with the Oakland Raiders. The Southern winners are:

Troy Edwards, Louisiana Tech, 1998

Josh Reed, LSU, 2001

Calvin Johnson, Georgia Tech, 2006

CHAPTER 4

THE COACHES

If the South looks upon its college football players as Saturday's warriors, it only follows that the men who coach the game are treated with the respect and deference accorded great generals. The men who shaped the great Southern game came from many different walks of life, but all had some things in common: an unshakable belief in themselves and their ability to do the job; a strong commitment to excellence, which they also demanded of those around them; and an utter contempt for losing and for those who were willing to tolerate it in any form.

For those who won, the rewards were significant. In the South, the successful college football coach was as powerful as any politician or university president—in some cases, even more powerful.

Over the past 100 years, the job of the Southern college football coach has evolved from a chore once handled by college professors in their free time to today's high-profile, demanding—and rewarding—career.

When Vince Dooley became the head coach at Georgia in 1964, his base pay was $12,500 per year. In January 2007 Alabama signed its new coach, Nick Saban, to an eight-year contract worth $32 million.

"But," said Dooley, who retired after the 1988 season, "to whom much is given, much is also expected. And that is particularly true in coaching."

Here are some of the legendary coaches who put passion into Southern Fried Football.

ROBERT C. "BOBBY" BOWDEN
SAMFORD, WEST VIRGINIA, FLORIDA STATE
1959–62, 1970–Present

In 1943 13-year-old Bobby Bowden was stricken by rheumatic fever, and with it came one of the toughest ordeals a teenager could face: six months of complete bed rest followed by a year's confinement in order to completely recover.

"There was no television, no video games, no computer," Bowden said. "Just me and my radio."

On the radio Bowden would listen to what he would later call "a play-by-play" of World War II. In his mind the young Bowden envisioned war battles and the strategies of the great generals who fought them.

Florida State's Bobby Bowden joined the 300-win club with a 12–0 national championship team in 1999. Photo courtesy of the *Atlanta Journal-Constitution*.

The interest in strategy formed in those months of confinement created the foundation that made Bowden one of the most successful coaches in college football history.

The 2008 season will be Bowden's 33rd at Florida State University and his 43rd as a head football coach. He is one of only five NCAA Division I-A coaches to win 300 games. On that short list, only Bowden and Penn State's Joe Paterno are still active.

A native of Birmingham, Alabama, Bowden grew up in the shadow of historic Legion Field and fulfilled a lifetime dream when he played as a freshman quarterback for the University of Alabama. But Bowden found something he loved more than Alabama football, and that was the lovely Ann Estock, his childhood sweetheart. So after just one semester at Alabama, Bowden came back to Birmingham, married Ann, and transferred to Howard College, now Samford University.

He was only 29 years old when he became head coach at Samford, where he stayed for four seasons. After serving as an assistant coach at Florida State and West Virginia, Bowden became the head coach at West Virginia in 1970. In 1976 Bowden took on the challenge of building a program at Florida State.

At Florida State Bowden inherited a program that had won just four games over the previous three seasons, including an 0–11 record in 1973.

Bowden said that he never imagined staying at Florida State for the long haul.

"I figured we would build the program up for a few years and then a bigger opportunity would come along," he said.

Bowden turned Florida State into the job of a lifetime.

In just his second year, Florida State won 10 games. In his fourth year, the Seminoles were 11–1 and earned a trip to the Orange Bowl.

In 1987 Bowden's dream job at the University of Alabama opened up, and he was very tempted to go back home and walk the same sideline where his hero, Bear Bryant, had won so many games.

"But it didn't work out," Bowden said. "Guess I was meant to stay here."

Florida State is certainly glad Bowden stayed. That same year, 1987, Bowden's teams began one of the most impressive strings of success in the history of college football. For 14 consecutive seasons Florida State posted 10 wins or more and finished in the final top five of the Associated Press poll.

For years Bowden kept an empty picture frame in his office that was reserved for his first perfect team. Bowden filled that frame in 1999. He joined the 300-win club on October 23 by beating Clemson, which was coached by his son, Tommy. The Seminoles went on to an 11–0 regular season, a No. 1 national ranking, and then beat No. 2 Virginia Tech 46–29 in the Sugar Bowl to give Bowden his second national championship.

On October 25, 2003, Florida State beat Wake Forest 48–24 to give Bowden his 339th career victory. That put him ahead of Paterno and made Bowden Division I-A's all-time winner. He enters the 2008 season with 373 career victories, just one ahead of Paterno.

Just about every honor that can come to a college football coach has already been bestowed on Bowden. In 2004 the field at Florida State's Doak Campbell Stadium was officially named Bobby Bowden Field. In December 2006, the College Football Hall of Fame waved its normal three-year waiting period after retirement and inducted Bowden.

The Fellowship of Christian Athletes honors a football player each year for his success on the field, in the classroom, and in his community with an award named after Bobby Bowden.

Bowden, who will turn 79 on November 8, 2008, shows no signs of slowing down. Since that impressive 14-year run ended in 2000, Bowden's teams have not been quite as successful. His 2006 and 2007 teams both went 7–6. But Bowden is determined to get the Seminoles back on top before he steps down for good.

He says he will coach as long as his health holds out.

"After you retire, there's only one big event left," said Bowden. "And I ain't ready for that."

School	Years	Record
Samford	1959–62	31–6–0
West Virginia	1970–75	42–26–0
Florida State	1976–Present	300–87–4
Total	(through 2007)	373–119–4

ACC championships (12): 1992, 1993, 1994, 1995, 1996, 1997, 1998, 1999, 2000, 2002, 2003, 2005

National championships (2): 1993, 1999

Alabama legend Paul "Bear" Bryant announces his retirement on December 15, 1982. Photo courtesy of the Atlanta Journal-Constitution.

PAUL "BEAR" BRYANT

Maryland, Kentucky, Texas A&M, Alabama
1945–1982

The end of the 1957 season represented one of the lowest points in the University of Alabama's proud football history. The Crimson Tide finished their fourth straight losing season with an embarrassing 40–0 loss to Auburn, their hated rival. Then, to add insult to injury, Auburn was declared national champions.

The tenure of coach J.B. "Ears" Whitworth, whose teams were 4–24–2 in three seasons, had been a disaster. Something had to be done.

That something happened three days after the loss to Auburn when Paul W. Bryant, an end on Alabama's 1934 Rose Bowl team, agreed to leave Texas A&M and come back to Tuscaloosa as head coach of the Crimson Tide.

Bryant had actually agreed to take the job a month before in secret meetings with key Alabama officials. Bryant left Texas A&M with seven years remaining on his contract. When asked why he would leave a lucrative job to take over a program in trouble, Bryant simply said: "Mama called."

Over the next 25 years at Alabama, Bryant dominated Southern college football like no man before or since, posting 232 wins and only 46 losses, 13 Southeastern Conference championships, 24 straight bowl games, and six national championships.

But the numbers don't reveal the true size of the shadow that Bear Bryant cast over the game for an entire generation. To this day, when people talk about Bryant, they usually spend more time praising the man than the football coach.

"He was the most impressive man I've ever been close to," said the late John Forney, Alabama's radio broadcaster from 1953 to 1983. "When he walked into a room a hush came over it."

ESPN broadcaster Ron Franklin agrees: "When he walked in a room, it was like his presence got their 30 seconds before he did. There was just something really special about him."

Bryant's philosophy of coaching was simple: he was willing to pay the price to win and demanded that those around him—players, coaches, managers, and university presidents—do the same. He was relentless, but he never pushed anybody harder than he pushed himself.

"Coach Bryant could get more out of his people than anybody I have ever known," says Danny Ford, who played for Bryant from 1967 to 1969 and later became head coach at Clemson and Arkansas. "He expected you to win and you expected to win for him."

Bryant's knack for winning inspired a grudging respect among his fellow coaches. Jake Gaither, the Hall of Fame coach from Florida A&M, paid Bryant the ultimate compliment when he said, "He could take his'n and beat your'n, and take your'n and beat his'n."

One of 12 children, Bryant grew up poor on a farm in Moro Bottom, Arkansas. His nickname came at age 14 when he wrestled a bear on stage in Fordyce, Arkansas. He grappled with the bear for only a few minutes, but the nickname stuck with him for a lifetime.

On November 28, 1981, Bear Bryant won his 315th game, breaking the major college record of 314 wins set by Amos Alonzo Stagg. Stagg needed 57 years to set the record. Bryant did it in just 37 years.

Bear Bryant coached one more season before announcing his retirement. On December 29, 1982, he coached his last game, a 21–15 win over Illinois in the Liberty Bowl.

Toward the end of his career, Bryant was constantly asked when he would retire, and he usually uttered the words that will live forever: "Retire? Hell, I'd probably croak in a week!"

His words were prophetic. On January 26, 1983, just 42 days after he announced his retirement from coaching, Bear Bryant died at age 69.

School	Years	Record
Maryland	1945	6–2–1
Kentucky	1946–53	60–23–5
Texas A&M	1954–57	25–14–2
Alabama	1958–82	232–46–9
Total	38 years	323–85–17

SEC championships (14): 1950, 1961, 1964, 1965, 1966, 1971, 1972, 1973, 1974, 1975, 1977, 1978, 1979, 1981

National championships (6): 1961, 1964, 1965, 1973, 1978, 1979

Georgia Tech legend Bobby Dodd. Photo courtesy of the *Atlanta Journal-Constitution.*

ROBERT LEE "BOBBY" DODD

GEORGIA TECH

1945–66

General Robert R. Neyland, Tennessee's legendary coach, knew that Bobby Dodd, his All-America quarterback, was going to be a good coach someday. Neyland assumed it would be at Tennessee.

But Dodd broke Neyland's heart and changed a lot of college football history in 1931 when he rejected offers from Tennessee and Duke and went to Georgia Tech as an assistant to Bill Alexander.

He never left. Bobby Dodd remained at Georgia Tech as an assistant coach (1931–44), head coach (1945–66), athletics director (1950–76), and a consultant to the school's alumni association until his death on June 21, 1988, at age 79.

In 22 seasons as a head coach, Dodd won 165 games, two SEC championships, and one national championship (1952). From 1951 to 1953 his teams put together a 31-game winning streak.

But Dodd not only won games, he also won the hearts and minds of several generations of Georgia Tech players and fans.

"He was one of the smartest, most innovative people I have ever met," said the late Kim King, who was the quarterback on Dodd's last team in 1966. "He was a man truly ahead of his time."

The word most often used to describe Dodd was *unconventional.* While Dodd was a protégé of Neyland, his approach to the game was very different from the General's. Neyland believed in long, hard practices in order to drill fundamentals into his players. Dodd believed practice should be fun and should merely sharpen the skills already possessed by the players.

"Coach Dodd believed that you should never leave your best effort out on the practice field," said the late Ray Beck, who played for Dodd from 1949 to 1951 and is a member of the College Football Hall of Fame.

Dodd's approach to practice was particularly unconventional when he took his team to the 1947 Orange Bowl.

"As soon as we got to Miami, we assembled at the hotel and he took us to the beach to go swimming," said Red Patton, who played at Georgia Tech from 1947 to 1950. "We beat Kansas [20–14] and everyone was happy."

Dodd was also unconventional once the game started. Instead of pacing the sideline like other coaches, he would sit at one end of the field in a lawn chair and direct the game, as if he were enjoying a day at the beach.

Dodd retired as Georgia Tech's head coach after the Orange Bowl on January 2, 1967. In 1993, he was inducted as a coach into the College Football Hall of Fame. He is one of only three men (along with Amos Alonzo Stagg and Tennessee's Bowden Wyatt) to reach the Hall of Fame as both a player and a coach.

School	Years	Record
Georgia Tech	1945–66	165–64–8

SEC championships (2): 1951, 1952
National championships (1): 1952

MIKE DONAHUE
AUBURN, LSU
1904–27

Three men are given the lion's share of the credit for bringing college football from the North and making it an institution in the South. They are John Heisman (Auburn, Clemson, Georgia Tech), Dan McGugin (Vanderbilt), and Mike Donahue, who won 99 games at Auburn from 1904 to 1922.

Donahue played quarterback for the great Walter Camp at Yale. Tiny in size (5'4") but huge in intellect, Donahue demanded that his players not only think hard but hit hard as well.

According to Wayne Hester's anthology on Auburn football, *Where Tradition Began*, Donahue was one of the most versatile faculty members in the history of the university. Not only did he coach football, but he also was the school's first basketball coach. He also coached baseball, track, and soccer. In his free time he taught classes in English, math, history, and Latin.

Mike Donahue, Auburn's Hall of Fame coach. Photo courtesy of Auburn SID.

Donahue took a year off from coaching football in 1907 to concentrate on his duties as Auburn's athletics director. But he couldn't stay away from the game, and he returned as head coach for the 1908 season. He subsequently led Auburn to some of its greatest successes on the football field.

In a stretch that lasted from 1913 to 1915, Donahue's teams went 23 straight games without a loss and outscored their opponents 600–13.

After the 1922 season, Donahue decided to leave Auburn and become head coach at LSU, where he was not as successful. He stepped down as head coach after five seasons to become a golf professional at a local country club.

Donahue got back into coaching at Spring Hill College in Mobile, Alabama, and then returned to LSU in 1937 as director of intramurals.

In 1951 Donahue was inducted into the College Football Hall of Fame. He died in 1958 at age 84.

School	Years	Record
Auburn	1904–06, 1908–22	99–35–5
LSU	1923–27	23–19–3
Total	23 seasons	122–54–8

Georgia coach Vince Dooley (1964–88) won 201 games and six SEC titles. Photo courtesy of the Atlanta Journal-Constitution.

VINCE DOOLEY
GEORGIA
1964–88

November 22, 1963, the day President John F. Kennedy was assassinated in Dallas, is a date that lives in infamy. It is doubly remembered in Georgia, thanks to another event that occurred on that same day and changed the course of University of Georgia football history.

Just hours before those terrible shots rang out in Texas, Joel Eaves, the head basketball coach at Auburn, agreed to become the next athletics director at Georgia. On December 4, Eaves made his first major decision by hiring Vince Dooley as the Bulldogs' new head football coach.

It was not a popular choice with the Georgia alumni, who wanted a big-name coach to bring Georgia out of its football doldrums. Georgia's fans had suffered through three straight losing seasons under coach Johnny Griffith, who replaced future Hall of Fame member Wally Butts after the 1960 season. Griffith was fired with a 10–16–4 record.

Eaves, always known for an independent streak, went against the alumni and hired Dooley, a 31-year-old assistant to Auburn coach Shug Jordan. Dooley had played football and basketball at Auburn and had served a stint in the Marine Corps before returning to Auburn to begin his coaching apprenticeship.

"I was convinced he had all the tools it took to be a head coach," Eaves would say later. "And he wouldn't panic."

So, for a salary of $12,500 per year, Dooley became Georgia's new head football coach. Twenty-five years later he retired with 201 victories, six SEC championships, and one national championship.

There was no mystery to Dooley, no fancy slogans or secrets to success. Dooley believed in organization. He believed in discipline. And most of all he believed in preparation.

"If you've haven't done the preparation on Monday through Friday, there's nothing magical you can do on Saturday to get your team ready to play the game," Dooley often said. "Teams are most confident when they know they are prepared."

Dooley's greatest success came in the four seasons from 1980 to 1983 when his teams won 43 games and lost only four, earned three SEC championships, and won a national championship in 1980.

In 1988, after a 9–3 season, Dooley retired as head football coach to become Georgia's full-time athletics director. Under his guidance Georgia became one of the country's most successful college athletics programs. In the 1998–99 academic year Georgia won four national championships and finished second to Stanford as the nation's best athletics program.

Only Alabama's Bear Bryant won more SEC championships than Dooley's six.

As the 2008 season approaches, Dooley is one of only 18 Division I-A coaches to record more than 200 career victories. In 25 years Dooley had only one losing season (1977).

Dooley was inducted into the College Football Hall of Fame in December of 1994. He retired as Georgia's athletics director on June 30, 2004, ending a 41-year relationship with the school.

The Dooley legacy continues with his youngest son, Derek, who is the head coach and athletics director at Louisiana Tech.

School	Years	Record
Georgia	1964–88	201–77–10

SEC championships (6): 1966, 1968, 1976, 1980, 1981, 1982
National championships (1): 1980

John Heisman, the coach for whom the Heisman Trophy is named. Photo courtesy of the *Atlanta Journal-Constitution.*

JOHN HEISMAN
AUBURN, CLEMSON, GEORGIA TECH
1895–1919

Had John Heisman's life gone according to plan, he never would have been a coach and never would have had college football's highest honor named after him. But fate, in the form of an accident, stepped in and changed everything.

Heisman, the son of a German immigrant, fell in love with football as a Brown University undergraduate. His love for the sport grew at the University of Pennsylvania, where he played while earning his law degree.

While playing for Penn in the old Madison Square Garden, Heisman's eyes were injured by the Garden's galvanic lighting system. Doctors prescribed a two-year rest for his eyes, which required him to put his law career on hold. In the interim, Heisman decided to try coaching.

His decision changed the face of college football in the South. Heisman coached at eight different colleges, but forged his legend at Auburn (1895–99), Clemson (1900–03), and Georgia Tech (1904–19). He posted winning records at all three stops before returning to Penn in 1919.

A perfectionist who was both rigid and innovative, Heisman could not stand mistakes, especially fumbles. He would often stand holding a football under his arm and say: "Better to have died as a small boy, than to fumble this football."

The contradictions in Heisman's personality were legendary. While he played the role of the tough, autocratic football coach on the field, he fancied himself to be an actor and would wander out at night to get ice cream for his pet poodle, Woo. And even though he portrayed himself to be above common human emotion, it was a grudge that led him to set up the most humiliating defeat ever devised for an opponent.

Heisman also coached baseball at Georgia Tech, and in the spring of 1916, Tech lost 22–0 to a team of professionals pretending to be players from Cumberland College. That fall Heisman lured the Cumberland football team to Atlanta with an all-expenses-paid trip plus $500. Georgia Tech won the game 222–0.

Heisman wanted to finish his coaching career at Georgia Tech. But during a divorce settlement in 1919, he agreed not to live in the same city as his wife, Evelyn. She chose Atlanta, and Heisman went back to Pennsylvania.

Heisman retired from coaching in 1926 to become the director of athletics for the Downtown Athletic Club in New York. He died on October 3, 1936. Two months later the DAC awarded its first Heisman Trophy, which today still goes to the nation's most outstanding college football player.

School	Years	Record
Auburn	1895–99	12–4–2
Clemson	1900–03	19–3–2
Georgia Tech	1904–19	102–29–7
Total	24 seasons	133–36–11

National championships (1): 1917

RALPH "SHUG" JORDAN

AUBURN

1951–75

In 1947 Jordan's one goal in life was to return to his alma mater as head football coach. When Auburn passed him over in favor of Earl Brown, a former All-American at Notre Dame, Jordan did nothing to hide his feelings.

"If they don't think an Auburn man can do the job, they ought to close the joint down," he said.

Brown won only three games in three seasons at Auburn. The 1950 team, Brown's last, was 0–10.

In 1951 the Auburn trustees had the good sense to finally hire Jordan, but the proud coach, who still held a grudge because he had not been chosen at first, had to be goaded into formally applying for the job.

In the rough-and-tumble world of college football coaches, Jordan was known as a Southern gentleman throughout his 25 years at Auburn. But no one ever accused Jordan of being "soft." Whenever Jordan felt he or his players were not receiving their proper due, he would rise up with righteous indignation, like a fire-breathing minister admonishing his flock for their sins.

Auburn Hall of Fame coach Ralph "Shug" Jordan. Photo courtesy of the *Atlanta Journal-Constitution.*

In November 1971 Auburn quarterback Pat Sullivan all but locked up the Heisman Trophy with an unforgettable performance against Georgia when he completed 14 of 24 passes for 248 yards and four touchdowns. After the game a reporter had the bad judgment to suggest that despite his efforts that day, Sullivan still might not receive college football's highest award.

"Maybe not," bellowed Jordan, "But if someone else does get it, I'll bet he's Christ reincarnated!"

Jordan, a deeply religious man, then regained his composure.

"Now I'll be up all night saying Hail Marys. Let's just say if someone else gets it, he'll have to be...uh...magnificent."

Sullivan did go on to win the Heisman Trophy, Auburn's first.

In *When Tradition Began*, a history of Auburn football published by the Birmingham News, author Wayne Hester recalls Jordan's final years leading up to his 1975 retirement. Opposing recruiters were spreading word that his health was failing. Some of that talk was coming from Alabama, Auburn's hated rival, where coach Bear Bryant was enjoying one of the most successful decades in college football history. Tired of the talk, Jordan, according to Hester, took a not-so-veiled shot at his counterpart across the state. Jordan said, "At least I don't climb up in a four-story tower and holler through a bullhorn like a plantation owner working his slaves."

So while Shug Jordan struck a grandfatherly pose in public, he would never back away from anybody once he stepped into the fire of competition.

"Coach Jordan was a true gentleman, but he had a mean, cold streak to do what he had to do," said Liston Eddins, who played defensive end from 1973 to 1975.

Jordan's teams won 176 games and produced 20 All-Americans. His 1957 team went undefeated and won the national championship. In fact, it was a 40–0 beating of Alabama in the finale of the 1957 season that forced the Crimson Tide to hire Bryant, who would torment Auburn (and the rest of the SEC) for the next 25 years.

In April 1975 Jordan decided that his 25th season at Auburn would be his last. He served on the Auburn University Board of Trustees until his death in July 1980. In 1982 Jordan was inducted into the College Football Hall of Fame.

His career at Auburn, and his life, can be summed up in what he called "My Seven *D*s of Success:"

1. Discipline
2. Desire to Excel
3. Determination
4. Dedication
5. Dependability

6. Desperation

7. Damn It Anyway

School	Years	Record
Auburn	1951–75	176–83–6

SEC championships (1): 1957
National championships (1): 1957

DAN MCGUGIN

VANDERBILT

1904–17, 1919–34

The most successful period in Vanderbilt's football history was three minutes away from never happening. That's how close Dan McGugin came to taking another job in 1904.

Vanderbilt had asked Fielding Yost of Michigan for help in finding a new football coach. Yost, in turn, contacted McGugin, one of his brightest players and a recent graduate of the Michigan law school.

McGugin wrote Vanderbilt and expressed his interest in the job but did not receive an immediate reply. In the interim McGugin received a telegram from Western Reserve University in Cleveland offering him the head coaching job for $1,000 a year and asking for an immediate reply. With no response from Vanderbilt, McGugin wired back and accepted Western Reserve's offer.

When McGugin returned to his room on campus, there was a telegram from Vanderbilt offering him a job at $850 a year. McGugin really wanted to go south and decided that if he could stop the telegram to Western Reserve, he would take Vanderbilt's offer. If not, he would go to Ohio.

Vanderbilt's Dan McGugin won 197 games in 30 years as coach. Photo courtesy of Vanderbilt SID.

McGugin ran to the telegraph office and stopped the message just three minutes before it was scheduled to be delivered.

It turned out to be the most important three minutes in Vanderbilt football history. Over the next 31 years McGugin and Vanderbilt dominated Southern college football, winning 197 of 271 games.

McGugin had a number of traits that made him a good football coach. His strongest was an uncanny ability to inspire his players.

Though McGugin was a graduate of the Michigan law school, he would not hesitate to invoke Southern pride as a motivational tool, particularly when his teams faced opposition from the North. He did it against Yale in 1910 (see introduction) and again when Vanderbilt tied Michigan 0–0 in 1922. Michigan's Yost, who had by then become McGugin's brother-in-law, was less than impressed.

"That McGugin and his phony accent," Yost said. "Before he came to Vanderbilt he'd never been farther South than Toledo."

McGugin's 30 Vanderbilt teams not only won 72.6 percent of their games but also outscored their opponents by a whopping 6,662 to 1,668, an average margin of victory of 18.4 points.

Citing health problems, McGugin ended his coaching career after the 1934 season. He died in 1936 at age 56. In 1951 he was inducted into the College Football Hall of Fame.

School	Years	Record
Vanderbilt	1904–34*	197–55–19

*McGugin did not coach the 1918 season while serving in World War I, where he achieved the rank of lieutenant colonel.

GENERAL ROBERT R. NEYLAND

TENNESSEE
1926–34, 1936–40, 1946–52

It was the University of Tennessee's inability to beat state rival Vanderbilt and coach Dan McGugin that caused school officials to take a step that would forever change the school's football history. In 1926, after losing 18 of its last 22 games against Vanderbilt, Tennessee hired then-Captain Robert R. Neyland as its head coach. He was only 34.

Neyland took the discipline and strategy he learned in the military and brought it to the football field, and he got great results. Over the next 26 years, with two breaks for active military service, Neyland won 173 games while losing only 31 as the head coach of the Volunteers.

Neyland won with a simple formula. He firmly believed that great defense, a sound kicking game, and the elimination of mistakes were the keys to victory. He also believed that constant repetition in practice was the only way to make a football team operate like a well-oiled machine on game day.

He applied a clearly defined set of principles to the game of football. One of the first principles was "The head coach must remain a little aloof from the players and, to a certain extent, from the coaches."

Neyland believed such detachment was necessary to maintain discipline. There was never any doubt that Neyland saw the Tennessee football team as his army and himself as the general in command.

"The General was always in complete control," says John Michels, who played for Neyland from 1949 to 1952. "He never got excited. He was highly organized and a great disciplinarian."

"The General was not the easiest guy to work with on Monday through Friday, but on Saturday he was a fatherly figure," said Herky Payne (1949–51). "On Saturday he was a warm man who gave you a lot of confidence."

Tennessee coach Robert Neyland in 1947. Photo courtesy of the *Atlanta Journal-Constitution.*

That confidence, Neyland believed, came from thorough preparation, not from emotional speeches in the locker room before the game.

"Proper mental attitude on game day stems almost entirely from attitudes built up over a considerable period of time," Neyland once wrote. "Pregame harangues, as a rule, do more harm than good. Inspiration at zero hour is a poor thing to rely on."

Neyland was not, however, above a little psychological gamesmanship. Before the 1928 game with Tennessee, he approached Alabama coach Wallace Wade. Neyland asked if Wade would mind shortening the second half if his team, a decided underdog, fell too far behind. Neyland said he didn't want his players to get too discouraged in defeat.

Wade smiled and said he would shorten the game if necessary.

Tennessee ran the opening kickoff back for a touchdown and upset Alabama 15–13.

In 1929, the week before the big game with Vanderbilt, Neyland sent 10 of his starting players to scout the Commodores against Georgia Tech in Nashville. Problem was, Tennessee had a game that same day against Carson-Newman. Neyland didn't care. He sent his starters to watch Vanderbilt and the Volunteers scrubs beat Carson-Newman 73–0. The next week Tennessee beat Vanderbilt 13–0.

Neyland won five SEC championships, and at times, Tennessee completely dominated the other teams in the South. From 1938 through 1940, the Volunteers won 31 games and lost only two, a run that included a 22-game winning streak. The Vols lost only once in 1950 and went through the 1951 regular season unbeaten and won the national championship.

Because of illness, Neyland made the 1952 season his last as Tennessee's coach. The Volunteers went to the Cotton Bowl, but Neyland was too sick to coach in the game. After his retirement as coach,

Neyland became Tennessee's athletics director, a position he held until his death on March 28, 1962. He was elected into the College Football Hall of Fame in 1956.

Appropriately Tennessee's football stadium, which regularly draws more than 107,000 fans, is named after Robert R. Neyland.

School	Years	Record
Tennessee	1926–34, 1936–40, 1946–52	173–31–12

SEC championships (5): 1938, 1939, 1940, 1946, 1951
National championships (3): 1938, 1940, 1951

The 10 Basic Principles of General Robert R. Neyland

1. The head coach must remain a little aloof from the players and, to a certain extent, from the coaches.
2. The first qualification of a head coach is to possess a cool head so that he may see things in their true relation to each other and so in their proper perspective. There are things in football of which the head coach alone can comprehend the importance.
3. His first principle must be to calculate what he must do to win and see if he has the necessary means to surmount the obstacles with which the enemy will oppose him. Once the decision is made, see that all do their respective parts to earn the victory.
4. Football is composed of nothing but accidents. The great art is to profit from such accidents. This is the mark of genius.
5. It follows that all plans must be made to minimize our own mistakes and to magnify the effect of the opponents' mistakes.
6. On the nature of the struggle between two equal teams: the difference is never physical but invariably mental.
7. It is important to keep the squad eternally aware of the very nature of football and so not dismayed when things are going wrong.
8. To defeat a weak opponent is not the problem. The problem is to win when he is as good or better than you.
9. Almost all close games are lost by the losers, not won by the winners.
10. Proper mental stance on game day stems almost entirely from attitudes built up over a considerable period of time. Pregame harangues, as a rule, do more harm than good. Inspiration at zero hour is a poor thing to rely on.

EDDIE ROBINSON

GRAMBLING

1941–97

Some people are well into adulthood before they find their calling in life. Eddie Robinson was unique; he found his passion in the third grade.

Grambling coach Eddie Robinson. Photo courtesy of the *Atlanta Journal-Constitution.*

That's when a local high school football coach brought his team to Robinson's elementary school in an effort to sell season tickets. While his classmates focused on the players in their fancy uniforms, Robinson's eyes were riveted on the coach.

"I liked the way he talked to the team. I liked the way he could make us all laugh," Robinson recalled. "I liked the way they respected him."

By the time Robinson was in the ninth grade he was organizing and coaching teams in the neighborhoods around his home in Baton Rouge, Louisiana.

At the age of 21 Robinson was a college graduate working at a feed mill for 25¢ an hour. A relative told him that the Louisiana Negro Normal and Industrial Institute was looking for someone to coach football, basketball, and baseball at a starting salary of $63.75 a month. Based on the hours he would be putting in, Robinson knew he would definitely be taking a cut in pay if he got the job.

"But coaching was all I ever wanted to do," he said.

That decision launched one of the most successful and most distinguished careers in the history of college football. When Eddie Robinson became coach at Louisiana Negro Normal, which would later become Grambling, the Japanese had not yet bombed Pearl Harbor. When he retired in 1997 the man they all called "Coach Rob" had won 408 games.

The sheer numbers are staggering:

- He is one of only two college coaches in history at any level of football to win 400 games. John Gagliardi, who is still going strong after 55 seasons at St. John's (Minnesota), has 453 victories.
- He won or shared 17 Southwestern Athletic Conference (SWAC) championships and nine Black College Football National Championships.
- During his 57-year career, 210 of Robinson's players found their way onto NFL rosters.

But the numbers don't even begin to tell the whole story.

Like any coach, Robinson wanted to win, but he cared more about turning out good men who would become good husbands and fathers.

Former player Tremaine Jackson once said that if a player used incorrect English on the practice field, Robinson would stop the workout and correct the player on the spot. He did not tolerate profanity from his players, on or off the field. When traveling to and from games, Robinson insisted his players wear jackets and ties. He required his players to take etiquette classes from Grambling's home economics department so that they knew how to behave in public.

When Grambling did not field a team in 1943 or 1944 due to World War II, Robinson coached the local high school football team. One day, the father of Robinson's star running back came to practice wanting to take his son home to pick cotton. Robinson responded by taking his whole team to the fields. Once the cotton was picked, the running back was allowed to return to practice. Grambling High School went on to win a state championship that season.

"The football players are the most important people in the world to me," he said. "Without them, there would be no me."

Robinson also said that his greatest accomplishment was not winning 408 games, but going for 57 years with "one job and one wife." Robinson married Doris, his high school sweetheart, the same year he came to Grambling.

When Robinson took over at Grambling, it had 175 students and five buildings. He made the school, and himself, internationally famous.

In 1997 Robinson retired from coaching at age 78. The National Football Foundation and College Hall of Fame waived its customary three-year waiting period and immediately inducted him that December.

"No one has ever done or ever will do what Eddie Robinson has done for this game," said Penn State coach Joe Paterno. "Eddie Robinson and Jake Gaither [of Florida A&M] stand alone. Our profession will never, ever be able to repay Eddie Robinson for what he has done for the country and the profession of football."

Robinson died on April 3, 2007, at age 88.

School	Years	Record
Grambling	1941–97	408–165–15

SWAC championships (17): 1960, 1965, 1966, 1967, 1968, 1971, 1972, 1973, 1974, 1975, 1977, 1978, 1979, 1980, 1983, 1985, 1994

Black College National Championships (9): 1950, 1967, 1972, 1974, 1975, 1977, 1980, 1983, 1992

STEVE SPURRIER

DUKE, FLORIDA, SOUTH CAROLINA

1987–Present

With 14 conference championships and six national championships, no coach has dominated the SEC like Alabama's Paul "Bear" Bryant. It can, however, be argued that next to Bryant, no coach has had a greater impact on the SEC than Steve Spurrier.

When Spurrier came to Florida, his alma mater, as head coach in 1990, the SEC was still a league where the successful teams ran the ball first and passed only when necessary.

Spurrier, who affectionately became known as "the Head Ball Coach" turned the SEC on its ear with a wide-open, sophisticated passing attack that became known as the "Fun 'n Gun" offense.

Over the next 12 years Spurrier's teams at Florida rewrote all of the passing records in the SEC. In the process the Gators dominated the SEC like no other team since the 1970s Alabama dynasty.

In the 12 seasons from 1990 to 2001, Spurrier's teams won 122 games, six SEC championships, and one national championship in 1996. In his first

Steve Spurrier, who won six SEC championships at Florida, returned to college football in 2005 as the head coach at South Carolina. Photo courtesy of the University of Florida.

season, 1990, Florida finished first in the SEC with a 6–1 record but was not eligible to win the conference championship due to NCAA sanctions that were levied against the previous coaching staff.

Spurrier is the only coach in SEC history who has posted 10 or more wins in six straight seasons (1993–98).

In the 12 seasons Spurrier was at Florida, the Gators were an unprecedented 87–14 against SEC competition.

"If you played quarterback for Coach Spurrier, you knew that if you just listened and did what he said, you would be successful," said Danny Wuerffel, the 1996 Heisman Trophy winner. "Coach Spurrier's teams played with a great deal of confidence. That's because he was confident."

Spurrier's confidence was very refreshing for what had always been a pretty buttoned-down league. Spurrier was not above tweaking an opposing coach on the week of a big game if he felt that it would give him an edge.

"Absolutely the most competitive person I've ever met in my life," said Norm Carlson, a longtime sports information director at Florida and noted Gator football historian. "It didn't matter what the game was—football, golf, or table tennis. He was in it to win."

And it is clear that Spurrier changed the face of Southern college football on a very grand scale.

"When Steve Spurrier brought his passing attack to the SEC, the rest of the schools in the league had to adjust to him," said former SEC commissioner Roy Kramer, himself a former coach. "Everybody had to open up their offenses or they would never score enough points to beat him."

The 1966 Heisman Trophy winner at Florida, Spurrier got into coaching after a 10-year pro career as a player. After a year at Florida and a year at Georgia Tech as an assistant coach, Spurrier became the offensive coordinator at Duke, where his wide-open style got its first national attention.

After three seasons as the head coach of the Tampa Bay Bandits of the USFL, Spurrier returned to Duke as head coach and, in 1989, won the ACC championship.

The Florida program had fallen on hard times when Spurrier was lured back to his alma mater in 1990. When Spurrier arrived, Florida had never won an SEC championship and had never won 10 games in a season. Spurrier won six SEC titles, played in the national championship game twice, and posted nine seasons of 10 wins or more.

In 2002 Spurrier decided to take a shot at the NFL, signing a five-year contract for $5 million a season to coach the Washington Redskins. It was a bad experience, as Spurrier went 7–9 and 5–11 and then decided that the pro game was not for him.

There was a move to bring Spurrier back to Florida after Ron Zook, his replacement, was fired midway through the 2004 season. But Spurrier decided to take on the challenge of rebuilding at South Carolina, which had never won an SEC championship since joining the league in 1992.

Spurrier's 2007 South Carolina team started 6–1 and was ranked as high as No. 6 in the nation before losing its final five games to finish 6–6. It was only the second nonwinning season in his 18 years as a college head coach.

Spurrier made no excuses. He never does.

"We just weren't very good in the second half of the season," Spurrier said when it was over. "We had plenty of chances to win more games. But we didn't play well and we didn't coach well. We have no one to blame but ourselves."

Spurrier, who turned 63 on April 20, 2008, enters the 2008 season convinced that he will eventually win an SEC championship at South Carolina, which would be the perfect ending to a storybook career.

"We have everything we need at South Carolina to win a championship," Spurrier said. "It's just a matter of time."

School	Years	Record
Duke	1987–89	20–13–1
Florida	1990–2001	122–27–1
South Carolina	2005–Present	21–16
Total	18 seasons	163–56–2

ACC championships (1): 1989
SEC championships (6): 1991, 1993, 1994, 1995, 1996, 2000
National championships (1): 1996

FRANK THOMAS

ALABAMA

1931–46

After Wallace Wade decided to leave Alabama for Duke in 1930, the search began for a coach to continue the Crimson Tide's winning tradition. Alabama found its man in Frank Thomas, a short, quiet man with a very large and innovative football mind.

Thomas was a quarterback on Knute Rockne's Notre Dame teams of 1921 and 1922. After graduating from the Notre Dame law school in 1923, he set out to establish a coaching career. Thomas was an assistant at Georgia when Wade recommended that he be hired for the 1931 season.

Over the next 16 seasons Thomas won 81 percent of his games (115–24–7), two national championships (1934, 1941), and four SEC championships, and he made three trips to the Rose Bowl.

A brilliant tactician who had an uncanny ability to make adjustments during the course of a game, Thomas is best remembered for introducing the South to the "Notre Dame box," a shifting, wide-open offense unlike anything opponents had ever seen.

Harry Gilmer, an All-American halfback for the

Alabama coach Frank Thomas (1931–46). Photo courtesy of the *Atlanta Journal-Constitution*.

Crimson Tide in 1945, recalls a pregame speech where Thomas emotionally implored them to play for the honor of those who had worn the Alabama jerseys before them. At the end of this impassioned plea, it dawned on Thomas that the team was wearing brand-new, lightweight jerseys—not the heavy woolen jerseys he had referred to in his speech.

"The last thing he made us do before the game was get off the bus and put on those old, woolen, hot jerseys," said Gilmer, who was the SEC Player of the Year in 1945 and is a member of the College Football Hall of Fame.

Thomas's nervous personality made him do strange things before big games.

In *Century of Champions,* author Wayne Hester recalls that in 1933, just prior to Thomas's first win over Tennessee, Frank stuck the lighted end of a cigar in his mouth. Before another game, according to Hester, Thomas was so nervous that he literally urinated in his pants. A player saw what was happening and asked Thomas about it. "Aw, yeah, I'm just nervous," he said.

Thomas's nervousness would eventually catch up with him. In 1945 he was diagnosed with high blood pressure, and by 1946 he was in such poor health that he had to coach the entire season while riding around in a homemade cart. He retired after that season at age 48.

When the College Football Hall of Fame was established in 1951, Thomas was one of the charter members. He died on May 10, 1954.

School	Years	Record
Alabama	1931–46	115–24–7

SEC championships (4): 1933, 1934, 1937, 1945
National championships (2): 1934, 1941

JOHN VAUGHT

MISSISSIPPI

1947–70, 1973

In January 1947, 37-year-old John Vaught had a difficult decision to make.

Mississippi head coach Harold "Red" Drew was leaving after just one season to become head coach at Alabama, replacing Frank Thomas. Vaught could go with Drew to Alabama, one of college football's most successful programs, or stay in Oxford and take over as head coach. The Rebels had just completed a difficult 2–7 season, and the immediate future looked uncertain. Both jobs would pay about $12,000 per year.

With Drew's other assistants in the car waiting to take him to Tuscaloosa, Vaught decided to remain in Oxford to see if he could make it as a head coach.

It turned out to be the most important decision in the history of Ole Miss football. Vaught remained as the Rebels' head coach for 25 seasons. In that span he won 190 games, six SEC championships, and three national championships. To this day, Vaught's tenure is considered the golden age of football at Ole Miss.

The sixth of 11 children who grew up together on a Texas farm, Vaught possessed a number of qualities that made him a successful head coach. At an early age, he learned the importance of hard work, discipline, and attention to detail from his grandmother.

In Vaught's book, *Rebel Coach*, he writes that when he lived with his grandmother she would not tolerate anything that was not done perfectly. If he mowed the lawn improperly, she would make him mow it again and again until it was done to her standards of perfection.

"I didn't realize it at the time, but Grandmother taught me the qualities of good leadership," Vaught wrote. "She taught me that something half done was a failure, and that fits my coaching philosophy."

Vaught was a master of game preparation, a quality he learned from coach Francis Schmidt when he was a player at Texas Christian from 1929 to 1932. Schmidt was obsessive about everything, but especially game preparation. During practice one day he forced his team to run a play 72 consecutive times until they got it right.

Mississippi coach John Vaught. Photo courtesy of the *Atlanta Journal-Constitution.*

Schmidt was one of the first coaches to study films of opponents and would invite Vaught, a smallish offensive guard, into the physics lab to watch with him. Vaught began using film to prepare for every possible situation he might face in a game, a method he used throughout his career.

As head coach at Ole Miss, Vaught got off to a strong start. With the help of quarterback Charlie Conerly and end Barney Poole, Ole Miss upset Kentucky and coach Bear Bryant 14–7 in Vaught's first game. The Rebels went on to finish the regular season 8–2 and win the SEC championship.

The Sugar Bowl extended an invitation to Ole Miss in 1947, but during the previous summer Vaught had agreed to send his team to the new Delta Bowl in Memphis to play Texas Christian. Vaught wanted to help the Delta Bowl get started and liked the idea of playing against his alma mater. Ole Miss fans wanted Vaught to break the contract with the Delta Bowl, but he remembered another lesson his grandmother taught him: always keep your word. Ole Miss played TCU in the Delta Bowl, winning 13–9.

Vaught's teams in 1959, 1960, and 1962 were named national champions by various wire services, and his 1959 team was voted the SEC Team of the Decade.

On January 13, 1971, the 61-year-old stepped down as head coach on the advice of his doctor. But in 1973 a stunning series of events brought Vaught out of retirement. After the Rebels started 1–2, which included a 17–13 loss to Memphis State, both head coach Billy Kinard and athletics director Frank "Bruiser" Kinard were abruptly fired. Vaught took over both positions and coached the team for the rest of the season, winning five of the remaining eight games.

After winning his final game, a 38–10 decision over Mississippi State, Vaught retired again as coach—this time for good. He remained as athletics director until 1977, and he was inducted into the College Football Hall of Fame in 1979.

Coach John Vaught died on February 3, 2006, at age 96.

School	Years	Record
Mississippi	1947–73	190–61–12

SEC championships (6): 1947, 1954, 1955, 1960, 1962, 1963
National championships (3): 1959, 1960, 1962

WALLACE WADE

ALABAMA, DUKE

1923–50

If it had not been for the poor timing of a search committee at Kentucky, Alabama could have been deprived of the man who established the great Crimson Tide tradition.

In 1923 Wallace Wade, an assistant at Vanderbilt, was up for the head-coaching job at both Kentucky and Alabama. Wade visited Kentucky first, and after the interview the search committee asked him to step outside while they had a discussion. They left Wade out in the hall for three hours.

Wade, a temperamental man who did not take such slights lightly, stormed into the room and announced that he was going to Alabama. He further vowed that no team of his would ever—*ever*—lose to Kentucky.

Wade made good on that promise during his brilliant career at Alabama, where he was 61–13–3 in eight years, and at Duke, where he was 110–36–7 in 16 seasons.

In those 24 seasons his teams met Kentucky a total of 11 times and won each time.

Ironically Wade was called "the Bear" some 35 years before Paul "Bear" Bryant came to Alabama in 1958. But when Wade's players called him "Bear" it was not with affection. Wade was rough and tough, and he was a total disciplinarian.

But he got results. In his third season Wade took Alabama to the Rose Bowl, where the Crimson Tide upset Washington 20–19 in one of the biggest wins ever for Southern football. That season Wade also led Alabama to the first of its 12 national championships. The next season Alabama went back to the Rose Bowl, tying Stanford and winning another national championship.

Then Alabama faced three straight difficult seasons (5–4–1, 6–3, 6–3), at least by Alabama standards. Wade could not understand the criticism he was receiving in light of his national championships in 1925 and 1926. Feeling unappreciated, he announced in April 1930 that he had accepted an offer from Duke and would leave after the next season. Wade went out with his guns blazing as Alabama

Duke coach Wallace Wade (left) left the school in 1942 to serve in World War II. Photo courtesy of the *Atlanta Journal-Constitution.*

went 10–0, won the Rose Bowl, and captured another national championship.

At Duke Wade won 110 games in 16 years. He took the Blue Devils to the Rose Bowl and won six conference championships.

In 1942, at the age of 52, Wallace left Duke and joined the army in order to fight in World War II. He fought in the Battle of Normandy and received the Bronze Star.

After four seasons away from coaching, Wade came back to Duke in 1946 and retired after the 1950 season.

In *Century of Champions,* author Wayne Hester tells of the day in 1980 when 88-year-old Wallace returned to the Alabama campus for a reunion of his 1930 Rose Bowl team.

When he arrived in Tuscaloosa, Wallace was driven directly to Bear Bryant's practice field. Bryant, in the waning years of his career, came down from his famous tower and gathered the Alabama players around him. Then Bryant pointed to Wade and said, "Boys, this man standing here is responsible for the great tradition of Alabama football."

Wallace Wade died on October 6, 1986, at age 94. He was inducted into the College Football Hall of Fame in 1955.

School	Years	Record
Alabama	1923–30	61–13–3
Duke	1931–50*	110–36–7
Total	24 seasons	171–49–10

*From 1942 to 1945, Wade did not coach because he was serving in World War II.

Southern Conference championships (10): 1924, 1925, 1926, 1930, 1933, 1935, 1936, 1938, 1939, 1941
National championships (3): 1925, 1926, 1930

THE BEST OF THE REST

Arkansas coach Frank Broyles. Photo courtesy of the *Atlanta Journal-Constitution.*

Here are 25 more coaches who have earned special places in the history of Southern college football.

William Alexander took over at Georgia Tech when John Heisman left Atlanta for Pennsylvania in 1920. He stayed 25 seasons, winning 134 games and a national championship in 1928. He also had the vision to hire Bobby Dodd away from Tennessee and General Bob Neyland for the exorbitant sum of $300 a month. As a student, assistant coach, head coach, and athletics director, Alexander was on the campus of Georgia Tech for 44 years. He was inducted into the College Football Hall of Fame in 1951.

Frank Broyles played for Bobby Dodd at Georgia Tech and was an offensive coordinator for the Yellow Jackets when he was named head coach at Missouri in 1957. After one season at Missouri Broyles was named head coach at Arkansas.

In 19 seasons at Arkansas Broyles won 144 games, seven Southwest Conference championships, and the 1964 national championship. Broyles retired as coach after the 1976 season but remained as athletics director, a post he held until his retirement on December 31, 2007.

Wallace Butts, "the Little Round Man," won four SEC titles and 140 games in 22 seasons at Georgia. He developed 12 All-Americans including Fran Tarkenton, the Hall of Fame quarterback, and running backs Frank Sinkwich and Charley Trippi. In 1997 Butts was posthumously inducted into the College Football Hall of Fame.

Marino Casem, better known as "the Godfather," had a brilliant career as both a coach and an administrator. He was the head coach and athletics director for 22 seasons at Alcorn State.

Georgia coach Wally Butts with Fran Tarkenton (No. 10) and Pat Dye (No. 60) in 1959. Photo courtesy of the *Atlanta Journal-Constitution.*

In 1986 he became athletics director at Southern University, which became the best overall program in the SWAC. He was inducted into the College Football Hall of Fame in 2003.

Jerry Claiborne won 179 games in a 28-year career with stops at Virginia Tech, Maryland, and Kentucky. Claiborne played for Bear Bryant at Kentucky and began his head coaching career at Virginia Tech in 1961. He was named Coach of the Year in three different conferences: Southern (1963), ACC (1973, 1975, and 1976), and SEC (1983). Claiborne won three straight ACC titles at Maryland (1974–76), and his 1976 Maryland team finished 11–1. Claiborne was inducted into the College Football Hall of Fame in 1999. Claiborne died on September 24, 2004, at age 72.

Doug Dickey was a star player at the University of Florida but began his head coaching career at Tennessee in 1964. After going 4–5–1 in his first season, Dickey posted five straight seasons of eight wins or more. Dickey then returned to his alma mater where he coached for nine seasons. After four years in private business, Dickey went back to Tennessee as athletics director, a position he held for 18 years. Dickey was inducted into the College Football Hall of Fame in 2003.

Bill Dooley, brother of Hall of Fame coach Vince Dooley of Georgia, won 161 games in 26 seasons at North Carolina, Virginia Tech, and Wake Forest. His greatest success was at North Carolina where he won three ACC championships (1971, 1972, and 1977). He retired after coaching his final season at Wake Forest in 1992.

Pat Dye was an All-American guard at Georgia but did his coaching apprenticeship as an assistant to Bear Bryant at Alabama from 1965 to 1973. He coached for six seasons at East Carolina and one at Wyoming before becoming head coach at Auburn in 1981. Dye won 99 games and four SEC championships in 12 seasons at Auburn. He had a Heisman Trophy winner in Bo Jackson in 1985 and, as athletics director, was responsible for bringing the game with Alabama to the Auburn campus for the first time in history. Dye retired from coaching after the 1992 season. He was inducted into the College Football Hall of Fame in 2005.

Jake Gaither coached for 25 years and won 203 games at Florida A&M. His 84.4 winning percentage is sixth all-time among college coaches. In a quote that has been repeated often, Gaither wanted his players to be "mo-bile, a-gile, and hos-tile." He was inducted into the College Football Hall of Fame in 1975. He died in 1994 at age 90.

Ray Graves won 70 games in 10 seasons at Florida (1960–69) and was inducted into the College Football Hall of Fame in 1990. Graves spent 13 seasons as an assistant to Bobby Dodd at Georgia Tech.

Frank Howard was the colorful coach at Clemson for 30 years. He won 165 games and a million more hearts for his beloved Tigers. He won eight conference championships (Southern and ACC). He passed away on January 28, 1998, at age 85. He was inducted into the College Football Hall of Fame in 1989.

Billy Joe was a very successful coach at Cheyney State and Central State before taking over at Florida A&M in 1994. Joe took the Rattlers to six straight appearances in the Division I-AA playoffs. Only Grambling's Eddie Robinson won more Black National Championships than Joe, who was inducted into the College Football Hall of Fame in 2007.

Roy Kidd coached his alma mater, Eastern Kentucky, for 39 seasons (1964–2002), winning 315 games. He took the Colonels to 17 NCAA Division I-AA playoff appearances and won the national championship in 1979 and 1982.

Harry Mehre was the Notre Dame center who snapped the ball to the fabled Four Horsemen when they were sophomores in 1922. Mehre became head coach at Georgia in 1928 on Rockne's recommendation. After 10 years and 59 wins at Georgia, Mehre went to Ole Miss for eight seasons.

Harry Mehre. Photo courtesy of the *Atlanta Journal-Constitution.*

Charlie McClendon played for Bear Bryant at Kentucky and then went on to win 137 games in 18 seasons (1962–79) as the head coach at LSU. Affectionately known as "Cholly Mac," McClendon died on December 6, 2001, at age 78. The practice facility at LSU is named after him.

Allyn McKeen remains the most successful coach in Mississippi State history, winning 76 percent of his games (65–19–3) in nine seasons (1939–48). The Tennessee graduate took the Bulldogs to the Orange Bowl after a 10–0 season in 1940. He was inducted into the College Football Hall of Fame in 1991.

Alabama coach Bear Bryant with his friend, LSU's Charlie McClendon. Photo courtesy of the *Atlanta Journal-Constitution.*

Johnny Majors won a national championship at Pittsburgh (1976) before returning to Tennessee, his alma mater, in 1977. Majors won three SEC championships at Tennessee before leaving after the 1992 season and finishing his career back at Pittsburgh. He won 185 games in 29 seasons as a head coach. Majors was inducted into the College Football Hall of Fame as a player in 1987.

John Merritt won 232 games in 31 years at Jackson State and Tennessee State. Known as "Big John," Merritt had seven teams that won Black College National Championships and had five teams that finished their seasons undefeated. Among the 144 players Merritt sent to the NFL was Ed "Too Tall" Jones. Merritt died in 1983 and was inducted into the College Football Hall of Fame in 1994.

Bill Murray took over at Duke when Wallace Wade retired in 1951, and the Blue Devils just kept on winning. He won 93 games in 15 seasons at Duke and captured seven conference titles. Under Murray, Duke beat Nebraska in the 1955 Orange Bowl and beat Arkansas in the 1961 Cotton Bowl.

Jess Neely coached at Clemson for only nine seasons (1931–39) but had a profound effect on the Tigers program. In 1939, his final season, Clemson went 9–1, beating Boston

Georgia Tech's Bobby Dodd (right) with Rice coach Jess Neely in 1960. Photo courtesy of the *Atlanta Journal-Constitution.*

Erk Russell was the defensive coordinator at Georgia for 17 seasons (1964–80) before leaving to resurrect the football program at Georgia Southern. Photo courtesy of Georgia Southern University/Sports Information.

From left to right, Oklahoma's Bud Wilkinson, Maryland's Jim Tatum, and Kentucky's Bear Bryant in 1952. Photo courtesy of the *Atlanta Journal-Constitution.*

College in the Cotton Bowl, the school's first bowl appearance ever. The Tigers finished 12th in the final Associated Press poll, its first top 20 season. Neely left Clemson and spent the next 27 years at Rice, where he led the Owls to four Southwest Conference championships. He retired with 207 career wins. He was inducted into the College Football Hall of Fame in 1971.

Erk Russell was one of the most beloved and respected coaches in the history of college football. After 17 successful years as Vince Dooley's defensive coordinator at Georgia (1964–80), Russell left to resurrect the football program at Division I-AA Georgia Southern. By 1985 Russell won the first of his three national championships at Georgia Southern. Russell retired after his 1989 team went 15–0 and won the national title. Russell, with his clean-shaven head, was one of the best motivators the game has ever known. He died on September 8, 2006, at age 80.

Clark Shaughnessy won 149 career games but is best remembered as the most successful coach in Tulane history. He won 59 games in 10 seasons with records of 8–1 in 1924 and 9–0–1 in 1925. He was inducted into the College Football Hall of Fame in 1968.

Jim Tatum won 100 games in a career that was tragically cut short. Tatum took over at Maryland in 1947 and won 73 games in nine seasons. In 1951 the Terps went 10–0 and upset No. 1 Tennessee in the Sugar Bowl. In 1953 Maryland went 10–1 and was declared national champions. In 1955 Maryland posted another 10-win season under Tatum. He left for North Carolina, his alma mater, in 1956, but in the summer of 1959 Tatum died suddenly from Rocky Mountain Spotted Fever.

Thad "Pie" Vann, of Southern Miss, lettered four years in baseball and football at Ole Miss. In

1937 he came to Southern Mississippi as a line coach and baseball coach and never left. Vann became head football coach for the Golden Eagles in 1949 and held the post for 20 years, winning 139 games. He captured the mythical Small College National Championship in 1958 and 1962. He was inducted into the College Football Hall of Fame in 1987.

George Welsh took over at Virginia in 1982 and led the Cavaliers to the most successful period in school history. From 1987 to 1999 Virginia posted 13 consecutive seasons of seven wins or more. In 1990 Welsh led Virginia to the nation's No. 1 ranking and a berth in the Sugar Bowl. Welsh coached at Virginia for a total of 19 seasons, winning 134 games and taking the Cavaliers to 12 bowl games. He won two ACC championships. Welsh also won 55 games as the head coach at Navy, where he finished third in the Heisman Trophy voting as a player in 1955. He was inducted into the College Football Hall of Fame in 2004.

Chapter 5

GREAT TEAMS
Southern Fried Football's All-Time Teams and Dynasties

THE TOP 25
1. Sewanee, 1899 (12–0)

The Tigers from Tennessee went 12–0 in 1899, but that's not why this team is number one. In November 1899 Sewanee took the ultimate road trip, playing five games in six days. Not only did the Tigers win them all, but all five wins were by shutouts. The Tigers began their trip at Texas (12–0) and then beat Texas A&M (10–0), Tulane (23–0), LSU (34–0), and Ole Miss (12–0) by a combined score of 91–0. Before the trip, Sewanee had beaten Georgia, Georgia Tech, and Tennessee. After the trip Sewanee closed out the season with a 71–0 win over Cumberland, an 11–10 win over Auburn (the only

The Sewanee team of 1899 won five games in six days, all by shutouts and all on the road. Photo courtesy of Sewanee SID.

team to score on the Tigers all season), and a 5–0 win over North Carolina. As a result, Sewanee confidently declared itself the champion of Southern college football.

2. OLE MISS, 1959 (10–1)

Ole Miss was so good in 1959 that despite having suffered one loss, the team was named SEC Team of the Decade by the Associated Press. Coach John Vaught knew this team had a chance to be special, but he didn't know that his 1959 Ole Miss team would close out the season just two yards short of perfection. The Rebels were deep at every position and had two future Hall of Fame players in quarterback Jake Gibbs and fullback Charlie Flowers. The team was undefeated and ranked No. 3 in the nation when it traveled to play No. 1 LSU, the defending national champion, on Halloween night. The world will always remember Billy Cannon's 89-yard punt return that gave LSU a 7–3 lead. What the world doesn't remember is that the Rebels drove all the way down to the LSU 2-yard line inside the final minute. On fourth down Ole Miss was stopped, and LSU won the game. The Rebels went on to finish 9–1 and were able to avenge their only loss of the season by beating LSU 21–0 in the Sugar Bowl.

3. DUKE, 1938, (9–1)

The Blue Devils, led by future Hall of Fame center Dan Hill and Coach Wallace Wade, went through the regular season unbeaten and unscored upon. That earned the Blue Devils a trip to the Rose Bowl,

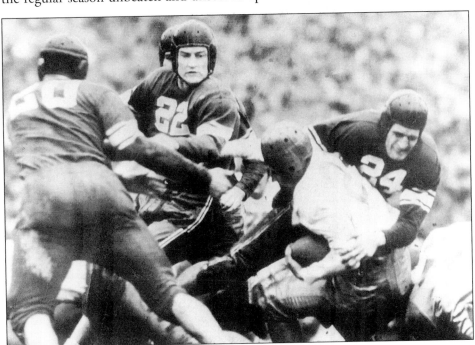

The 1938 "Iron Dukes" did not allow a point during the regular season. Photo courtesy of Duke SID.

the first postseason game in school history. Duke led 3–0 after a field goal early in the fourth quarter. Then Southern California drove the length of the field with three quick passes and scored a touchdown with only 40 seconds left, to win 7–3.

Despite that disappointing loss, the Iron Dukes, as the team became known, are remembered as one of the greatest teams in Southern football history.

4. TENNESSEE, 1938 (11–0)

Many fans believe this was Tennessee's best team under legendary coach Robert Neyland. The Volunteers gave up 10 points in their first two wins against Sewanee and Clemson and were not scored on again during the rest of the season with the exception of a 14–6 win over LSU in their sixth game. Tennessee was declared the national champion by several services after a 10–0 regular season, and then went on to snap Oklahoma's 14-game winning streak with a 17–0 win in the Orange Bowl. Future Hall of Fame players George "Bad News" Cafego and Bowden Wyatt (who later became head coach at Tennessee) were the stars.

5. ALABAMA, 1934 (10–0)

Coach Frank Thomas, who took over for Wallace Wade in 1931, led the 1934 Crimson Tide team to the Rose Bowl in only his fourth season as head coach. With the passing combination of Dixie Howell to Don Hutson, the best of that era (or any era, some might say), the Crimson Tide rolled to a 9–0 regular-season record and then beat Stanford 29–13 in Pasadena. The 1934 Alabama team outscored its regular-season opponents 316–45, and only one team, Tennessee, came within 20 points of the Tide. After falling behind Stanford 7–0 in the Rose Bowl, Howell and Hutson dazzled the crowd with 22 unanswered points in the second quarter. Famed sportswriter Grantland Rice called it "one of the greatest all-around exhibitions football has

George "Bad News" Cafego led the great Tennessee team of 1938. Photo courtesy of Tennessee SID.

Alabama coach Frank Thomas (left) with starting quarterback Dixie Howell in 1934. Photo courtesy of the *Atlanta Journal-Constitution.*

ever known." Howell and Hutson went on to the College Football Hall of Fame, as did the other end on the 1934 team, Paul "Bear" Bryant.

6. MARYLAND, 1951 (10–0)

Maryland's 1953 team won the national championship, but many Terrapins fans still believe the 1951 team, led by quarterback Jack Scarbath and head coach Jim Tatum, was better. Offensive guard Bob Ward, at the bruising weight of 165 pounds, was a first-team All-American. Dick "Little Mo" Modzelewski was an All-American defensive lineman. Dick's brother Ed ("Big Mo") made several All-America teams at running back. The Terps did not play a ranked team during the regular season, beating eight of nine opponents by 19 points or more. Over the objections of Southern Conference officials, the No. 3–ranked Terps accepted a bid to play No. 1 Tennessee in the Sugar Bowl. The Volunteers were 10–0 and had already been declared national champions. Maryland jumped out to a 21–0 lead against the stunned Volunteers and won the game 28–13. The beating was so thorough that Robert Neyland, the famed Tennessee coach, said after the game, simply, "We were soundly beaten by a superior team."

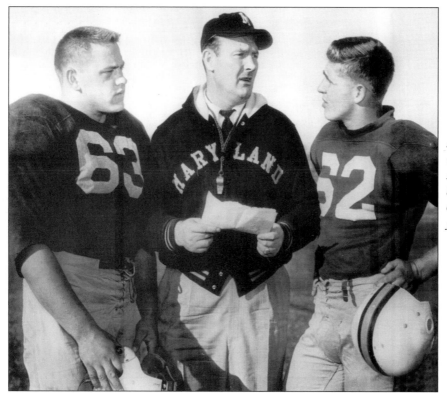

Maryland coach Jim Tatum with All-Americans Dick Modzelewski (left) and Jack Scarbath in 1951. Photo courtesy of the *Atlanta Journal-Constitution.*

7. TENNESSEE, 1951 (10–1)

If the national championship had been decided after the bowls, Tennessee would have won it all in 1950. The Volunteers lost their second game of the season to Mississippi State (7–0) and then rolled through the rest of the schedule, beating No. 3 Texas, 20–14, in the Cotton Bowl while No. 1 Oklahoma and No. 2 Army were also losing. As it turned out, the disappointment of 1950 set the stage for a 10–0 regular season in 1951. The Vols were led by running back Hank Lauricella, the Heisman Trophy runner-up that year, and Doug Atkins, a member of both the College and Pro Football Halls of Fame. Tennessee was declared the national champion after the regular season and missed a perfect season by losing to Maryland 28–13 in the Sugar Bowl.

8. ALABAMA, 1992 (13–0)

Even after a 12–0 regular season that included a 28–21 victory over Florida in the first SEC Championship Game, No. 2 Alabama appeared not to have much of a chance against No. 1 Miami in the Sugar Bowl. The Hurricanes were the defending national champions and had the Heisman Trophy winner in quarterback Gino Torretta. The Crimson Tide had not won a national championship since 1979, but third-year coach Gene Stallings said his team was not an underdog. Stallings was right. Thanks to a brilliant game plan devised by defensive coordinator Bill "Brother" Oliver, Alabama hounded Torretta and defeated Miami 34–13. Led by defensive ends Eric Curry and John Copeland, seven players on Alabama's defense made one of the various All-SEC teams.

9. GEORGIA TECH, 1952 (12–0)

Bobby Dodd called it "the best team I ever coached" and with very good reason. The Yellow Jackets, with two future Hall of Fame linebackers in George Morris and Larry Morris, gave up double-digit points in only one game, a 17–14 win over Florida. In its other 11 games, Georgia Tech allowed a total of only 45 points. Still, there were some anxious moments along the way. Quarterback Pepper Rodgers had to kick a field goal in the fourth quarter to beat Florida. Jakie Rudolph, a 5'7", 155-pound running back, had to tackle Alabama's Bobby Marlow on fourth down on the

Georgia Tech's 1952 national champions had six All-Americans (left to right): Leon Hardeman, George Morris, Buck Martin, Bobby Moorehead, Pete Brown, and Hal Miller. Photo courtesy of Georgia Tech SID.

Running back Leon Hardeman was one of six All-Americans on Georgia Tech's 1952 team. Photo courtesy of the Georgia Institute of Technology/Sports Information.

4-yard line to preserve a 7–3 win. Georgia Tech then went on to defeat unbeaten Mississippi 24–7 in the Sugar Bowl. The AP and UPI polls named Michigan State, which had finished 9–0 but not played in a bowl game, the national champion, but the International News Service awarded the honor to the Yellow Jackets.

10. Georgia, 1942 (11–1)

Arguably the best team in Georgia's football history, the 1942 Bulldogs had what became known as the "Dream Backfield" of Frank Sinkwich, the Heisman Trophy winner that season, and Charley Trippi, who received the Maxwell Award as college football's best player in 1946. The Bulldogs rolled through nine straight opponents, including a sound 21–10 beating of No. 1 Alabama in Atlanta. On November 21 Georgia was ranked No. 1 when it traveled to Columbus, Georgia, to play Auburn. Georgia was a heavy favorite against Auburn, which had a 4–4–1 record, but lost 27–13 in one of the biggest upsets in the history of both schools. Still, Georgia closed out the regular season with a 34–0 win over No. 2 Georgia Tech. The Bulldogs then went on to the Rose Bowl where they beat UCLA 9–0. Georgia was named national champion in six polls recognized by the NCAA.

11. Tennessee, 1998 (13–0)

In 1998, the year after the departure of quarterback Peyton Manning, many Volunteers fans worried that the program would sag. Instead Tennessee went 13–0, won its second straight SEC championship, and then beat Florida State in the Fiesta Bowl for the national championship, the school's first since 1951. But it wasn't easy. Three times the Volunteers had to rally from behind in the fourth quarter to win. In the opener, a 34–33 victory over Syracuse, the Vols had to drive the length of the field to set Jeff Hall up for a field goal as time expired. Hall also kicked a field goal in overtime to beat Florida 20–17. The offense was led by the big-play combination of quarterback Tee Martin and wide receiver Peerless Price, while the defense was anchored by linebacker Al Wilson.

Auburn's 1957 team went 10–0 and won the national championship. Photo courtesy of Auburn SID.

12. AUBURN, 1957 (10–0)

Coach Ralph "Shug" Jordan thought his seventh Auburn team would be special if he could find a quarterback. Having kicked his number one quarterback off the team for disciplinary reasons, Jordan turned to left-hander Lloyd Nix, who had been a halfback the season before, and the rest was Tigers history. Nix knew his job was not to win the game but to keep from making mistakes so the team would not lose it. He could afford to play conservatively because Auburn's defense, led by Zeke Smith, the 1958 Outland Trophy winner, was tremendous. Before the season ended, Auburn had shut out six opponents and the other four were held to just seven points each. The offense did only what it had to do. The Tigers scored seven points against Tennessee, six against Kentucky, three against Georgia Tech, and six against Georgia—and won all four games. Unranked when the season began, Auburn was No. 1 by the final regular-season game with Alabama. The Tigers then went out and pounded Alabama 40–0 and were named consensus national champions. Ironically, it was this beating by Auburn that forced Alabama to go to Texas A&M and hire Paul "Bear" Bryant as its head coach. Despite Auburn's successful season, the team did not play in a bowl game due to NCAA penalties.

13. FLORIDA STATE, 1993 (11–1)

For six straight seasons leading up to 1993 Florida State had won 10 or more games and finished in the final top four of the polls. But in spite of all that success, Coach Bobby Bowden did not have a national championship to show for it. Critics were beginning to say that Bowden, in his 18th season at Florida

Florida State quarterback Charlie Ward leads the Seminoles to a win over Nebraska in the 1994 Orange Bowl. Photo courtesy of Florida State SID.

State, couldn't win the big one. Every year the Seminoles lost a big game, usually against Miami, that kept Florida State out of the national championship hunt. It had apparently happened again in 1993 when No. 1 Florida State lost to No. 2 Notre Dame 31–24 on November 13. Even Bowden conceded at the time that losing a big game so late in the season made it almost impossible to get back into the national championship race. But then fate stepped in.

The following week Notre Dame, now ranked No. 1, was stunned by Boston College 41–39 at home and dropped to No. 3 in the polls. Florida State, which had only dropped to No. 2 after the Notre Dame loss, jumped back up to No. 1 in the Associated Press poll and stayed there. Florida State then played No. 2 Nebraska in the Orange Bowl for the national championship and won, 18–16, although it did not happen without some drama. Nebraska seemed to have won the game when Byron Bennett kicked a 27-yard field goal with 1:16 left to give the Cornhuskers a 16–15 lead. But Florida State quarterback Charlie Ward, the Heisman Trophy winner, drove the Seminoles into position for a 22-yard field goal by Scott Bentley with 21 seconds left to give Florida State the lead. Bowden had to hold his breath as Nebraska's Bennett missed a 45-yard field goal on the last play of the game.

14. LSU, 1958 (11–0)

After Paul Dietzel had won only 11 games in his first three seasons as LSU's head coach, no one had any reason to think that the Tigers would be anything special in 1958. The Tigers were young, with only three seniors among the top 55 players. But Dietzel knew better. He had some weapons, beginning with junior running back Billy Cannon, who would go on to win the Heisman Trophy the next year. Dietzel also had talented depth, so much so that he fielded two separate offenses: the White Team (the first team) and the Gold Team, which was later shortened to "Go Team." Dietzel called his defense the

The LSU Chinese Bandits of 1958. Photo courtesy of LSU SID.

Chinese Bandits, after the old *Terry and the Pirates* comic strip that called Chinese Bandits "the most vicious people in the world." With these three units LSU marched through the regular season 10–0. LSU was named the national champion, but there were some rough spots along the way. Against Florida the Tigers needed a 29-yard field goal in the final three minutes to win the game 10–7. They held Ole Miss out of the end zone after the Rebels had reached the LSU one-foot line and went on to win 14–0. In a game against Mississippi State, LSU scored the winning touchdown in the third quarter to win 7–6. LSU beat Tulane 62–0 to win the national championship, which, in those days, was announced by the wire services at the end of the regular season. LSU closed out its most memorable season with a 7–0 win over Clemson in the Sugar Bowl.

15. OLE MISS, 1960 (10–0–1)

With the bulk of the 1959 team returning, including quarterback Jake Gibbs, the Rebels expected to win another SEC championship and compete for the national title. And that's exactly what they did, topping off an undefeated season with a 14–6 win over Rice in the Sugar Bowl. The Rebels only encountered two anxious moments along the way: on October 22 in Little Rock, Allen Green kicked a 39-yard field goal on the last play of the game to beat Arkansas 10–7; and a week later Green kicked a 41-yard field goal with six seconds left to tie LSU 6–6. That was the only mark on Mississippi's record that

Quarterback Jake Gibbs led Ole Miss to a win over LSU in the 1960 Sugar Bowl. Photo courtesy of Mississippi SID.

season. After they won the Sugar Bowl the Rebels were ranked No. 2, but later that day No. 1 Minnesota was upset 17–7 by Washington in the Rose Bowl, and Ole Miss won the Grantland Rice Trophy, which goes to the national champion selected by the Football Writers Association of America.

16. Clemson, 1981 (12–0)

Clemson had gone 6–5 in 1980 and as a result were not ranked in any preseason polls for 1981. Danny Ford, Clemson's 33-year-old coach, led his team to a 14–6 record in his first two seasons, and some fans wondered if he was the right guy for the job. But all those doubts were put to rest when Clemson went through the regular season undefeated and beat Nebraska in the Orange Bowl to win the school's first national championship in any sport. Clemson finished the year as the only undefeated, untied team in the country and had wins over three top 10 teams—Georgia (13–3), North Carolina (10–8), and Nebraska (22–15). Clemson won with a defense that forced 41 turnovers in 12 games, still a school record. The Tigers had five different players earn All-America honors, including linebacker Jeff Davis, the team's spiritual leader, who was inducted into the College Football Hall of Fame in 2007. Four players from this Clemson team went on to become NFL first-round draft choices, and 22 have played in the NFL.

17. FLORIDA STATE, 1999 (12–0)

Coach Bobby Bowden will remember the 1999 season for a lot of reasons. On November 8 the grandfather of 21 turned 70 years old. On October 23 Bowden became only the fifth coach in the history of Division I football to win 300 games, a milestone reached after beating Clemson, coached by his son, Tommy, 17–14 in the first-ever father-son coaching showdown. But on January 4, 2000, the Florida State team gave its coach the best present of all, a 46–29 win over No. 2 Virginia Tech in the Sugar Bowl. The win gave Bowden his second national championship and his very first undefeated season as a head coach. The 1999 team was not Bowden's most talented by a long shot, but because the players had to face so much adversity, it was one of his closest teams. The previous January, the Seminoles lost to Tennessee 23–16 in the Fiesta Bowl, losing the national title with it. "That day, this group of guys dedicated themselves to getting back in this position again," Bowden said. Then, star receiver Peter Warrick, the Heisman Trophy favorite, was arrested on charges of theft. Warrick was allowed to return to the team after a two-game suspension. Led by junior quarterback Chris Weinke, the 27-year-old former pro baseball player, Florida State rallied from a 29–28 deficit in the second half of the Sugar Bowl to win comfortably over the Hokies. Weinke threw four touchdown passes, and Warrick went out in a blaze of glory as he caught two touchdown passes and returned a punt for a third.

Florida State became the first team to begin a season at No. 1 and stay there since the Associated Press created its preseason poll in 1950.

18. FLORIDA, 1996 (12–1)

As is often the case, the seeds that blossomed into Florida's first national championship team were sown in disappointment. The season before, the Gators had gone through the regular season 12–0, winning their fourth SEC championship in that decade. But in the national championship game against Nebraska in the Fiesta Bowl, the Gators were humiliated 62–24. It was then that coach Steve Spurrier decided to make some changes. He brought in Bob Stoops of Kansas State, which had the nation's No. 1 defense the year before, to serve as the team's new defensive coordinator. That defense, plus a high-powered offense led by Heisman Trophy winner Danny Wuerffel and future NFL receivers Reidel Anthony, Ike Hilliard, and Jacquez Green, put the Gators into the race for the national title in 1996. Still, Florida needed some good fortune to get in position to win the championship. The Gators were 10–0 and ranked No. 1 when they traveled to No. 2 Florida State on November 30. Wuerffel took a severe pounding from the Florida State defense that day, and the Seminoles prevailed, 24–21. Florida, which dropped to No. 4 in the polls after the loss, thought it had lost a chance at the national championship, but then fate stepped in. On December 7 Florida beat Alabama 45–30 for the SEC championship. Earlier that day, No. 3 Nebraska was shocked 37–27 by unranked Texas in the Big 12 championship game. No. 2 Arizona State was committed to play Ohio State in the Rose Bowl, so Sugar Bowl officials took the Gators, who had moved up to No. 3, in a rematch with No. 1 Florida State. On January 1 No. 2 Arizona State lost to Ohio State, meaning the Sugar Bowl on January 2 would be for the national championship. Using a shotgun formation against the strong Florida State pass rush, the Gators dominated Florida State 52–20 to win the national title.

19. MIAMI, 1991 (12–0)

The Hurricanes won four national championships from 1983 to 1991. But a strong case can be made that the 1991 squad was Miami's best during this incredible dynasty. The Hurricanes went 12–0 against a schedule that included four teams in the top 10. They capped off this strong performance with a solid 22–0 thumping of No. 11 Nebraska in the Orange Bowl. Miami started the season ranked No. 3 and moved to No. 2 after a 31–3 win over Arkansas in their season opener. The Hurricanes were still No. 2 when they traveled to Florida State and knocked off the No. 1 Seminoles 17–16. Miami moved into the No. 1 spot in the next Associated Press poll and stayed there through its victory in the Orange Bowl. Miami was named the national champion in the AP media poll while Washington, which had beaten Michigan in the Rose Bowl to finish 12–0, was No. 1 in the CNN/*USA Today* Coaches poll. The 1991 Miami team had five first-team All-Americans plus junior quarterback Gino Torretta, who went on to win the Heisman Trophy in 1992. The bulk of this Miami team returned the following season, and the Hurricanes again went 11–0. They were denied their second straight national title with a loss to Alabama in the Sugar Bowl.

Herschel Walker, Georgia. Photo courtesy of the *Atlanta Journal-Constitution.*

20. GEORGIA, 1980 (12–0)

After Georgia went 6–5 in 1979, few thought they could even compete for the SEC championship in 1980. But a freshman running back named Herschel Walker and a group of players who had a knack for winning close games enabled the Bulldogs to go 12–0 and win the national title. Georgia had to rally from a 15–2 deficit to beat Tennessee 16–15 in the opener. The Bulldogs needed a miracle 93-yard touchdown pass from Buck Belue to Lindsay Scott to beat Florida 26–21 in November. Georgia finished the regular season 11–0 and then beat Notre Dame 17–10 in the Sugar Bowl for the national title.

21. MARYLAND, 1953 (10–1)

In 1953 Maryland had lost quarterback Jack Scarbath and defensive tackle Dick Modzelewski from the great teams of 1951 and 1952. While coach Jim Tatum thought his team's No. 6 preseason ranking was a little ambitious, he privately told friends that this Maryland team had a chance to be very, very good—and he was right. Led by quarterback Bernie Faloney and a defense that posted six shutouts, Maryland went 10–0 during the regular season with impressive wins over Mississippi (38–0) and Alabama (21–0). During the season, Maryland's defense gave up a total of only 31 points while scoring 298. The 1953 Terps were declared the national champions in the three major polls. Maryland hoped to round out the season with a win over Oklahoma in the Orange Bowl. But in the days leading up to the game in Miami, Faloney reaggravated a knee injury in practice and could not play. Without Faloney the Maryland offense could not move the ball and thus lost 7–0 to Bud Wilkinson and the Sooners. Still, the 1953 team is considered one of the best in Maryland history.

22. GEORGIA TECH, 1928 (10–0)

When Georgia Tech scheduled Notre Dame for a series of games from 1922 to 1929, fans thought coach Bill Alexander had lost his mind. But Alex, as he was affectionately known, knew exactly what he was doing. "They will beat us nine out of 10, but in losing, we will learn a lot of football," he told the *Atlanta Journal*. "And when we win, it will be a mighty sweet victory." That sweet victory came in 1928 when the Yellow Jackets beat Knute Rockne and the Fighting Irish 13–0 in Atlanta. Georgia Tech used that game as the springboard to a 10–0 season and a national championship honor from the International News Service. Georgia Tech completed the season with an 8–7 win over California in the Rose Bowl, which included one of the most infamous plays in college football history. California's

Wrong Way Riegels. Photo courtesy of Georgia Tech SID/California SID.

Roy Riegels picked up a Georgia Tech fumble but ran 66 yards the wrong way and was finally stopped on his 1-yard line. Tech then blocked a punt for a safety and took a 2–0 lead. These turned out to be the winning points for Georgia Tech's perfect season. Coach Alexander and center Peter Pund went on to be elected to the College Football Hall of Fame.

23. ALABAMA, 1978 (11–1)

If you want to start an argument with a group of Alabama fans, ask which of Bear Bryant's 1970s teams was the best. Alabama won 103 games and three national championships in the '70s, and seven of those 10 teams won 11 games or more. For sheer guts and determination, it would be hard to beat the Crimson Tide of 1978. Alabama began that season at No. 1, but when the Crimson Tide lost to Southern California 24–14 on September 23, some thought Alabama's chance for a national championship was gone. Bryant, however, would not let his team quit and promised that if they kept working, Alabama could still win the national title. Alabama rolled through the rest of its schedule to finish 10–1 and earned a chance for the national championship against Penn State in the Sugar Bowl.

The Crimson Tide led 14–7 late in the game when Penn State drove down to the Alabama goal line. On fourth down, Penn State decided to go for the touchdown. Just prior to the play, Alabama tackle Marty Lyons talked to Penn State quarterback Chuck Fusina.

"How far do you have to go?" asked Lyons.

"About 10 inches," Fusina responded.

Lyons smiled: "Then you better pass."

Penn State didn't pass, sending tailback Mike Guman over tackle. Alabama linebacker Barry Krauss met Guman head to head and knocked him back, stopping the drive and saving the game for Alabama.

Bryant, who went on to coach just three more seasons, called the goal-line stand "something I will never forget."

24. MIAMI, 1987 (12–0)

In 1986 Miami fielded one of the best college football teams ever. The No. 1 Hurricanes went through the regular season 11–0 but then lost to No. 2 Penn State 14–10 in the Fiesta Bowl for the national championship. With the exit of quarterback Vinny Testaverde, the Heisman Trophy winner, Miami's ability to get back into the national championship was questionable. But the Hurricanes, who started the season ranked No. 10, used a 26–25 win over No. 3 Florida State to propel them to an 11–0 regular season. When Miami arrived at the Orange Bowl to play No. 1 Oklahoma, the Hurricanes were ranked No. 2. With sophomore quarterback Steve Walsh, fullback Melvin Bratton, and wide receiver Michael Irvin leading the way, Miami knocked off Oklahoma 20–14 for the national title. It was the first-ever

Kentucky coach Bear Bryant with quarterback Babe Parilli (left) and tackle Bob Gain in 1950. Photo courtesy of the Atlanta Journal-Constitution.

undefeated season for Miami and the first national title for head coach Jimmy Johnson. Defensive back Bennie Blades and defensive end Daniel Stubbs were consensus All-Americans that year.

25. KENTUCKY, 1950 (11–1)

After coaching one year at Maryland, Paul "Bear" Bryant left the Terps to become Kentucky's head coach in 1946. His goal was to bring the first SEC football championship to basketball-crazy Kentucky. It only took five seasons for Bryant to give the school its best football season ever. With two future Hall of Fame players—Babe Parilli and Bob Gain—leading the way, Kentucky went through the regular season 10–1 and won the SEC championship. The only blemish on the team's record was a 7–0 loss to Tennessee in Knoxville in the last game of the regular season. With a 5–1 conference record, Kentucky won the SEC championship over Tennessee, which was 4–1 after a 7–0 loss to Mississippi State. On January 1, Bryant coached the biggest win in school history—an upset of No. 1 Oklahoma, which broke the Sooners' 31-game winning streak.

HONORABLE MENTIONS (IN CHRONOLOGICAL ORDER)

LSU, 1908 (10–0): The Tigers, led by quarterback E.G. "Doc" Fenton, scored 442 points in 450 minutes of play in an era when touchdowns only counted five points.

Alabama, 1925 (10–0): Crimson Tide won its first national championship and beat Washington 20–19 in the Rose Bowl in a game that put Southern college football on the map.

Tulane, 1925 (9–0–1): After an undefeated season that included a tie with Missouri, the Green Wave turned down a chance to go to the Rose Bowl.

Florida, 1928 (8–1): The Gators led the nation in scoring, but a loss to Tennessee in Knoxville cost them a chance to go to the Rose Bowl.

Alabama, 1930 (10–0): Wallace Wade's last Alabama team won the national championship, including a 24–0 win over Washington State in the Rose Bowl.

Tulane, 1931 (11–1): Tulane finished the regular season undefeated with eight shutouts but lost to Southern California in the Rose Bowl.

Tennessee, 1939 (10–1): The Volunteers were unbeaten and unscored upon until they lost 14–0 to Southern California in the Rose Bowl.

Tennessee, 1940 (10–1): After another undefeated regular season, the Vols lost to Boston College 19–13 in the Sugar Bowl.

Mississippi State, 1940 (10–0–1): The Bulldogs were tied by Auburn 7–7 but beat Georgetown in the Orange Bowl.

Duke, 1941 (9–1): The Blue Devils went through the regular season undefeated but lost to Oregon State 20–16 in the Rose Bowl, which was played that year in Durham, North Carolina.

Georgia, 1946 (11–0): After sitting out two seasons to serve in World War II, running back Charley Trippi returned to Georgia to close out his brilliant career by leading the Bulldogs to a glorious undefeated season, which included a win over North Carolina in the Sugar Bowl.

Alabama, 1945 (10–0): The great Harry Gilmer led the Crimson Tide to a perfect season, including a 34–14 win over Southern Cal in the Rose Bowl.

Clemson, 1948 (11–0): Frank Howard's Tigers won the Southern Conference championship and beat Missouri in the Gator Bowl.

Clemson, 1950 (9–0–1): A tie against South Carolina (which finished 3–4–2) kept the Tigers from playing for the national championship.

Auburn, 1958 (9–0–1): Only a 7–7 tie with Georgia Tech kept the Tigers from a perfect season.

Ole Miss, 1962 (10–0): The Rebels gave up only 53 points in 10 games on the way to a national championship.

Arkansas, 1964 (11–0): The Razorbacks beat Nebraska 10–7 in the Cotton Bowl to win their first national championship.

Arkansas, 1965 (10–1): The Razorbacks went 10–0 during the regular season. Their 22-game winning streak was broken by a 14–7 loss to LSU in the Cotton Bowl.

Alabama, 1966 (11–0): Alabama should have won its third straight national championship with this team, led by quarterback Ken Stabler. Instead Notre Dame, which had a 10–10 tie against Michigan State, won the national title.

Alabama, 1971 (11–1): The Crimson Tide's only loss this year was to national champion Nebraska in the Orange Bowl.

Alabama, 1973 (11–1): The Crimson Tide's only loss was 24–23 to Notre Dame in the Sugar Bowl. Alabama was still named UPI national champions.

Arkansas, 1977 (11–1): The Razorbacks, under first-year coach Lou Holtz, upset No. 2 Oklahoma 31–6 in the Orange Bowl.

North Carolina, 1980 (11–1): The Tar Heels, led by future superstar linebacker Lawrence Taylor, lost only to Oklahoma in the regular season.

North Carolina linebacker Lawrence Taylor went on to a Hall of Fame career with the New York Giants. Photo courtesy of the *Atlanta Journal-Constitution.*

Georgia, 1982 (11–1): The Bulldogs, with Heisman Trophy winner Herschel Walker, lost the national championship game to Penn State (27–23) in the Sugar Bowl.

Miami, 1983 (11–1): This team started the Hurricanes' dynasty. Miami opened the season with a 28–3 loss to Florida and never lost again. On January 2 Howard Schnellenberger's team was ranked No. 3 when it played No. 1 Nebraska in the Orange Bowl. Miami stopped a two-point conversion to beat the Cornhuskers 31–30 and win their first of five national titles during the next 18 seasons.

Miami, 1986 (11–1): Led by Heisman Trophy winner Vinny Testaverde, the Hurricanes lost the national championship to Penn State (14–10) in the Fiesta Bowl.

Florida State, 1987 (11–1): The Seminoles' only loss was to Miami (26–25) on a failed two-point conversion attempt. Miami won the national championship.

Miami, 1988 (11–1): The Hurricanes' only loss this season was 31–30 to Notre Dame, the eventual national champion.

Miami, 1989 (11–1): Despite a loss to Florida State, the Hurricanes still won the national championship in Dennis Erickson's first year as coach.

Georgia Tech, 1990 (11–0–1): Only a tie with North Carolina kept the UPI national champions from perfection.

Auburn, 1993 (11–0): First-year coach Terry Bowden led the Tigers to an unbeaten season, but Auburn did not go to a bowl because of NCAA sanctions.

Florida, 1995 (12–1): Thanks to a great Gators' offense, Florida went undefeated until a 62–24 loss to Nebraska in the Fiesta Bowl.

Florida State, 1997 (12–1): Only a 32–29 loss to Florida in the last game of the regular season kept the Seminoles from playing for the national title.

Virginia Tech, 1999 (11–1): The Hokies, led by redshirt freshman quarterback Michael Vick, went undefeated and won the Big East championship while dominating every regular-season opponent but one (West Virginia, 22–20). Ranked No. 2, Virginia Tech played Florida State for the national championship in the Sugar Bowl and lost, 46–29.

Miami, 2000 (11–1): This was the best Miami team that never got a shot at the national title. The Hurricanes lost at Washington 34–29 in the second game of the season but did everything else it was asked to do, beating No. 1 Florida State (27–24) and No. 2 Virginia Tech (41–21) on the way to a 10–1 regular season. Despite its win against Florida State, the BCS formula picked the Seminoles (11–1) to play Oklahoma for the national championship. Florida State lost 13–2 and Miami dominated Florida 37–20 in the Sugar Bowl.

Miami, 2001 (12–0): Coach Butch Davis, who had rebuilt the Miami program, left for the Cleveland Browns after the 2000 season and was replaced by Larry Coker. But these Hurricanes never slowed down, beating their opponents by an average of 32.9 points per game. Featuring players such as QB Ken Dorsey (Maxwell Award winner), running back Clinton Portis, and tight end Jeremy Shockey, this Miami team is considered one of the school's best ever. They certainly proved it in the BCS championship game against Nebraska in the Rose Bowl, jumping out to a 34–0 lead at halftime before winning 37–14.

Miami, 2002 (12–1): The Hurricanes were 12–0 and riding a 34-game winning streak when they played Ohio State for the BCS national championship at the Fiesta Bowl. Despite five turnovers and a game-ending injury to running back Willis McGahee, Miami thought it had won the game when Glenn Sharpe batted away a fourth-down pass in the first overtime. But Miami was called for pass interference, which allowed Ohio State to score and send the game into the second overtime, where the Buckeyes won 31–24.

Georgia, 2002 (13–1): Mark Richt's second team at Georgia won the Bulldogs' first SEC championship since 1982. But it didn't come without some drama. The Bulldogs needed a 19-yard touchdown pass from David Greene to Michael Johnson on fourth down with just 1:25 left to beat Auburn 24–21 and advance to the SEC championship game. After beating Arkansas 30–3 for the conference title, Richt had his first meeting with his mentor, Florida State coach Bobby Bowden, in the Sugar Bowl. Georgia won 26–13 to post its first 13-win season.

LSU, 2003 (13–1): Nick Saban's fourth LSU team turned out to be his best as the Tigers beat No. 3 Georgia for the SEC championship, 34–13, and then went on to beat Oklahoma 21–14 in the BCS championship game at the Sugar Bowl. The only loss on the schedule was a 19–7 defeat to Florida on October 11 in Baton Rouge. The Tigers then closed with eight straight wins to give the school its second national title.

Auburn, 2004 (13–0): In a normal season, an undefeated SEC team would get a chance to play for the national championship. But in 2004 Southern California and Oklahoma started the season ranked No. 1 and No. 2, respectively, in the major polls and never lost. Auburn, featuring running backs Ronnie Brown and Carnell "Cadillac" Williams, played its way to No. 3 and could never get any higher. The Tigers beat ACC champion Virginia Tech in the Sugar Bowl to finish their first perfect season since 1993.

The Gators won the national championship in 2006 under coach Urban Meyer; it was only his second year at Florida. Photo courtesy of the University of Florida.

Florida, 2006 (13–1): Urban Meyer's second year as coach brought the Gators their second national championship. Florida lost only once, that coming at Auburn (27–17). But winning this championship was not easy. The Gators had to block a field goal on the last play of the game to beat South Carolina, who was led by their old coach (Steve Spurrier), 17–16. Florida beat Arkansas 38–28 for the SEC championship and, after No. 2 Southern California lost to UCLA on the same day, the Gators jumped to No. 2 and played No. 1 Ohio State in the BCS championship game. Florida dominated the Buckeyes 41–14 in Glendale, Arizona, to win the national title.

LSU, 2007 (12–2): This is the only team on this list with two losses, but the Tigers of 2007 are very deserving. LSU lost during the regular season to Kentucky (43–37) and Arkansas (50–48). Both losses came in triple overtime. After the heart-breaking loss to Arkansas on November 23, LSU thought its dreams of a national championship were over. But on December 1, when the Tigers beat Tennessee 21–14 for the SEC title, both No. 1 Missouri and No. 2 West Virginia lost. LSU was elevated to No. 2, and the Tigers, led by All-American defensive tackle Glenn Dorsey, beat No. 1 Ohio State 38–24 in the BCS championship game in New Orleans.

GLORY DAYS: THE SOUTH'S GREATEST DYNASTIES

Every school has a favorite period in its college football history. The following periods of success may not all qualify as dynasties in the classic sense, but they do generate the fondest memories for the fans of that particular school. Here are the best of those Southern dynasties (in alphabetical order).

ALABAMA, 1961–67 AND 1971–81

It's rare when one coach puts together two different dynasties at the same school. But Paul "Bear" Bryant, as the world now knows, was no ordinary coach. Bryant came to Alabama in 1958 and by 1961 he had won the first of his 13 Southeastern Conference titles and the first of his six national championships. Alabama had three national championships in the '60s and should have had a fourth when its 1966 team went 10–0 and thumped Nebraska (34–7) in the Orange Bowl. That national championship went to Notre Dame. After Alabama struggled in 1968, 1969, and 1970, some fans believed the game had passed Bryant by. Bryant installed the wishbone offense for the 1971 season and began an 11-year stretch where Alabama won 116 games, nine SEC championships, and three national championships.

> **Overall record:** 1961–67 (68–7–3); 1971–81 (116–15–1)
> **SEC championships:** 13
> **National championships (6):** 1961, 1964, 1965, 1973, 1978, 1979
> **Coach:** Paul "Bear" Bryant
> **Top players:** Lee Roy Jordan, Billy Neighbors, Paul Crane, Cecil Dowdy, Joe Namath, Johnny Musso, John Hannah, Leroy Cook, Ozzie Newsome, Marty Lyons, Barry Krauss, E.J. Junior, Ken Stabler, Dennis Homan, Steve Sloan, Ray Perkins, Woodrow Lowe

Pat Dye led Auburn to four SEC championships. Photo courtesy of the *Atlanta Journal-Constitution.*

AUBURN, 1983–89

When Pat Dye took over as Auburn's head coach in 1981, the Tigers had not been to a bowl game since 1974 and had lost eight straight games to Alabama, their bitter rival. Dye's timing for bringing the Auburn program back could not have been better. In Dye's second year he beat Alabama and Bear Bryant, his former mentor. Bryant retired after the 1982 season, and Dye used that opportunity to lead Auburn to its most consistent run with 67 wins in seven seasons and four SEC championships. The highlight of this stretch came on December 2, 1989, when Auburn upset No. 2 Alabama 30–20 to share the SEC championship. Dye coached three more seasons before retiring in 1992.

Overall record: 67–16–1
SEC championships (4): 1983, 1987, 1988, 1989
National championships: None
Coach: Pat Dye
Top players: Bo Jackson (1985 Heisman Trophy winner), Gregg Carr, Donnie Humphrey, Ben Tamburello, Brent Fullwood, Aundray Bruce, Kurt Crain, Stacy Searels, Tracy Rocker (1988 Outland, Lombardi winner), Walter Reeves, Benji Roland, Ed King

FLORIDA, 1990–2001

When 1966 Heisman Trophy winner Steve Spurrier took over as head coach in 1990, Florida had never won an SEC championship and had never won 10 games in a season. That quickly changed. Florida finished No. 1 in the SEC in Spurrier's first season in Gainesville but could not claim the SEC title because of NCAA sanctions levied against the previous coaching staff. Over the next six years Florida won five SEC titles 28–21 to Alabama in the SEC Championship Game. Alabama would go on to win the national championship. In 1996 Florida won its fifth SEC title in six years and then went on to beat Florida State in the Sugar Bowl for the school's first national championship.

When Spurrier left Florida after the 2001 season, it capped the most dominating run by a team in the SEC since Alabama in the 1970s. In a 12-year span Florida went 122–27–1 with six SEC championships and one national championship. In 12 seasons, Spurrier and the Gators went 87–14 against SEC competition, a winning percentage of .861.

Overall record: 122–27–1
SEC championships (6): 1991, 1993, 1994, 1995, 1996, 2000
National championships (1): 1996
Coach: Steve Spurrier
Top players: Huey Richardson, Shane Matthews, Will White, Brad Culpepper, Errict Rhett, Judd Davis, Kevin Carter, Jack Jackson, Jason Odom, Danny Wuerffel (1996 Heisman winner), Reidel Anthony, Ike Hilliard, Jacquez Green, Donnie Young, Jeff Mitchell, Rex Grossman, Alex Brown, Jabar Gaffney, Lito Sheppard, Lawrence Wright, Fred Taylor

FLORIDA STATE, 1987–2000

Given the parity in college football in the 21st century, it is highly unlikely that any team in the future will match Florida State's 14-year run from 1987 to 2000. For 14 consecutive seasons the Seminoles won at least 10 games and each year they finished in the top five of the final Associated Press poll. The run produced two Heisman Trophy winners (Charlie Ward in 1993, Chris Weinke in 2000) and a boatload of All-Americans. There was one undefeated season (1999) and seven seasons with only one loss. "I don't know if anybody will ever do that again," coach Bobby Bowden said. "It's pretty amazing when you think about it."

Year	Record	Final AP Ranking	Year	Record	Final AP Ranking
1987	11–1	2	1994	10–1–1	4
1988	11–1	3	1995	10–2	4
1989	10–2	3	1996	11–1	3
1990	10–2	4	1997	11–1	3
1991	11–2	2	1998	11–2	3
1992	11–1	2	1999	12–0	1
1993	12–1	1	2000	11–2	5

Overall record: 152–18–1
National championships (2): 1993, 1999
Coach: Bobby Bowden
Top players: Charlie Ward (1993 Heisman Trophy winner), Deion Sanders, LeRoy Butler, Marvin Jones, Terrell Buckley, Derrick Brooks, Corey Sawyer, Clifton Abraham, Clay Shiver, Peter Boulware, Reinard Wilson, Warrick Dunn, Chris Weinke (2000 Heisman winner), Peter Warrick, Corey Simon

GEORGIA, 1980–83

The dynasty lasted only four years, but for Georgia fans it was the most glorious four years in school history. It began in 1980 when Georgia was trying to rebound from a disappointing 6–5 season in 1979. Coach Vince Dooley believed his 1980 team had the chance to be special, but he needed to find one more piece to the puzzle. That piece turned out to be freshman running back Herschel Walker, who became an instant legend, leading the Bulldogs to a 12–0 season and the national championship. In 1981 Georgia went 10–2, losing to Clemson, the eventual national champion, and Pittsburgh, whom it played in the Sugar Bowl. In 1982, Georgia went 11–0 and was ranked No. 1 before it lost to No. 2 Penn State in the Sugar Bowl. In 1983, the year after Walker left to play professional football, Georgia almost won its fourth straight SEC title. But a 13–7 loss to Auburn and Bo Jackson gave the championship to the Tigers. By the time Georgia's run was over, the Bulldogs had won 43 games, three SEC championships, and one national championship.

Overall record: 43–4–1
SEC championships (3): 1980, 1981, 1982
National championships (1): 1980
Coach: Vince Dooley
Top players: Herschel Walker (1982 Heisman Trophy winner), Buck Belue, Lindsay Scott, Terry Hoage, Rex Robinson, Kevin Butler, Jimmy Payne, Freddie Gilbert, Jeff Sanchez, Tommy Thurson, Guy McIntyre, Eddie Weaver

GEORGIA TECH, 1951–56

After a disappointing 5–6 season in 1950, Coach Bobby Dodd decided to make some changes. He hired former Georgia Tech player Frank Broyles, who would later become head coach at Arkansas, to run the Georgia Tech offense. Ray Graves, who later became head coach at Florida, directed the defense. Broyles and Graves, plus talent that included future Hall of Fame players Ray Beck, George Morris, and Larry

Morris, created Georgia Tech's most consistent period of success. In six seasons the Yellow Jackets won 59 games, two SEC championships, and one national championship. In 1951, only a 14–14 tie with Duke at midseason kept the Yellow Jackets from posting an undefeated season. Georgia Tech finished No. 3 after beating Baylor in the Orange Bowl. That win set the table for 1952, when Georgia Tech went 12–0, including a 24–7 win over Mississippi in the Sugar Bowl.

Overall record: 59–7–3
SEC championships (2): 1951, 1952
National championships (1): 1952, International News Service
Coach: Robert Lee "Bobby" Dodd
Top players: Ray Beck, Pete Brown, Leon Hardeman, Buck Martin, Bobby Moorhead, Larry Morris, George Morris, Don Stephenson, Lamar Wheat, Hal Miller, Franklin Brooks, Allen Ecker

GRAMBLING, 1960–89

While the other dynasties listed here all played Division I-A football, Grambling's accomplishments under coach Eddie Robinson are simply too great not to include in the list of Southern dynasties. Robinson coached an unprecedented 55 seasons at Grambling, but he was particularly dominating in this 30-year stretch, winning 247 games, or an average of more than eight wins per season. The Tigers won or shared 16 Southwestern Athletic Conference championships and seven Black College National Championships.

Overall record: 247–76–8
SWAC championships: 16
Black College National Championships (7): 1967, 1972, 1974, 1975, 1977, 1980, 1982
Top players: Buck Buchanan, Ernie Ladd, Charlie Joiner, Alphonse Dotson, Frank Lewis, Richard Harris, James Harris, Gary Johnson, James Hunter, Doug Williams, Dwight Scales, Everson Walls, Sammy White, Willie Brown

LSU, 2003–07

LSU has a long and rich football tradition. But right now, Tiger fans will tell you, are the glory days. When LSU defeated No. 1 Ohio State on January 7, 2008, in New Orleans, the Tigers completed the best five-year run in school history: 56 wins, two SEC championships, and two BCS national championships. The dynasty began under coach Nick Saban, who left LSU after the 2004 season to become the head coach of the Miami Dolphins. Les Miles, the former head coach at Oklahoma State, took over and the Tigers just kept on winning. In three years under Miles LSU was 34–6.

And here is the most impressive thing about this great run by LSU. The Tigers didn't win the national championship in 2006, but they may have been the best team in the land at the season's end. The Tigers lost four first-round draft choices including quarterback JaMarcus Russell, the overall No. 1 pick from the 2006 team. Still, LSU came back in 2007 to finish 12–2 and win another national championship. Now *that's* reloading.

Year	Record	Final AP Ranking
2003	13–1	1
2004	9–3	16
2005	11–2	6
2006	11–2	3
2007	12–2	1

Overall record: 56–10
SEC championships (2): 2003, 2007
National championships (2): 2003, 2007
Top players: JaMarcus Russell (2006 Manning Award), Glenn Dorsey (2007 Outland Trophy), Ben Wilkerson, Corey Webster, Marcus Spears, LaRon Landry, Dwayne Bowe, Jacob Hester, Tyson Jackson, Ali Highsmith, Craig Steltz, Chevis Jackson

MIAMI, 1983–94, 2000–03

What makes the first Miami dynasty (1983–94) so impressive is that it took place under three different coaches. Howard Schnellenberger left after the 1983 national championship. Jimmy Johnson took over, won a national championship in 1987, and then became coach of the Dallas Cowboys after the 1988 season. Dennis Erickson won national titles in 1989 and 1991 and left after the 1994 season. Only twice in the 12 years of the first dynasty did the Hurricanes fail to win as many as 10 games. The 12-year run included two Heisman Trophy winners, an Outland Trophy winner, and a Lombardi Award winner.

Butch Davis took over in 1995 and went about the work of rebuilding the program's image on and off the field. His 2000 team went 11–1 but was denied the opportunity to play for the national championship despite beating Florida State, which did play for the title, in a head-to-head match-up. When Davis left for the Cleveland Browns after the 2000 season, he told a friend that he had left enough talent behind to win more than one national championship. Davis was very close to being right.

Offensive coordinator Larry Coker was elevated to head coach and the Hurricanes blew through a 12-game schedule to win the 2001 national championship. The following season the Hurricanes were undefeated and ranked No. 1 when they lost to Ohio State in double overtime (31–24) in the BCS championship game at the Fiesta Bowl. The loss snapped Miami's 34-game winning streak.

Overall record: 1983–94 (126–19); 2000–03 (46–4).
National championships (5): 1983, 1987, 1989, 1991, 2001
Coaches: Howard Schnellenberger (1979–83); Jimmy Johnson (1984–88); Dennis Erickson (1989–94); Butch Davis (1995–2000); Larry Coker (2001–06)
Top players: Jay Brophy, Jerome Brown, Vinny Testaverde (1986 Heisman winner), Bennie Blades, Danny Stubbs, Steve Walsh, Greg

Gino Torretta. Photo courtesy of Miami SID.

Mark, Russell Maryland (1990 Outland winner), Kevin Williams, Micheal Barrow, Gino Torretta (1992 Heisman winner), Warren Sapp (1994 Lombardi winner), Michael Irvin, Ray Lewis, Bryant McKinnie, Dan Morgan, Jeremy Shockey, Ken Dorsey, Willis McGahee, Sean Taylor, Kellen Winslow, Devin Hester.

MISSISSIPPI, 1954–63

For a 10-year stretch, John Vaught's Ole Miss Rebels were the team to beat, not only in the South, but in the nation as well. During that period, Vaught won five of the school's six SEC championships and all three of its national championships. With players like quarterback Jake Gibbs and fullback Charlie Flowers, who both went on to the Hall of Fame, Ole Miss won 90 games in 10 years. The 1959 team is considered to have been the best, having posted eight shutouts and losing only to LSU, 7–3, on Billy

Jake Gibbs, Mississippi's All-American quarterback, led the Rebels to a 10–0–1 season in 1960. Photo courtesy of Mississippi SID.

Cannon's famous 89-yard punt return. The Rebels avenged that loss two months later by beating LSU in the Sugar Bowl 21–0. The Ole Miss squad of 1959 was named the SEC Team of the Decade.

> **Overall record:** 90–13–4
> **SEC championships (5):** 1954, 1955, 1960, 1962, 1963.
> **National championships (3):** 1958, Dunkel; 1960, Football Writers Association; 1962, Litkenhous
> **Coach:** John H. Vaught
> **Top players:** Rex Reed Boggan, Paige Cothren, Jackie Simpson, Charlie Flowers, Jake Gibbs, Bill Ray Adams, Treva Bolin, Jim Dunaway, Kenny Dill, Jimmy Patton, Billy Brewer

TENNESSEE, 1938–40

General Robert R. Neyland won 173 games in 21 years as Tennessee's head football coach, but his coaching tenure was interrupted twice by military service. This three-year stretch represents the most dominating period of Neyland's legendary career. Tennessee posted three consecutive undefeated regular seasons, losing only to Southern California (14–0) in the January 1, 1940, Rose Bowl and to Boston College (19–13) in the January 1, 1941, Sugar Bowl. The Vols' defense was the hallmark of this incredible stretch. Of the 33 games Tennessee played in these three seasons, the Volunteers posted 26 shutouts, setting an NCAA record with 17 straight regular-season shutouts and 71 straight quarters without giving up a point. In 1939 Tennessee did not give up a point during the entire regular season and then lost to Southern California 14–0 in the Rose Bowl. Duke is the only other team to do that, in 1938.

Four players from these three teams went on to the College Football Hall of Fame. Various wire services awarded the national championship to Tennessee in 1938 and 1940.

Overall record: 31–2
SEC championships (3): 1938, 1939, 1940
National championships (2): 1938, Dunkel, Litkenhous; 1940, Dunkel, Williamson
Coach: Robert R. Neyland
Top players: George "Bad News" Cafego, Ed Molinski, Bob Suffridge, Bowden Wyatt, Abe Shires, Bob Fox, Johnny Butler, Ray Graves, Bob Woodruff

CHAPTER 6

GAME DAY
The Towns, the Traditions

Webster defines *tradition* as a set of customs transmitted from one generation to another. Tradition, more than anything else, is the cornerstone of college football in the South. Each college town has its own special set of traditions that make it a unique place to visit on a game day. Tennessee has its checkerboard end zones and the Volunteer Navy, Ole Miss has The Grove, Auburn has the Tiger Walk and Toomer's Corner, and Clemson has the Esso Club. These traditions are the glue that binds the generations of Southern college football fans to one another and keeps them coming back to their beloved campuses year after year. People in the South take these football traditions very, very seriously. To many fans, the renewal of these traditions each fall provides all the physical and emotional comfort of a warm blanket on a cold winter's night.

"As soon as the last bowl game is over in January, most of the people I know start counting the days until the next season gets here," said Brandon "Booger" Seely, a longtime Georgia fan from Albany. "A lot of us live and die until they kick it off again in the fall. A lot of friendships are built and maintained for a lifetime thanks to college football."

Game day routines in the South differ with each campus, but they do have several things in common.

Almost every hotel in a college town in the South requires a two-night-minimum stay during football weekends, meaning that fans wanting a room have to pay for both Friday and Saturday nights. Many hotels in Southern college football towns make a significant portion of their yearly income during those six or seven football weekends when they are totally booked and, because of the demand, are able to charge premium rates.

This policy guarantees that the pregame party begins in earnest on Friday night. These celebrations can get a little rowdy, as Alabama coach Bear Bryant found out in 1976 when his team played at Georgia. The Crimson Tide had won the SEC championship in 1975 and was favored to do it again in 1976. But Georgia and its fans had been getting ready for their October 2 game with Alabama since the end of spring practice the previous April. When the Alabama team arrived in Athens on the Friday before the

Georgia fans, like most fans around the South, can get a bit rowdy at times. Photo courtesy of the *Atlanta Journal-Constitution.*

game, the Georgia fans were waiting for them.

Bryant made the mistake of housing his team at the Athens Holiday Inn, just a few blocks from Georgia's Sanford Stadium. Word of the team's location got out, and about midnight some "enthusiastic" Georgia fans parked their cars outside the area of the hotel where the Crimson Tide players were trying to sleep. The fans turned on their headlights and began blaring their horns to wake up the Alabama players. The commotion got so out of hand that Bryant finally ordered his troops to take their mattresses out of the rooms and sleep in the hall.

The next day Georgia won the game 21–0. The Bulldogs finished the regular season 10–1 and won their first SEC championship since 1968.

"That's one of the biggest differences I've seen between football in the South and football anywhere else," said Frank Broyles, the former head coach at Arkansas who recently retired as the school's athletics director. "On game day, the South has the most aggressive fans in America. In other parts of the country, fans are there to enjoy the game. But in the South, the fans believe they are there to participate!"

Because the supply of hotel rooms in a Southern college football town can never match the demand, some fans become very possessive of those rooms once they have acquired them. Some fans take this possessiveness to the extreme.

"We had a man who had been staying in the same room with us for at least 20 years," says Leroy Dukes, the former manager of the Ramada Inn in Athens. "Unfortunately, one year he died during the off-season. Come fall, the man's son showed up saying he was there to claim his daddy's room. He just assumed that the room would be passed down to him after his daddy died."

But the one tradition that all Southern College football towns have in common is tailgating.

Tailgating is the term used to describe the pregame and postgame ritual of eating, drinking, and socializing with one's fellow fans. The name comes from the practice of opening the tailgate to a station wagon or pickup truck and spreading out the food for all to share.

Fans all over the country practice some form of tailgating, but those who follow Southern college football have turned it into nothing less than an art form. Just like the players on the field want to be the best, Southern fans want their tailgating parties to be bigger and better than anyone else's.

In the Grove, the most popular tailgating spot at Ole Miss, it is not unusual to see a complete buffet spread on a white linen tablecloth. The tablecloth is often held in place by a silver candelabra.

At Clemson or South Carolina, you'll often see fans enjoying a Low Country Boil, a delicious combination of shrimp, potatoes, corn, crab, and sausages cooked to perfection in one huge pot.

At Auburn and Alabama, fans start up their barbecue grills well before dawn on game day and by lunch produce some of the best eats on the planet.

At LSU they put a Cajun twist on tailgating, and the jambalaya and crawfish etouffee flow freely.

But all tailgating parties in the South, regardless of their locale, must have a few basics: fried chicken, potato salad, deviled eggs, pimento cheese sandwiches (no crust on the bread, please!), pecan pie, and plenty of iced tea (sweet, of course!) to wash it all down. Some fans choose beverages a little on the harder side of iced tea, and by kickoff these hardy souls already have on their "game faces." Sometimes fans get so involved in the fun of tailgating that they forget about the game.

"Our folks make a mad rush for the gates a few minutes before kickoff," said the late Bob Bradley, Clemson's longtime sports information director. "They've just got to have that last glass of bourbon and that last chicken leg."

After the game Southern fans begin their second round of tailgating to celebrate the victory or drown their sorrows in defeat. Many will stay around for an hour or more in order to let the traffic thin out. Then it's time to pack up the food and the folding chairs and begin what, for some fans, is a very long drive home. Of course the drive seems a lot shorter after a win than after a loss.

Here is a look at just some of the Southern college football towns where game day is always something magical.

GAME DAY AT GEORGIA

The Revolutionary War had barely been over two years when the University of Georgia was founded in 1785. The nation's first state-chartered university is located in Athens, approximately 75 miles north of the state capital in Atlanta, and has an undergraduate enrollment of more than 33,000.

The Bulldogs fans love to tailgate at Georgia, which has earned the reputation as being one of the most beautiful campuses on which to enjoy a fall football Saturday. For almost 80 years, fans have been turning out to support their troops at Sanford Stadium, which was named after the late S.V. Sanford, the former president of the university. The stadium was dedicated on October 12, 1929, with a 15–0 upset of Yale, one of college football's national powers at the time.

The stadium, which had an original seating capacity of 30,000, has been expanded and renovated many times in its history and now seats 92,746, the second largest capacity in the SEC. It is the fifth largest stadium in Division I-A football.

Surrounding the field is a row of English privet hedge. The original hedges were installed in 1929 and removed when the stadium hosted the women's soccer competition during the 1996 Summer Olympics.

Playing "between the hedges" has never been easy for opposing teams. Since 1929 Georgia is 301–103–11 (.739 winning percentage) at home.

"Between the Hedges" at Georgia's Sanford Stadium. Photo courtesy of Georgia SID.

Here are a few other reasons why game day at Georgia is special:

The Arch: This gateway to the lovely Georgia campus was installed in 1964. For years, upperclassmen did not allow freshmen to walk under the arch. Officially the tradition has ended, but some freshmen still keep it alive.

The Chapel Bell: In the 1890s freshmen were ordered by upperclassmen to ring this bell until midnight to celebrate a Georgia victory. Today the bell is still intact, and students and fans remain after every home win to take turns ringing it.

Silver Britches: Under coach Wally Butts (1939–60) Georgia's teams wore silver pants as part of their uniform. When Vince Dooley became head coach in 1964, he changed the uniform to include white pants. But in 1980 Dooley decided to go back to the silver pants, or "britches" as he called them. That year Georgia went 12–0 and won the national championship. With the exception of a few games, Georgia has worn the silver britches since.

UGA I–VI: The most recognized mascot in all of college football is the English Bulldog UGA (pronounced ugh-ga)

The historic Arch is the gateway to the University of Georgia. Photo courtesy of Georgia SID.

that has been Georgia's official mascot since 1956. UGA I was born on December 2, 1955, and appeared on the Georgia sideline the following fall. In 1997 UGA V, the most famous of the lineage, appeared on the cover of *Sports Illustrated* as college football's best mascot. UGA V also appeared in the movie *Midnight in the Garden of Good and Evil*, which was directed by Clint Eastwood. UGA V retired prior to the 1999 season and was replaced by his son, UGA VI. He is the biggest of all the UGA mascots, weighing 65 pounds, 20 pounds heavier than his father. UGA VI will enter the 2008 season with a record of 77–27.

"Glory, Glory": Sung to the tune of "The Battle Hymn of the Republic," "Glory, Glory" has been the official Georgia fight song since 1915:

Glory, Glory to Old Georgia
Glory, Glory to Old Georgia
Glory, Glory to Old Georgia
G-E-O-R-G-I-A

Often, the last line of the song is replaced with "And to Hell with Georgia Tech."

The Dawg Walk: The tradition was started in 2001 by current Georgia coach Mark Richt as a way to fire up his players. About two hours before the game the Georgia Redcoat Band creates a human corridor down the middle of a parking lot on the West side of Sanford Stadium. Georgia's players arrive at the area in buses and walk through the band and thousands of Georgia fans as they enter the stadium.

How 'Bout Them Dawgs!: Georgia fans began using the phrase to greet one another in the 1970s, but the phrase became ultrapopular after Georgia won the 1980 national championship.

Redcoat Band: Known for their uniforms, which feature brilliant red coats, the Georgia band plays a big part on game day in Athens. After the Dawg Walk, the band enters Sanford Stadium through the West entrance to begin the pregame ceremonies. After the game, in one of Georgia's long-standing traditions, the Redcoat Band remains in the stadium for a brief concert, including "Tara's Theme" from *Gone With the Wind*. This concert, which concludes with the school fight song, officially marks the end to game day at the University of Georgia.

GAME DAY AT AUBURN

Located about 55 miles north of the Alabama state capital of Montgomery, Auburn University has long been known as "the Loveliest Village on the Plain." Never is this more true than on a football Saturday.

The town has only about 50,000 residents, but more than 85,000 fans turn out for each home game at Jordan-Hare Stadium. The stadium is named for former coach Ralph "Shug" Jordan (1951–75) and Cliff Hare, a member of Auburn's first football team who went on to become a dean in the School of Chemistry.

The stadium was dedicated in 1939 with 7,500 seats and 10 years later was named after Hare. The facility was renamed Jordan-Hare Stadium in 1973, two years before Jordan retired as head coach. The most recent expansion, completed in 2004, moved Jordan-Hare Stadium's capacity to 87,451.

In 2005, prior to the annual "Iron Bowl" game with Alabama, the turf where Auburn plays officially became Pat Dye Field in honor of the man who coached the Tigers for 12 seasons (1981–92) and won four SEC championships.

Auburn got its nickname, "Tigers," from a line in an Oliver Goldsmith poem, "The Deserted Valley" which reads: "where crouching Tigers await their hapless prey." The town of Auburn got its name from the same poem.

Here are just a few of the things that make game day at Auburn special:

The Tiger Walk: A couple of hours before each home game, Auburn's players walk from Sewell Hall, the school's athletics dormitory, to Jordan-Hare Stadium, several hundred yards away. Fans line either side of Donahue Drive to form a human corridor. This tradition serves to get both fans and players fired up before the game.

The largest Tiger Walk, which began in the early 1960s, was prior to the Alabama game on December 2, 1989, when more than 20,000 attended.

"War Eagle!": The battle cry for all Auburn faithful was born on February 20, 1892, when Georgia and Auburn met for the first time in college football history at Atlanta's Piedmont Park. According to a popular legend, a member of the Auburn faculty brought with him an eagle that the man had raised since his days in the Civil War. After Auburn's first touchdown, the eagle broke loose from its handler and soared above the crowd. When the

Aubie, the Auburn mascot, gets a push. Photo courtesy of the *Atlanta Journal-Constitution.*

"War Eagle!" Auburn's eagle, named Tiger, guards the sideline. Photo courtesy of the *Atlanta Journal-Constitution.*

fans saw the familiar figure, they shouted "War Eagle" and a tradition was born. Auburn still has a golden eagle named Tiger on the sideline for each game as the school's official mascot. A student dressed in a tiger costume and going by the name Aubie shares the sideline with Tiger.

When one Auburn fan greets another on game day, they don't say hello. They simply shout "War Eagle."

Auburn fans celebrate a big victory by "rolling" Toomer's Corner. Photo courtesy of Auburn SID.

Toomer's Corner: This corner, located in the center of town where the university campus meets the town of Auburn at the intersection of Magnolia Avenue and College Street, is the official gathering place after a home football game. Students, fans, players, and sometimes even coaches join together to roll the trees with toilet paper to celebrate a big victory.

GAME DAY AT LSU

On a campus rich with tradition, one of the most enduring events at Louisiana State University is night football at Tiger Stadium. LSU started playing under the lights in 1931, and over the years, a Saturday night in Baton Rouge has been one of the most intimidating atmospheres for opponents in all of college football. Since 1960 LSU is 192–62–4 under the lights at home. The Tigers are 17–22–3 during the day at home.

"You were at a distinct disadvantage when you went into Baton Rouge to play," said Ron Franklin, ESPN's longtime college football voice. "Nine times out of 10 they wanted you to take the field first and feel the sense of terror. Because when they came out of the South tunnel, the night erupted. Their players were lifted by it as well."

The tailgating scene at LSU games is unique to all of college football. With New Orleans located about an hour down Interstate 10, the pregame meal has a Cajun flair instead of the usual fried chicken and potato salad found in most places around the South.

In the best Mardi Gras tradition, fans arrive in Baton Rouge as early as Thursday evening for a Saturday night game. To walk across campus on Friday night is to enjoy a smorgasbord of smells that include crawfish, boiled shrimp, and jambalaya. In 1996, ESPN named LSU's tailgating scene as the best in all of college football.

Mike the Tiger. Photo courtesy of LSU SID.

Here are just a few of the other sights and sounds you'll enjoy on a football weekend at Baton Rouge:

Mike the Tiger: Since 1935, a real Bengal tiger has been on the LSU sidelines as the school's official mascot. Today's Tiger, Mike VI, lives in a plush permanent residence just north of the stadium that includes a pool and a glass-encased area where fans can watch him. Before the game, Mike is placed in a rolling cage and parked just outside the opposing locker room so players from the other team must walk by. The sight can be a little intimidating. One year Mike was particularly feisty when Alabama arrived and, according to legend, coach Bear Bryant had a student feed Mike a steak laced with tranquilizers. Mike VI made his debut on October 6, 2007, during a nationally televised game with Florida.

Tiger Rag: One of the most popular pregame rituals is when LSU's Golden Band from Tigerland marches down North Stadium Drive into Tiger Stadium. Once the band takes the field it remains silent until it suddenly pounds out the first few notes of the Tiger Rag—"Hold...That...Ti-Ger! Hold...That...Ti-Ger"—which causes the crowd to erupt. "That sound," noted a veteran sportswriter, "will make the hair stand up on a dead man's chest."

Victory Hill: Two hours before each home game, the Tigers walk down a hill near the Journalism school, down North Stadium Drive, and into Tiger Stadium accompanied by the Golden Band from Tigerland and the Golden Girls. Coach Curley Hallman started the tradition in 1990, and each coach since has continued it.

White Jerseys: Unlike other schools in the South, LSU prefers to wear white jerseys for home games. This was a tradition that dated back to the 1950s and ended in 1983 when the NCAA ruled that home teams must wear dark jerseys. When Gerry DiNardo became head coach in 1995, he lobbied the NCAA to make an exception in order to bring the tradition back to LSU. The NCAA passed a rule that said teams could wear white jerseys at home if the visiting team agreed, and the only team not to agree over the years has been Vanderbilt, DiNardo's former employer that still held a grudge because he left the school. Instead of going with its old purple jerseys against Vanderbilt, DiNardo introduced gold ones, and LSU won the game 35–0.

The Earthquake: How loud can it get in Tiger Stadium? On October 8, 1988, after LSU scored the winning touchdown against Auburn, the explosion of sound was so great that it registered on the LSU geology department's seismograph.

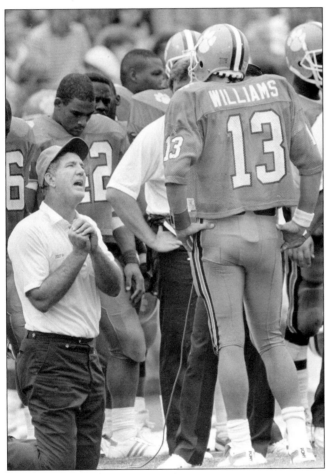

Clemson coach Danny Ford pleads with quarterback Rodney Williams in 1987. Photo courtesy of the Atlanta Journal-Constitution.

GAME DAY AT CLEMSON

You don't have to wonder if you're on the right road to Clemson, South Carolina. Just a few miles from the city limits on Highway 76, a series of orange tiger paws leads visitors to one of the most unique places in all of college football. Rising up at the foothills of the Blue Ridge Mountains and near the shores of scenic Lake Hartwell, Clemson is located in the northwestern corner of the state, just two hours north of Atlanta.

Clemson's population is only a little over 14,000, but on Saturdays more than 81,000 fans pack Memorial Stadium, better known as Death Valley, making it the second largest city in the state just behind Columbia, the capital.

Going into the 2008 season Clemson has won or shared 13 Atlantic Coast Conference titles. But its shining moment in football came in 1981 when the Tigers won their first and only national championship. Every year fans fill Memorial Stadium hoping the Tigers will make another run at the title.

Here are some of the sights and sounds you'll experience on a game day at Clemson.

Howard's Rock: Mounted on a pedestal on a grassy hill at the east end of Memorial Stadium, this rock from Death Valley, California, was given to Frank Howard, Clemson's legendary coach from 1940 to 1969. Howard wanted to throw the rock away, but one of his assistants convinced him to keep it. Looking for something to motivate his team, Howard brought out the rock prior to a game with Virginia in 1966.

Howard said his players could touch the rock for good luck, but only under the following conditions. "I said all them that was going to give me 110 percent could touch my rock, and if they weren't going to give me 110 percent, keep your filthy hands off my rock," said Howard, who died in 1996.

Not everyone was enthralled with Coach Howard and his rock.

"I got a letter from a lady over at Travelers Rest, South Carolina, who said, 'Coach, if you believed more in the Lord than you do that rock, you'd be a much better football coach,'" said Howard.

Running Down the Hill: ABC broadcaster Brent Musburger once termed it "the most exciting 25 seconds in college football." About 10 minutes

Touching Howard's Rock before kickoff is a Clemson tradition. Photo courtesy of Clemson SID.

before kickoff, the Clemson team leaves the locker room under the west stands and buses around the stadium to the east side of the stadium, where there is a grassy hill about 100 feet long that leads directly to the playing field. At a given signal, a cannon is fired, the band plays Tiger Rag, and the team charges down the hill as the crowd goes wild. The tradition started in 1942, and for all but 15 home games since, the Clemson team has run down the hill. For the record, Clemson is 6–9 when it doesn't run down the hill, 238–83–7 (73.6 percent) when it does. In 1967 touching Howard's Rock at the top of the hill officially became part of the pregame ceremonies.

Esso Club: Not all the partying at a Clemson game goes on in the parking lots around the stadium. At Clemson, fans gather before and after the game at the Esso Club, a converted gas station that has become the area's most popular watering hole and a Southern institution.

"The Esso Club is a place where professors used to go to get a cold beer when nobody else in town had one," said the late Bob Bradley, the former sports information director at Clemson.

The Esso club now has its own website: www.theessoclub.com.

The Graveyard: Clemson has beaten a lot of ranked teams at home. But at its practice fields, which are just across the street from Memorial Stadium, it has constructed a "Graveyard" to celebrate victories over ranked teams on the road. Since 1948, Clemson has posted 19 road victories over ranked teams. In 2004, 2005, and 2006 Clemson had road victories over No. 10 Miami (24–17), No. 19 South Carolina (13–9), and No. 6 Florida State (27–20).

Tiger Mascot Pushups: Since 1954 a Clemson student dressed in a Tiger suit has served as the school's mascot. After every Clemson score, the mascot does pushups to match the current number of Tiger points. If Clemson scores and goes ahead 7–0, the mascot does seven pushups. If the team scores again and goes up to 14–0, the mascot does 14 pushups. The record number of pushups for one game was 465 by Ricky Capps during an 82–24 win over Wake Forest in 1981.

GAME DAY AT SOUTH CAROLINA

Football fans say there is a special place in heaven reserved for all fans of South Carolina football—for they have certainly been through hell here on earth.

South Carolina players run through the smoke during the "2001" pregame ceremony. Photo courtesy of South Carolina SID.

No group of fans has suffered so much and yet been so supportive of a college football program. Going into the 2008 season, the 117th in school history, South Carolina has had only nine years of eight victories or more, and three of those have come since 2000. In more than a century of football, only once (1984) has South Carolina won 10 games in a season.

Still, every year Gamecock fans flock to Williams-Brice Stadium in Columbia, the capital of the Palmetto State. During the 1999 season, the first for new coach Lou Holtz, South Carolina fans set a record by purchasing 53,000 season tickets. That was after a 1–10 season in 1998. In 1999 the Gamecocks were 0–11, but the fans kept coming.

South Carolina fans were rewarded for their patience in 2000 and 2001 when Holtz took the Gamecocks to back-to-back Outback Bowls, where they played Ohio State twice and beat the Buckeyes both times.

South Carolina has won only four bowl games in its history but is ranked in the top 20 nationally in attendance each year.

"We have the greatest fans in the world," said Holtz, who retired as head coach after the 2004 season and was replaced by Steve Spurrier. "We raise more money per win than any school in America."

The tailgating scene at the State Fairgrounds, directly across the street from the stadium, is as good as any you will find in the South. But a word of advice: get there early. There are basically only two roads into the stadium area and more than 80,000 fans must use them.

Here are just a few of the things you need to know about game day at South Carolina:

2001: When Joe Morrison took over as head coach at South Carolina in 1983, he wanted to find something that would bring excitement into Williams-Brice Stadium at the beginning of each game. Thus he instituted this tradition. In the moments prior to the South Carolina team taking the field, the public address system begins to blare out the opening notes to the theme song from *2001: A Space Odyssey*. As the music plays, the crowd's enthusiasm builds. When the music hits the highest note, the Gamecocks rush onto the field through a tunnel of smoke, and the crowd goes wild.

The Chicken Curse: Legend has it that former governor and U.S. Senator "Pitchfork" Ben Tillman, who founded Clemson University, South Carolina's archrival in the state, is responsible for this curse. As a farmer, Tillman felt the bluebloods who attended South Carolina looked down their collective noses at him and his people. Over the years, Tillman's curse has been used to explain why South Carolina has experienced so many disappointments in athletics.

Among the disappointing events attributed to the curse:

- In 1984 South Carolina was 9–0 and would have risen to No. 1 with a win over Navy, a heavy underdog. Instead the Gamecocks lost 38–21, ending their hopes of a national title.
- The death of Morrison by a heart attack in 1989.
- A loss at home against the Citadel, a Division I-AA school, in 1990.

The Cockaboose: South Carolina fans take a backseat to no one when it comes to creativity in tail-gating. In 1990 a couple from Columbia decided to put to good use a set of abandoned train tracks that run along one side of Williams-Brice Stadium. They installed 22 rail cars, decorated to the hilt and out-fitted with all the amenities such as running water, air conditioning, and cable television, them out to the serious tailgaters among the Gamecocks fans.

Florida players celebrate their win over Alabama in the 1994 SEC Championship Game. Photo courtesy of AP/Wide World Photos.

GAME DAY AT FLORIDA

Until 1990 the University of Florida had always had a good, but not great, college football tradition.

But all that changed when Steve Spurrier, a Heisman Trophy winner at Florida in 1966, returned to Gainesville to become head coach.

Before Spurrier took over in 1990, Florida had never won an SEC championship in football. Spurrier won five SEC titles in his first seven seasons at Florida and a total of six championships in his 12 seasons as the head coach. In 1996, with Heisman Trophy quarterback Danny Wuerffel at the controls, Florida won its first national championship.

But what Spurrier did at Florida in the '90s went beyond mere wins and losses. He changed the attitude of Florida's entire fan base and made game day in Gainesville, Florida, very special.

At the end of the 1991 season, his second at Florida, Spurrier came up with a most appropriate nickname for Ben Hill Griffin Stadium. He labeled it "the Swamp" because, Spurrier said, "That's where Gators live. We feel comfortable there, but we hope our opponents feel tentative. A swamp is hot and sticky and can be dangerous."

Since 1990 the Swamp has been one of the toughest venues in all of college football for opponents, as the Gators have posted a record of 100–12.

With the warm weather and a campus surrounded with palm trees, Florida offers a pregame and postgame tailgating scene that is unlike just about any other in the South.

Here are but a few things that make game day at Florida a unique experience:

"We Are the Boys from Old Florida": At the end of the third quarter at each Florida home game, Gator fans stand arm-in-arm, swaying back and forth while singing this tune, which dates back to World War II.

Over the years attempts to make it more politically correct were overwhelmingly voted down by male and female students alike. Today, the words remain unchanged:

We are the boys from old Florida...
F-L-O-R-I-D-A...
Where the girls are the fairest...
The boys are the squarest...
Of any old state down our way...
We are all strong for old Florida...
Down where the old Gators play...
In all kinds of weather...
We'll all stick together...
For F-L-O-R-I-D-A...

Mr. Two Bits: George Edmundson, a retired insurance salesman from Tampa who attended every Florida game dressed in saddle oxford shoes, a yellow oxford-cloth shirt, and a blue-and-orange tie, earned his nickname because before each game he ran to the middle of the field holding a crumpled sign that read "Two Bits" and began to lead the most recognized cheer in college football. Edmundson retired as Mr. Two Bits after the 1998 season but still comes back for special Florida games such as those against Tennessee and Florida State.

"He-e-e-e-e-r-e Come the Gators!": In 1964, Jim Finch, the Gators' public address announcer, began this tradition of stretching out the word "Here" for approximately 20–25 seconds as the Florida players take the field. The Ben Hill Griffin Stadium crowd grows louder and louder, and after that long "Here," the PA announcer finishes with a quick "Come the Gators!" By then the Florida crowd is going crazy.

North End Zone: The north end zone of Ben Hill Griffin Stadium was rebuilt in 1991, raising capacity to 83,000. This reconstruction also made the Florida

Florida's Mr. Two Bits, George Edmundson. Photo courtesy of Florida SID.

Stadium one of the loudest in all of college football. The Victory Bell, which was once on the battleship USS *Florida*, was installed in the north end zone in the 1930s, when the ship was decommissioned. Fans and students ring the bell after each home win. In 2003 the stadium underwent a $50 million renovation that increased capacity to over 90,000 and made it one of the best football facilities in the country.

GAME DAY AT GEORGIA TECH

To attend a game day at the Georgia Institute of Technology, known as one of the leading technological universities in the world since its founding in 1888, is to partake in a totally different kind of college football experience.

Whereas most campuses in the South are located in smaller towns and have stadiums surrounded by wide-open spaces, Georgia Tech's campus spreads across more than 300 acres of prime real estate in the heart of downtown Atlanta. In most college towns around the South, only pine trees tower above the rim of the stadium. At Georgia Tech's Bobby Dodd Stadium at Historic Grant Field, fans see overhead the skyscrapers that mark the Empire City of the South.

Georgia Tech's stadium was originally built in 1913, making it the oldest on-campus stadium in Division I-A football. Georgia Tech students built the original west stands, which seated 5,000 fans at the time.

The stadium was originally named Hugh Inman Grant Field after the deceased son of John W. Grant, a member of the Georgia Tech Board of Trustees and a well-known Atlanta merchant, who donated $15,000 toward the stadium's construction costs.

In the more than 90 years of its existence, the stadium has undergone several renovations, and in 1988 Georgia Tech added to it the name Bobby Dodd, its Hall of Fame coach who retired in 1966.

Parking is limited on the narrow streets around Bobby Dodd Stadium, so game day traffic can be quite a nightmare. Some fans take MARTA, Atlanta's commuter rail system, which runs from the suburbs. Other fans choose to drive to the campus several hours before the game so that they can take part in a street fair held on Bobby Dodd Way, right behind the north entrance to the stadium.

Fraternity houses and residence halls line Fowler Street and Techwood Drive, the two streets on either side of Bobby Dodd Stadium. After a big Georgia Tech victory those houses keep the party going and music blaring well into the wee hours of the morning.

On the night of November 3, 1990, the Georgia Tech students living in those houses had their finest hour. Earlier that day, several hundred miles away in Charlottesville, Virginia, Georgia Tech had upset No. 1 Virginia 41–38 in one of the greatest games ever played in the South. Immediately after the game, Georgia Tech students stormed into an empty Bobby Dodd Stadium and tore down the goal posts and, while holding them aloft, did a victory parade in the streets.

Georgia Tech's famed "Ramblin' Wreck." Photo courtesy of Georgia Tech SID.

One goal post was tossed into a bonfire set at the corner of Techwood Drive and Bobby Dodd Way.

In *Focused on the Top*, Jack Wilkinson's book on Georgia Tech's 1990 national championship season, Tech president Patrick Crecine was philosophical about the antics of his fire-wielding students on that fateful night.

"Maybe someone learned something about thermodynamics," Crecine said. "Heat rises."

Welcome to game day at Georgia Tech. Here are just a few traditions you can enjoy:

Ramblin' Wreck (the car): This restored 1930 Model A Ford Sports Coupe has been leading the Georgia Tech team onto the field at home games since September 30, 1961. Ted J. Johnson, a former Delta pilot, had restored the car as a gift to his son and later donated it to the school. The car was restored again in 1982 under the supervision of Tech alumnus Pete George, a manager of the Ford assembly plant near Atlanta.

"Ramblin' Wreck" (the song): With the possible exception of the Notre Dame fight song, this is the most recognized tune in college football. It is so well known that, according to Georgia Tech records, Richard Nixon and Nikita Khrushchev sung it in their historic face-to-face meeting in Moscow in 1959.

If you're going to visit Georgia Tech, learn the lyrics. It's a big part of game day on the Flats, as the school is also known:

I'm a Ramblin' Wreck from Georgia Tech
And a hell of an engineer
A helluva, helluva, helluva, helluva, hell of an engineer
Like all the jolly good fellows
I drink my whiskey clear
I'm a Ramblin' Wreck from Georgia Tech
And a hell of an engineer.

Rat Caps: Since 1915 all members of the freshman class at Georgia Tech have worn these gold-colored caps. The term *rat* was originally used for first-year military students but was later expanded to include all freshmen. The freshmen decorate their rat caps with winning football scores written right side up and losing scores written upside down.

George P. Burdell: He won't be there in body, but he will be there in spirit. In 1927 Georgia Tech student Ed Smith decided to play a prank and enroll a fictitious classmate, George P. Burdell, in some classes. He took the ruse to the point of actually turning in papers for Burdell. Other students joined in the fun over the years, keeping Burdell enrolled until he eventually got a bachelor's degree from Georgia Tech. In 1969, when registration became computerized, students feared that Burdell's attendance string would end. But Burdell beat the system and registered for all 3,000 classes at Georgia Tech.

The Varsity: Located on North Avenue, just two blocks from the stadium, the Varsity is one of the South's most famous drive-in restaurants and serves as a gathering place for fans before and after the game. The Varsity is famous for its onion rings and its counter-service people who will always greet you with "Whaddaya have?"

There is also the Varsity lingo, which has developed over the years between Varsity employees and customers:

Varsity employee: "Whaddaya have?"

Customer: "I want two dogs walkin' through the garden, a ring, a fry, and a PC."

Translation: "I want two chili dogs to go, with slaw, some onion rings, some french fries, and a container of chocolate milk."

GAME DAY AT TENNESSEE

Located in East Tennessee near the foot of the Smoky Mountains, Knoxville is a relatively small city (population 177,000).

But on those fall Saturdays when Tennessee plays at home, the seat of Blount County swells with an additional 100,000-plus fans who turn out to watch their beloved Volunteers do battle.

The capacity of Neyland Stadium/Shields-Watkins Field is 102,037, which is fourth among on-campus football facilities behind Michigan, Penn State, and Ohio State. During the 2007 season Tennessee was fourth nationally in average attendance with 103,918 fans per game.

The stadium is named after legendary coach Bob Neyland, the man most responsible for establishing the school's tradition in football, and Colonel W.S. Shields, the president of Knoxville's City National Bank, who provided the initial capital to build the original facility. Shields added the name of his wife, Alice Watkins, when the field was completed in 1921.

Tennessee became known as the "Volunteer State" in the 19th century because of the willingness of its men to fight in the War of 1812 and in the Mexican War. So it was only fitting that the teams of the state's largest university, founded in 1794, would take on that name.

Tennesseans are proud of their heritage and proud of a football tradition that dates back to 1891. Like most Southerners, Volunteers fans live for football season. When the Pride of the Southland Band marches onto the field, and the players dressed in orange and white run through the block "T," fans know, as legendary radio announcer John Ward always said right before kickoff, "It's football time in Tennessee!"

Here are just a few of the game day traditions at Tennessee:

Volunteer Navy: In 1962 radio broadcaster George Mooney had grown weary of Knoxville's heavy traffic on game days. So he got creative, taking his small boat down the Tennessee River and docking it just across Neyland Avenue in the shadow of Neyland Stadium. The idea caught on and the "Volunteer Navy" was born.

Today, more than 200 boats make their way down the river on game day. For big games, some dock several days early because, in Big Orange Country, as the vast majority of Tennessee is known, it's never too early to put on your game face.

Tennessee's Volunteer Navy docks near Neyland Stadium before every game. Photo courtesy of Tennessee SID.

Tennessee's checkerboard end zones. Photo courtesy of Tennessee SID.

Tennessee's mascot, Smokey, the bluetick hound. Photo courtesy of Tennessee SID.

Checkerboard End Zones: The checkerboard design on the end zones at Neyland Stadium was introduced in the mid-1960s when Doug Dickey became head coach. The orange and white checkerboard end zones, which are unique to Tennessee, went on hiatus for a while when the school switched from natural grass to artificial turf in 1968. In 1989, Tennessee brought back the checkerboard end zones, which remain in place to this day.

Smokey: The bluetick coonhound, a native dog to the state, became Tennessee's official mascot in 1953. During halftime of the Mississippi State game that season, several dogs were paraded in front of the students, who voted with their applause. When "Blue Smokey," a hound owned by the Reverend

Bill Brooks, was introduced he howled loudly. The fans loved it and a bluetick coonhound named Smokey has been the mascot ever since.

Over the years there have been nine Smokeys and each has been among the most beloved figures in the state. Smokey VIII retired after the 2003 Chick-fil-A Bowl and was replaced by Smokey IX for the 2004 season.

Block T: One of the most recognizable symbols in college football, the Block T was added to the Tennessee football helmet by coach Doug Dickey in 1964. Just prior to each game, the Pride of the Southland Band forms a Block T with the bottom facing the Tennessee tunnel. The Tennessee team then runs through the T onto the field.

"Rocky Top": Tennessee has several official fight songs, but "Rocky Top," an old country bluegrass tune, has become the unofficial fight song. Some advice: if you don't like this song, do not go to Tennessee home games. No band plays its fight song during the course of the games more than Tennessee plays "Rocky Top":

Wish that I was on ol' Rocky Top,
down in the Tennessee Hills
Ain't no smoggy smoke on Rocky Top,
ain't no telephone bills
Once I had a girl on Rocky Top,
half bear, other half cat,
Wild as mink and sweet as soda pop,
I still dream about that.

Once two strangers climbed ol' Rocky Top
Lookin' for a moonshine still
Strangers ain't come down from Rocky Top
Reckon they never will

Chorus:
Rocky Top, you'll always be,
Home sweet home to me,
Good ol' Rocky Top,
Rocky Top, Tennessee
Rocky Top, Tennessee
(Words and lyrics by Boudleaux Bryant and Felice Bryant)

GAME DAY AT OLE MISS

Few places in the South have more charm than Oxford, Mississippi, home of the University of Mississippi, which is affectionately known as Ole Miss.

Located about an hour south of Memphis, Tennessee, Oxford combines small-town warmth with an intellectual, literary, and artistic community that is second to none. Many writers such as William Faulkner, Willie Morris, and John Grisham have called Oxford home and have drawn inspiration from its tree-lined streets and eclectic community.

The University of Mississippi was founded in 1844 under a unique set of circumstances. When Oxford was founded in 1840, the city's officials hoped that it would someday be the site of the state university of Mississippi. Looking for every edge, the founders named their city Oxford, after the famous university city in England. The strategy paid off. By a vote of 58–57, the state legislature put the university in Oxford.

The name Ole Miss has been synonymous with the university for over 100 years. It first surfaced as the winning entry in a contest to name the school yearbook. The name eventually became so popular that it became linked with the school itself.

Over its 164-year history, Ole Miss has seen both success and turmoil. In 1962 riots broke out on campus and the National Guard was called to restore order when James Meredith attempted to become the first African American student to attend the university. But out of that adversity, Ole Miss has emerged as a school strongly committed to the best possible education for all.

One reason why the people of the state have pulled together is their love of football and those special fall Saturdays in Oxford. But the thing that sets Ole Miss apart, more than the Grove or any of its other great traditions, is the love its alumni and the people of the state have for the institution. It has been said that Ole Miss is not just a location on a map, but a place in the heart. The late Frank E. Everett Jr., an Ole Miss grad, wrote this tribute to his alma mater many years ago:

> *There is valid distinction between The University and Ole Miss even though the separate threads are closely interwoven.*
>
> *The University is buildings, trees, and people. Ole Miss is mood, emotion, and personality. One is physical, and the other is spiritual. One is tangible and the other intangible.*
>
> *The University is respected, but Ole Miss is loved. The University gives a diploma and regretfully terminates tenure, but one never graduates from Ole Miss.*

Here are just a few of the things that make game day at Ole Miss special:

The Grove: A 10-acre park on campus that is the center of the pregame tailgating scene in Oxford. On game day, fans begin arriving at the Grove at 7:00 AM, regardless of the kickoff time. In just a few hours, the entire space is filled with tents, tables, chairs, and anything else necessary for a pregame

Before each home game, the Ole Miss players take their "Rebel walk" through the Grove. Photo courtesy of Mississippi SID.

tailgate party. About two hours before each game, the Ole Miss team leaves Kinard Hall and walks across campus to Vaught-Hemingway Stadium. Fans line up along the Grove to form a human corridor for the players. In 1998 the "Walk of Champions" Arch was erected where the Ole Miss players begin their walk to the stadium.

The Grove has been named the number one tailgating scene in all of college football by *Sports Illustrated* and *The Sporting News*.

The Lyceum: Built in 1848, the year the university held its first classes, the Lyceum was the state of Mississippi's first public building dedicated to higher education. Named after a tract of earth where Aristotle taught in ancient Greece, this building serves as the historic focal point of the Ole Miss campus and contains the offices of the chancellor and other key administrators. Built in the Greek Revival style with six columns, the Lyceum is a popular meeting place for fans on game day at Ole Miss.

Vaught-Hemingway Stadium: Even though Oxford is the home of Faulkner, its football stadium was originally named for a Hemingway. Judge William Hemingway (1869–1937) was a professor of law at Ole Miss and the longtime chairman of the university's Committee on Athletics. On October 16, 1982, the name of John Vaught, the most successful coach in Ole Miss history (1947–70, 1973), was added to the stadium.

In 1915 Ole Miss students built the first grandstand at the site of the current stadium. The stadium has grown over the years, and in 2002 it was expanded to a capacity of 60,580. The largest crowd to ever watch a game at Vaught-Hemingway Stadium was the 62,552 who turned out to see quarterback Eli Manning play his last home game against LSU on November 22, 2003.

No. 38: This number is worn each season by the Ole Miss player who wins the Chucky Mullins Courage Award. The award is given each spring at Ole Miss by the Phi Beta Sigma fraternity in honor of Mullins, a Rebel football player who suffered a paralyzing injury in a game with Vanderbilt on October 28, 1989. Mullins died from complications in May 1991. He was 21 years old.

The speed limit is 18 mph: As you travel around The Grove, you'll notice that the speed limit is always 18 mph. That is the jersey number of Archie Manning, the Rebels' legendary quarterback whose sons Peyton (Tennessee) and Eli (Ole Miss) went on to be great quarterbacks as well. Peyton Manning of the Indianapolis Colts was the MVP of the 2007 Super Bowl. Eli Manning of the New York Giants was the MVP of the 2008 Super Bowl.

"Hotty Toddy Cheer": This cheer is the favorite among Ole Miss fans:

"Hotty, toddy, gosh-a-mighty
Who the hell are we?
Flim flam, bim bam
Ole Miss, by damn!

GAME DAY AT FLORIDA STATE

While most Southern college football powers trace their roots all the way back to the 19th century, Florida State got a relatively late start in the sport. It didn't take long for the Seminoles and their fans to catch up and make game day in Tallahassee one of the most colorful and exciting in the South.

Located in the state capital of Tallahassee, the school was originally founded as a seminary. Later it became the Florida State College for Women. In 1947 the state legislature voted to make the school coeducational and to change the name to Florida State. With these changes came the understanding that football would also be coming to the campus.

Game day in Tallahassee has a little different feel than most game days in other college towns across the South. Tallahassee, located in the Florida panhandle just 20 miles north of the Gulf of Mexico, is certainly characterized by constant heat, which the Seminoles have used to their advantage over the years. Many schools outside of the South simply will not come to Tallahassee because their teams melt in the hot and humid weather September brings.

On September 26, 1998, Southern California came to Florida State. The game was close for a half, but in the final 30 minutes fans could see that the Trojans were wilting. Florida State won easily, 30–10.

"Now I remember why we don't like to come down here," said USC coach Paul Hackett after the game.

While Tallahassee has the Florida heat, its landscape includes the hills of Georgia and Alabama, its two neighboring states to the North. Many roads leading to the game have canopies of moss-draped oaks, giving an old Southern feel to one of the youngest institutions on the college football scene.

One more thing to keep in mind while you're visiting Florida State. The school uses "Seminoles" as its nickname, along with various other Native American references during game day, with the complete blessing and participation of the Seminole Tribe of Florida. Both parties believe Florida State's use of the symbols represents a tribute to a brave and proud people.

Florida State's Chief Osceola takes his pregame ride around Doak Campbell Stadium on Renegade. Photo courtesy of Florida State SID.

In 2005 the NCAA banned schools from using symbols and imagery that was "hostile or abusive" to Native Americans at its championships. Florida State was included on a list of schools that, according to the NCAA, were using such imagery. The backlash from Florida State fans and the Seminole Tribe of Florida was so severe that the NCAA granted Florida State a waiver from the new regulations.

Here are just a few things to look for on your game day trip to Tallahassee:

Chief Osceola and Renegade: The Seminoles have one of the most famous pregame traditions in all of college football. Just minutes before the kickoff, all eyes turn to the stadium's north end zone, where Chief Osceola, an FSU student carefully chosen and trained for this moment, leads the Florida State team onto the field while riding Renegade, his majestic Appaloosa.

After the coin toss, Chief Osceola rides Renegade back to midfield with a flaming spear above his head. As the crowd goes wild, Renegade rocks back on his hind legs and Chief Osceola plants the spear into the turf. The game is on.

The tradition began on September 16, 1978, before a home game against Oklahoma State. Over the years FSU has had 10 different riders and three different horses appear as Chief Osceola and Renegade.

War Chant: Shortly after kickoff, Florida State fans begin their famous war chant accompanied by the FSU Band, the Marching Chiefs. While fans sing the war chant, they also add the tomahawk chop motion in the air to the rhythm of the music.

Florida State players at the famed Sod Cemetery. Photo courtesy of Florida State University/Sports Information.

Sod Cemetery: When Florida State wins a big game on the road, someone digs up a piece of sod from the opposing field and brings it back to Tallahassee. The sod is buried in a "sod cemetery" located near the Florida State practice fields. A small monument marks each win. The tradition began in 1962 with an 18–0 win at Georgia. Florida State's most recent victory in a Sod Game came on November 3, 2007, when the Seminoles went on the road and beat No. 2 Boston College 27–17.

Doak Campbell Stadium: When it was built in 1950, Doak Campbell Stadium had a meager seating capacity of 15,000. Today it is a state-of-the-art facility that seats over 80,000. Named after Doak S. Campbell, the first FSU president, the stadium underwent its most recent renovation, which encased the entire structure in brick, in 1996. Now the noise of those 80,000 fans cannot escape. Florida State plays night games whenever possible, and on those nights, Doak Campbell Stadium is among the loudest in all of college football. In 2004 the name of the facility was changed to Bobby Bowden Field at Doak Campbell Stadium to honor the school's Hall of Fame coach.

Burt Reynolds: In 1954 Buddy Reynolds was a highly regarded freshman running back for Florida State. The native of West Palm Beach appeared headed for a very good football career until an auto accident left him with a bad knee. His football dreams over, Reynolds decided to try acting. Buddy Reynolds became Burt Reynolds and a huge star of movies and television, but he never forgot Florida State. He is a regular on the Florida State sideline during football season and has made significant contributions to the school's drama and film departments. Robert Urich, another famous actor, who appeared in the television show *Spenser: For Hire*, was an offensive lineman at Florida State in 1964 and 1965.

GAME DAY AT ALABAMA

Getting to a game day at Alabama is really pretty simple. You exit off I-20 at McFarland Boulevard, and then turn onto University Avenue. Then bear left on Paul W. Bryant Drive.

After about a mile you'll pass the Paul W. Bryant Museum. Across the way is Paul W. Bryant Hall. Finally you pass the Paul W. Bryant Conference Center and the Bryant-Denny Hospitality House before reaching your final destination: Bryant-Denny Stadium.

Obviously, Paul "Bear" Bryant, the Crimson Tide coach from 1958 to 1982, was pretty important at Alabama.

Nowhere else in America does the memory of one man dominate a place the way Bryant's does at the University of Alabama. Bryant died in 1983, less than two months after he had coached his last game, but his spirit still hangs over everything and everybody in Tuscaloosa.

The statue of Bear Bryant, who won 13 SEC championships and six national championships as Alabama's head coach, is a favorite gathering spot for Crimson Tide fans on game day in Tuscaloosa. Photo courtesy of the University of Alabama/Paul W. Bryant Museum.

While Bryant's influence remains strong at Alabama, there have been some major changes in how Crimson Tide fans celebrate game day.

During Bryant's career Alabama played at least three of its key games each year at Legion Field in nearby Birmingham. The stadium was bigger and Bryant believed that a strong presence in Birmingham, the center of financial and corporate power in the state, could only help his program.

But in 1999 school officials decided to move those big games back to Bryant-Denny Stadium. The stadium was named for the former coach and for former university president George H. Denny, whose leadership enabled the original facility to be built in 1929. That initial structure held 12,000 people. Two major renovations in 1998 and 2006 brought the seating capacity to 92,138.

The 2006 renovation included 10,000 additional seats plus a courtyard honoring all of Alabama's conference championships, national championships, and the four coaches (Wallace Wade, Frank Thomas, Bear Bryant, and Gene Stallings) who won national championships at Alabama. That courtyard is a favorite gathering place for fans before the game. Many come to have their pictures taken with Bryant's statue.

Here are just a few other things that make a football Saturday at Alabama special:

Dreamland: Located on the outskirts of Tuscaloosa, this modest but historic restaurant has a simple menu: barbecue ribs, white bread, and cold drinks. Don't even ask for coleslaw! Everyone, from royalty to common folk, who attends an Alabama football game must sooner or later make the pilgrimage to Dreamland.

The Paul W. Bryant Museum: A game day at Alabama, particularly for first-time visitors, is not complete without a visit to this museum, which not only traces the career of the former coach, but also provides a history of Alabama football dating back to 1892.

The Paul W. Bryant Museum traces the career of the famous coach and the history of Alabama football. Photo courtesy of the University of Alabama.

The Quad: The Quad is the central on-campus gathering place for pregame and postgame activities. At the edge of the Quad is Denny Chimes, a tower built in 1929 as a tribute to the university's president. Denny Chimes also serves as the standard meeting place for friends and family who arrive in Tuscaloosa from different parts of the state. On November 3, 2007, Alabama hosted LSU in Tuscaloosa. School officials estimated that 30,000 fans that didn't have tickets sat in the Quad and watched the game on television. They just wanted to be there.

The Million Dollar Band: Alabama's marching band travels in relative comfort now, but back in the 1920s the only way it could travel to the school's road games was by asking for contributions from the local merchants in Tuscaloosa. Turns out they were so good at fund-raising that W.C. Pickens, Alabama's football manager, tagged the group the "Million Dollar Band." The name has stuck until this day.

When the Million Dollar Band arrives at Bryant-Denny Stadium and plays the first five notes of the school fight song, "Yea Alabama," it is a sign for Crimson Tide fans everywhere that game day in Tuscaloosa has officially begun:

Yea, Alabama! Drown 'em Tide
Every Bama man's behind you, hit your stride
Go teach the Bulldogs to behave,
Send those Yellow Jackets to a watery grave

And if a man starts to weaken, that's his shame
For Bama's pluck and grit have writ her name in Crimson flame,
Fight on! Fight on! Fight on, men!
Remember the Rose Bowl we'll win then
Go! Roll on to victory! Hit your stride!
You're Dixie's football pride, Crimson Tide!
Roll Tide! Roll Tide!

CHAPTER 7

GREAT RIVALRIES

The passion of a Southern college football fan is fierce and indestructible, so it only stands to reason that when the passions of one group of fans encounters those of another, sparks fly. What is born of this collision of passions is a rivalry, the cornerstone of college football in the South. Each college football rivalry has its own history, its own record of greatness and controversy, of triumph and disappointment, and with each new season another chapter of that history is written. Every year schools get the opportunity to avenge a defeat or extend their domination over the others. In the South, college football rivalries turn friend against friend, brother against brother, and husband against wife—at least for a week. What's at stake that would put such a strain on these otherwise strong relationships?

Simple. It's called bragging rights.

More than anything, you want your team to win so that the jerk in your office (or in your family) won't be able to hold it over you for an entire year. Hell no. You want to hold it over your rival for an entire year.

Isn't this all a little childish? Perhaps. But in the South, folks would rather have bragging rights in college football than oil rights in the Middle East.

With these kinds of passions at work, it's no surprise that the great rivalries in the sport have given fans some of the best games and most unforgettable moments in college football history. Here are just a few of the greatest rivalries in Southern college football.

ALABAMA VERSUS AUBURN: IT LASTS 365 DAYS A YEAR
ALABAMA LEADS 38–33–1
To call what exists between state foes Alabama and Auburn a mere football rivalry would be like calling St. Patrick's Cathedral a nice little church.

Alabama-Auburn is, at its very core, a cultural war. The two sides simply use football to fight it.

When it comes to a single event that affects the entire fabric of a state, not only on game day but all year round, there is simply nothing like the annual Alabama-Auburn game.

"People talk about the Alabama-Auburn game on New Year's Day," said former Alabama coach Gene Stallings. "They talk about it on Christmas Day. They talk about it on the Fourth of July. It's the only game I've ever heard of where people talk about it 365 days a year. And if you don't live there, you couldn't possibly understand."

The two teams played 12 times from 1893 to 1907 but, befitting the rivalry, they did not play in 1908 because of contract disagreements and charges and countercharges of using illegal players. The feelings were so bitter that the two schools did not play again until 1948, and then only at the insistence of the Alabama state legislature.

A lot of bad feelings can build up after 40 years, and the two schools have been making up for it ever since. Every coach who has been thrust into the heat of this rivalry quickly learns that his success will be measured by one thing and one thing only: how he fares against Alabama or Auburn.

When Auburn lost two of the first three games to Alabama after the series was resumed, the school fired Earl Brown as coach and hired an Auburn man, Shug Jordan, who stayed for 25 years.

In 1957 Auburn beat Alabama 40–0 for its fourth straight win over the Crimson Tide. Auburn rubbed salt into Alabama's wound by also going 10–0 and winning the national championship that year. Alabama officials decided that they had had enough. A delegation went to Texas A&M and hired Alabama alumnus Paul "Bear" Bryant as its new coach. Bryant would be the dominant figure in Southern college football for the next 25 years, beating Auburn 19 times.

When Bryant and Alabama won nine out of 10 games from 1971 to 1981, Auburn's fans wondered if they would ever be competitive against the Crimson Tide again. Jordan had retired after the 1975 season having lost four of his last five to Alabama. His successor, Doug Barfield, went 0–5 against Alabama and was fired after the 1980 season.

Looking for someone to get Auburn back on top in the rivalry, the school hired Pat Dye, a former assistant to Bryant. Dye beat Bryant in his second season (1982), and not long after that Bryant retired. With Bryant gone and Auburn rejuvenated, the Tigers won four SEC championships between 1983 and 1989 and won six of their next eight meetings with Alabama.

Dye retired after the 1992 season, and the rivalry went back and forth for a while. Another major shift

Auburn coach Pat Dye (1981–92) played a major role in bringing the Alabama game to Auburn for the first time in 1989. Photo courtesy of the *Atlanta Journal-Constitution.*

in power came in 1999 when Tommy Tuberville left Ole Miss to become the head coach at Auburn. Tuberville has won seven out of nine meetings with Alabama and, as the 2008 season begins, Auburn has beaten Alabama six straight times.

When *Southern Fried Football* was first published in the fall of 2000, Alabama led its rivalry with Auburn by 10 games (36–26–1). That margin is now down to just five games.

Here are but a few of the great moments that these two teams have contributed to the history of Southern football:

1948: On December 4, the two teams met for the first time in 41 years. Sophomore Ed Salem threw three touchdown passes to lead Alabama to a 55–0 victory.

1967: Kenny Stabler ran 47 yards on a muddy field for a touchdown, giving Alabama a controversial 7–3 victory. It was controversial because Auburn coach Shug Jordan said afterward that Alabama blocker Dennis Dixon had tackled Auburn defender Gusty Yearout on the winning play.

1971: Alabama held Pat Sullivan, the Heisman Trophy winner that season, to the lowest yardage total of his career and won, 31–7.

1972: Trailing 16–3 with only nine minutes left, Auburn's Bill Newton blocked two Alabama punts and both blocked kicks were returned for touchdowns by David Langer. Auburn won the game 17–16 over the second-ranked Crimson Tide. For many Auburn fans this game still ranks as the greatest win in school history. Today the game is remembered simply as "Punt, Bama, Punt!"

Auburn's Tommy Tuberville enters the 2008 season with six straight wins over Alabama. Photo courtesy of Auburn University/Sports Information.

Auburn returned two blocked punts for touchdowns to upset Alabama in 1972. Photo courtesy of Auburn SID.

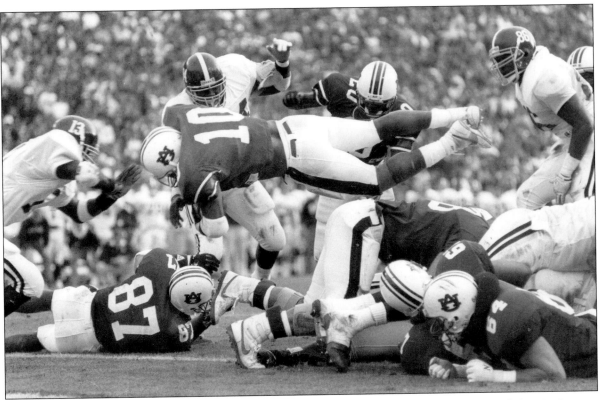

Auburn's James Joseph (No. 10) scores against Alabama in 1989. Photo courtesy of the *Atlanta Journal-Constitution.*

1982: Auburn beat Alabama 23–22, snapping the Crimson Tide's nine-game winning streak. No one knew that it would be Bear Bryant's last regular-season game as Alabama's head coach.

1985: Alabama's Van Tiffin kicked a 52-yard field goal as time ran out, and the Crimson Tide won 25–23.

1989: For sheer drama, nothing will match the 1989 game, the day Alabama finally came to Auburn. Since 1948, the game had been played at Birmingham's Legion Field, which Auburn people felt was a home stadium for the Crimson Tide.

Bryant and his successor, Ray Perkins, vowed that Alabama would never play at Auburn. But in 1989, after years of bitter negotiations, Alabama finally agreed to come to Jordan-Hare Stadium on December 2, 1989.

Alabama was undefeated and ranked No. 2. A win over twice-beaten Auburn would have put the Crimson Tide into the Sugar Bowl with a shot at the national championship. But Auburn won the game 30–20 in one of the most emotional afternoons in college football history.

That's when Alabama coach Bill Curry learned the true depth of the rivalry with Auburn. Despite a 10–1 regular season, Curry had lost his one game to the wrong opponent. He had won 26 games and taken Alabama to bowls in all three of his seasons as coach. But he was 0–3 against Auburn. The next season Curry was the head coach at Kentucky.

1992: Alabama dominated and won 17–0 in what would be Pat Dye's last game as Auburn's head coach. Alabama went on to win the national championship.

1993: Under first-year coach Terry Bowden, Auburn stunned Alabama 22–14 at Auburn to finish 11–0. Auburn could not play in a bowl game due to NCAA probation.

2001–Present: Alabama split games with Auburn in Dennis Franchione's two years (2001–02) as head coach. But when Franchione left suddenly for Texas A&M, Auburn and Tuberville took control of the rivalry and have won six straight games going into the 2008 season.

AUBURN VERSUS GEORGIA: BROTHER AGAINST BROTHER

AUBURN LEADS 53–50–8

When Auburn and Georgia played the South's first big football game in February of 1892, it is unlikely that any of the fans present in Atlanta's Piedmont Park knew the two teams would still be playing well into the 21st century.

When both schools have fielded teams, they have met every year since 1894, making it the longest continuous football rivalry in the South.

In 1897 Georgia disbanded its team for the rest of the season after a player was killed in the third game. Neither school had a team in 1917 or 1918 because of World War I. In 1943 Auburn did not have a team because of World War II. The two teams have played every season without interruption since 1944.

From 1916 until 1958 Auburn and Georgia played every game but one in Columbus, Georgia, near the Alabama state line. Starting in 1959, the game went to the respective campuses.

Going into the 2008 season, Auburn "officially" holds a 53–50–8 record in the series. Auburn's records give the Tigers an extra win because of the disputed game of 1899.

Reports indicate that Auburn held an 11–6 lead late in that game when play was suspended. Some stories say play was suspended because of darkness. Others claim it was because of an unruly crowd. In any event, the game went into the books as a 0–0 tie. Auburn later appealed, but the ruling was allowed to stand.

Despite the long-standing rivalry, the relationship between the two schools has always been good.

"It's hard to explain to others, but when Auburn and Georgia play it's like a game between you and your best friend," says former Georgia coach Vince Dooley, who holds two degrees from Auburn and played quarterback for the Tigers from 1951 to 1953.

Over the years a number of players and coaches have crossed the Alabama-Georgia state line to work at the other school. Pat Dye, who won 99 games as Auburn's coach from 1981 to 1992, was an All-American guard at Georgia in 1960. As Auburn's head coach, he recruited heavily in Georgia.

"When Auburn and Georgia play, it's like two brothers going at it in the backyard," said Dye. "I love my brother, but I want to whip him."

This unique relationship has brought about some of the more memorable games in Southern football history.

1942: Georgia was undefeated and ranked No. 1 with the dream backfield of Frank Sinkwich, the Heisman Trophy winner that season, and the great Charley Trippi. But the Bulldogs, looking ahead to a big showdown with No. 2 Georgia Tech, lost 27–13 to Auburn on November 21. It remains the biggest upset in the series.

1959: Georgia had lost six straight games to Auburn and was in danger of losing again, trailing 13–7 with less than a minute to go. With the ball at the Auburn 13-yard line, quarterback Fran Tarkenton kneeled in the Georgia huddle and drew up a play in the grass. Tarkenton hit Bill Herron for the touchdown on the next play. Georgia won 14–13 and captured its final SEC championship under coach Wally Butts.

1971: In one of the most hyped games ever between the two schools, Auburn's Pat Sullivan threw for 248 yards and four touchdowns as the No. 3 Tigers knocked off No. 6 Georgia 35–20 in Athens. Twelve days later, thanks to his performance against Georgia, Sullivan won the Heisman Trophy.

1982: Trying to clinch its third straight SEC championship, Georgia took a 19–14 lead against Auburn on a three-yard touchdown run by Herschel Walker in the fourth quarter. Auburn drove to the Georgia 9-yard line in the final seconds, but a fourth-down pass was knocked down by Jeff Sanchez in the end zone to preserve Georgia's victory.

1985: Bo Jackson had a 67-yard touchdown run against the Bulldogs in Athens and led Auburn to a 24–10 victory. Jackson finished the game with 121 yards, and that performance gave him the edge he needed to win the Heisman Trophy.

1986: Every rivalry needs some comic relief, and in 1986 it came to Auburn and Georgia. Using second-string quarterback Wayne Johnson, the Bulldogs upset the Tigers 20–16 at Auburn. The Georgia fans were so excited they stormed the field and began tearing up pieces of the turf to take back home. Auburn officials turned the water cannons on the Georgia fans hoping to get control of the situation. The 1986 game has since become known as "the Battle Between the Hoses." Ironically Kermit Perry, the Auburn official who decided to turn the water cannons on the Georgia fans, was a Georgia grad who ran track for the Bulldogs.

1994: Auburn had won 20 straight games under second-year coach Terry Bowden and was favored to make it 21 when 5–4 Georgia came to Jordan-Hare Stadium. Behind senior quarterback Eric Zeier, the Bulldogs rallied from a 23–9 deficit to tie the game 23–23.

Fran Tarkenton's touchdown pass to Bill Herron in the final seconds beat Auburn 14–13 in 1959. Photo courtesy of the *Atlanta Journal-Constitution.*

1996: The 100th game between Georgia and Auburn was one of the most exciting ever. Behind quarterback Dameyune Craig, Auburn dominated the first three quarters of the game, leading 28–14 going into the fourth quarter. But Georgia rallied and tied the score on the last play of regulation with Mike Bobo's 30-yard touchdown pass to Corey Allen. Georgia eventually prevailed in four overtimes, winning 56–49.

2000: Auburn quarterback Ben Leard, a native of Hartwell, Georgia, ran for a one-yard touchdown in overtime as the Tigers upset No. 13 Georgia 29–26. Auburn went on to beat Alabama 9–0 the following week to advance to the SEC championship game.

2002: Georgia trailed Auburn 21–17 when it faced a fourth and 15 at the Auburn 19-yard line with less than two minutes left. Georgia quarterback David Greene threw a perfect strike to Michael Johnson with only 1:25 remaining to give the Bulldogs a stunning 24–21 victory. The victory clinched the SEC East for Georgia, which went on to win its first SEC championship since 1982.

With the Sanford Stadium crowd energized by Georgia's new black jerseys, the Bulldogs dominated Auburn 45–20 in 2007. Photo courtesy of the University of Georgia/Sports Information.

2005: Trailing 30–28 and facing fourth down deep in his own territory, Auburn quarterback Brandon Cox threw a 63-yard completion to Devin Aromashodu. John Vaughn kicked a field goal with only six seconds left to beat Georgia 31–30.

2007: For the first time in its history, Georgia took the field for a game wearing black jerseys. Sanford Stadium was energized, and so were the Bulldogs, who rolled over Auburn 45–20.

ALABAMA VERSUS TENNESSEE: THE THIRD SATURDAY IN OCTOBER

ALABAMA LEADS 45–38–7

It was October 20, 1928, and for the first time in 14 years, Alabama and Tennessee met on the football field.

Alabama, in its sixth year under coach Wallace Wade, had been to the Rose Bowl in 1925 and 1926, winning the national championship both years. Tennessee had won 16 games and lost only one in its first two years under coach Robert R. Neyland, but the Vols had not faced a team as good as Alabama, which was heavily favored to win.

Prior to the game in Tuscaloosa, Neyland humbly walked up to Wade and asked if he would mind shortening the fourth quarter if Alabama were dominating the game, as most expected it would.

Neyland told Wade that he wanted to save his players from too much embarrassment. Wade said yes, he would allow Tennessee to save face.

Tennessee's Gene McEver ran the opening kickoff 98 yards for a touchdown and the Volunteers went on to win the game 15–13. The victory put Tennessee on the college football map, and the rivalry, which would become one of the richest in the South, was on.

Since that day in 1928, with a few exceptions, Tennessee and Alabama have met each year on the third Saturday in October. It is a rivalry so legendary that the late Al Browning, a longtime sportswriter in Birmingham, penned a book with that title.

Over the years, both schools have used this game as the true measuring stick of their respective teams. Here are but a few of the highlights in this legendary rivalry:

1932: Played in Birmingham, this game featured what many believe was the greatest punting duel of all time. Alabama's Johnny "Hurry" Cain averaged 48 yards on 19 kicks. Tennessee All-American Beattie Feathers averaged 43 yards on 21 kicks. Tennessee won the game 7–3 and went on to a 9–0–1 record and the Southern Conference championship.

1939: On October 21 in Knoxville, Tennessee beat Alabama 21–0 behind Johnny Butler's 56-yard touchdown run. The run, in which the sophomore running back went sideline to sideline, is still considered the greatest single play in the school's history. Tennessee went on to finish the regular season undefeated and unscored upon.

1965: Bear Bryant's defending national champions had already been upset by Georgia 18–17 in the season opener and were tied with Tennessee 7–7 in the final minutes of this game. The Crimson Tide drove inside the Tennessee 5-yard line and was setting up for the winning field goal when quarterback Ken Stabler lost track of the downs and threw the ball out of bounds to stop the clock—on the fourth down. Alabama gave up the ball, and the game ended in a tie. After the game, an angry Bryant kicked in the locker-room door.

1966: This time it was Tennessee's turn to have its heart broken. Trailing 11–10, the Vols drove deep into Alabama territory inside the final minute. Tennessee's Gary Wright missed a 20-yard field goal with 16 seconds left in the game, and the Crimson Tide held on. Both Wright and the Tennessee bench screamed at the officials, saying the field goal was good, but the ruling stood. Alabama went 11–0 that season, but Notre Dame was declared the national champion.

1971–81: With Alabama enjoying its greatest period of dominance ever, the Crimson Tide beat Tennessee 11 straight games. Only twice, in 1972 (17–10) and in 1976 (20–13), did Alabama win by less than double digits.

1982: Bryant won 16 of his 25 meetings against Tennessee, but not the last. On October 16 in Knoxville, Tennessee knocked off 5–0 Alabama, 35–28, to snap the Crimson Tide's 11-game winning streak. The Tennessee players carried coach Johnny Majors to the middle of the field to meet Bryant. No one knew it at the time, but it would be Bryant's last game against Tennessee.

1986–94: During these years Alabama reeled off a string of nine years without a loss. Alabama beat Tennessee eight times, and the teams tied 17–17 in 1993 in Birmingham when the Crimson Tide scored a late touchdown and a two-point conversion.

1995: After being dominated by Alabama for so long, the series began to turn in Tennessee's favor when Peyton Manning led the Vols to a convincing 41–14 win over the Crimson Tide in Birmingham. Tennessee went on to win seven straight games against Alabama. Over the next 13 games Tennessee won 10 times.

2003: It took almost five hours to play the game, but in the fifth overtime Tennessee batted down a fourth-down pass from Alabama's Brodie Croyle to win 51–43 in Tuscaloosa.

2005: In a classic defensive struggle, the score was tied 3–3 in the final moments in Tuscaloosa. Alabama quarterback Brodie Croyle completed a 43-yard pass to D.J. Hall down to the Tennessee 35-yard line. With 13 seconds left Jamie Christensen kicked a 31-yard field goal to give Alabama a 6–3 victory.

2006: For the second straight year it was a defensive battle that Alabama led 13–6 going into the fourth quarter. But Tennessee's James Wilhoit kicked a 27-yard field goal with 8:18 remaining, and then Arian Foster scored a touchdown with 3:28 left to give the Volunteers a 16–13 victory.

CLEMSON VERSUS SOUTH CAROLINA: STILL GOING STRONG AFTER BIG THURSDAY

CLEMSON LEADS 64–37–4

Officials from the University of South Carolina and Clemson College met in 1896 and decided to hold an annual football game between the two schools. But they wanted to do something different to make the game an event for the entire state to enjoy, so they agreed that instead of playing the game on a Saturday, it would be held on the Thursday during the annual State Fair in Columbia, South Carolina.

On November 12 South Carolina won the first game 12–7, and the tradition of Big Thursday was born.

Except for a one-year break in 1901 and a seven-year hiatus from 1903 to 1909 due to strained relations between the schools, South Carolina and Clemson played on Thursday each year until 1959. It was quite a celebration as students from both schools were excused from class in order to attend the game.

While the two teams played a number of great games, Big Thursday is best remembered for the events of 1946, when counterfeiters printed thousands of bogus tickets. The crowd finally stormed the gates and surrounded the field, standing as many as six deep.

The Big Thursday tradition ended after the 1959 game because Clemson's fans had grown tired of playing in Columbia every year. Clemson had just expanded its stadium by 18,000 seats and could now make more money playing at home.

But it didn't matter if the Clemson–South Carolina game was played on Big Thursday in Columbia or on a Saturday on the teams' respective campuses; it was and still remains one of the greatest rivalries in college football. Here are a few of the highlights:

Clemson coach Frank Howard kisses Big Thursday good-bye in 1959. Photo courtesy of Clemson SID.

1902: Because of a train accident, there was only one official available for the game. Not a single penalty was called, and South Carolina won 12–6. The night after the game a riot broke out between fans of the two schools. As a result, the teams did not play again until 1909.

1939: On October 19 future Hall of Fame player Banks McFadden rushed for 76 yards and threw for 85 more, leading the Tigers to a 27–0 win. Clemson went on to finish 9–1 and play in the Cotton Bowl, the first bowl in the school's history. The Tigers finished with a No. 12 national ranking, the team's first ranking in a final poll.

1947: Both teams scored three touchdowns, but Clemson's Mavis "Bull" Cagle missed two extra points, and South Carolina won 21–19 in what is still considered one of the better games in the series.

1948: With his team trailing 7–6 and only 4:15 remaining in the game, Clemson's Phil Prince blocked a South Carolina punt. Oscar Thompson picked up the ball on the 11-yard line and ran it in for a touchdown to give the Tigers a 13–7 win.

1961: A group of South Carolina students pretending to be Clemson players came onto the field and warmed up prior to this year's game. When Clemson's fans eventually discovered that it was not the real Clemson team but members of the Sigma Nu fraternity from South Carolina, some Clemson students went onto the field and fought with the imposters. State police were called in to restore order.

1962: Clemson's Rodney Rogers kicked a 24-yard field goal with 1:31 left to lift the Tigers to a 20–17 victory. The win was secured when South Carolina quarterback Dan Reeves was sacked on the last play of the game.

Jerry Butler's touchdown catch in the final moments helped Clemson beat South Carolina in 1977. Photo courtesy of Clemson SID.

1965: Clemson scored a touchdown with 40 seconds left to get within one point, 17–16. But instead of kicking the extra point to tie, Clemson faked the kick and tried a pass for two points. South Carolina linebacker Bobby Gunnels batted the ball away and South Carolina held on for the one-point win.

1977: Clemson was ranked No. 15 and was headed to the Gator Bowl when the team arrived in Columbia to play the Gamecocks. The Tigers led the game 24–0 only to have South Carolina rally and take a 27–24 lead. Clemson drove the length of the field and with 49 seconds left, Steve Fuller hit Jerry Butler, who made a leaping catch for a 20-yard touchdown to win the game. Butler's catch remains one of the most famous images from this rivalry.

1984: South Carolina was simply not ready to play Clemson, because the week before, the Gamecocks had lost to Navy, ending their undefeated season and taking away their shot at the Orange Bowl. The Gamecocks fell behind 21–3 before they finally woke up and rallied with a touchdown, a safety, and a field goal to come within six, 21–15. Quarterback Mike Hold then drove the Gamecocks 84 yards for a touchdown to tie the game with 54 seconds left. South Carolina missed the extra point, but Clemson was penalized for having 12 men on the field. This time the extra point was good, giving South Carolina the 22–21 win.

2000: This was one of the more controversial games in the series. South Carolina appeared to have won the game when it scored with 59 seconds left to take a 14–13 lead. But on third down and 12, Clemson quarterback Woody Dantzler threw a 49-yard pass to Rod Gardner. South Carolina fans swear to this day that Gardner pushed off to make the catch. Aaron Hunt kicked a 25-yard field goal with seven seconds left to give the Tigers a 16–14 victory.

2001: Playing in his final home game for South Carolina, quarterback Phil Petty stayed on the field despite injuring his shoulder in the second quarter. South Carolina took a 20–9 lead and then held on to win 20–15 and snap a four-game losing streak to the Tigers.

2004: Clemson won 29–7, but the game will be remembered for a fourth-quarter brawl between the two teams. Both teams finished 6–5 but were banned from going to bowls because of the fight. On the Monday after the game Lou Holtz officially retired as head coach. The next day Steve Spurrier was introduced as the new head coach at South Carolina.

2006: South Carolina had lost four straight games to Clemson, and it appeared the streak was going to increase to five as the Gamecocks trailed 28–14 in the third quarter. But South Carolina rallied and Ryan Succop kicked a 35-yard field goal with 7:51 left to give the Gamecocks a 31–28 lead. Clemson drove deep into South Carolina territory in the final moments, but Jad Dean missed a 39-yard field goal with 13 seconds left that would have tied the game.

2007: After losing by a field goal the year before, Clemson returned the favor in a game played in Columbia. South Carolina, which had lost four straight games after a 6–1 start, rallied from a 17–7 deficit and took a 21–20 lead with nine minutes left. But Clemson came back down the field behind quarterback Cullen Harper, and Mark Buchholz kicked a 35-yard field goal on the last play of the game to give the Tigers a 23–21 victory.

FLORIDA VERSUS FLORIDA STATE: THE SUNSHINE SHOWDOWN
FLORIDA LEADS 31–19–2

In 1947 the Florida state legislature proclaimed that the Florida State College for Women, located in Tallahassee, would become coeducational. That fall Florida State fielded its first football team and went 0–5. The most notable omission on the first Florida State schedule was the University of Florida.

Florida quarterback Danny Wuerffel dives into the end zone during a 31–31 tie at Florida State in 1994. Photo courtesy of Florida SID.

Florida wanted no part of the upstart school in Tallahassee. Athletics director Bob Woodruff was quoted saying that as long as he was at Florida the school would not play Florida State. The rationale was simple from Florida's perspective: the Gators had nothing to win by playing Florida State. Florida was the bigger school and had a stronger football tradition. The Gators were supposed to win. By playing Florida State, Florida would only enhance the visibility of a rival program and make recruiting against them in the state that much tougher.

Florida State, in turn, started flexing some of its political muscle. In 1955 a bill reached the floor of the legislature demanding that the schools play each other in all sports. But Florida had enough pull to get the bill voted down 19–15.

Governor Leroy Collins brought the two schools' athletics directors together and ordered them to schedule a game as soon as possible. Florida finally relented, and the first Florida–Florida State game was played on November 22, 1958.

On the opening kickoff of that game, Florida State's Bobby Renn took a handoff and rambled 78 yards. Florida State later scored to take a 7–0 lead and ignite the passion of the FSU fans. Florida came back to win 21–7, but on that day one the South's great rivalries was born.

Here are some of the highlights:

1964: After playing the first six games in Gainesville (all won by Florida with one tie) Florida State finally got the Gators to come to Tallahassee. Florida coach Ray Graves, in an attempt to mentally prepare his players to play at Florida State and keep the six-game unbeaten streak alive, put the words "Never, FSU, Never" on his team's practice jerseys. When Florida showed up for the game, the Gators players had the words "Go for Seven" printed on the front of their jerseys. But none of this gamesmanship worked for Florida as the Seminoles won 16–7 on the way to a 9–1–1 season.

1966: After losing at Florida 30–17 in 1965, Florida State again had a chance to win in Tallahassee. Trailing 22–19 with 26 seconds remaining, Florida State's Lane Fenner made a diving catch of a 55-yard pass near the boundary line of the end zone. The official on the play ruled Fenner out of bounds, touching off a huge argument. Florida prevailed by three points, but to this day, Florida State fans still insist that Fenner's catch should have been a touchdown.

1971: Florida State, in its first year under coach Larry Jones, came to Gainesville with a 5–0 record. Florida was rebuilding under second-year coach Doug Dickey and was 0–5, but Florida still won 17–15.

1994: The Seminoles and the Gators have twice played dramatic regular-season games only to get a rematch in the Sugar Bowl. In 1994, Florida dominated the rivalry game for almost three quarters, holding a 31–3 lead. But then Florida State rallied against a tired Gators defense, and the game ended in a 31–31 tie. Florida went on to beat Alabama in the SEC championship game and was then invited to play Florida State in the Sugar Bowl. This time the Seminoles won 23–17.

1996: Florida was undefeated and ranked No. 1 when the Gators traveled to Tallahassee to play No. 2 Florida State. The Seminoles pounded Florida quarterback Danny Wuerffel, the eventual Heisman Trophy winner, and won the game 24–21. That capped off an 11–0 season for Florida State and put the Seminoles into the Sugar Bowl where they played for the national championship. Florida State expected to play Nebraska for the title, but Nebraska lost to Texas in the Big 12 championship game. After Florida beat Alabama in the SEC championship game, the Gators moved to No. 3 in the rankings and got a rematch with Florida State in New Orleans. For this game coach Steve Spurrier put Wuerffel in the shotgun formation to slow down the Florida State rush. It worked, and the Gators dominated the Seminoles 52–20 to win the national championship.

1997: Florida State was undefeated and ranked No. 1 when it arrived at Florida's Swamp. The Seminoles knew that with a win they would be going to the Orange Bowl to play Nebraska for at least a share of a national championship. A field goal put Florida State in the lead, 29–25, with 2:38 left in the game. With only one more defensive stop Florida State would have had a perfect season. But on Florida's first play from scrimmage, quarterback Doug Johnson fooled the FSU secondary and hit Jacquez Green for a 63-yard completion. Two plays later Fred Taylor scored from one yard out, and the Gators won 32–29. Florida State coach Bobby Bowden later called it one of the most difficult defeats of his career.

1999: Florida State was 10–0 and ranked No. 1 when it came to Florida. The Seminoles knew that a win would put them in the BCS championship game in the Sugar Bowl. But it wasn't easy, as Florida led 16–13 midway through the third quarter. But then the Seminoles scored 17 unanswered points to take a 30–17 lead and eventually won 30–23, giving coach Bobby Bowden the first undefeated regular season of his career.

2003: In one of the wildest finishes in the series, Florida State's P.K. Sam caught a 52-yard touchdown pass from Chris Rix with only 55 seconds left as the Seminoles stunned Florida 38–34 in Gainesville. The lead changed hands four times in the fourth quarter. It was a game filled with emotion and questionable officiating. When the game was over, both teams had a big brawl at midfield. Because there was a three-way tie for the SEC East championship, and none of the league's tiebreakers could crown a champion, the BCS standings were used. Florida's loss knocked the Gators out of the SEC championship game, and Georgia went to Atlanta to play LSU.

2004: The day started well for Florida State as the school renamed the field at Doak Campbell Stadium in honor of coach Bobby Bowden. But it did not end well for the Seminoles, as Florida won 20–13 to give the Gators their first victory in Tallahassee since 1986. It was also the last game as Florida's head coach for Ron Zook, who had been fired in October, effective at the end of the season.

ALABAMA VERSUS GEORGIA TECH: A GREAT RIVALRY TURNS UGLY

ALABAMA LEADS 28–21–3

Alabama coach Paul "Bear" Bryant and Bobby Dodd, his counterpart at Georgia Tech, claimed to be friends. But the rivalry between the two schools took an ugly turn during the November 18, 1961, game in Birmingham.

In the fourth quarter, Georgia Tech's Chick Granning was running down the field under a Georgia Tech punt when Alabama's Darwin Holt, who was assigned to block the Tech player, threw an elbow to the face. Granning suffered a broken nose, a broken jaw, and lost five teeth. No penalty was assessed.

After the 10–0 win by Alabama, a war of words began in the newspapers in Atlanta and Birmingham. The Atlanta newspapers where highly critical of Bryant, accusing him of teaching dirty play. Bryant said the elbow thrown by Holt was unintentional. He further responded by showing the game film to writers in Alabama, pointing out the elbows that Georgia Tech had thrown.

The episode put a temporary strain on the relationship between Bryant and Dodd, who put an end to the series with Alabama after the 1964 game. The two teams would not play again until 1979, 13 years after Dodd retired.

The two teams played every year from 1979 to 1984 and have not played since. The schools have signed a two-year contract to meet again in 2013 and 2014.

Alabama's Bear Bryant (left) with Georgia Tech's Bobby Dodd in happier times. Photo courtesy of the *Atlanta Journal-Constitution.*

Here are some of the highlights of one of the South's great rivalries:

1952: Georgia Tech was 8–0 and ranked No. 2 when 7–1 Alabama came to Grant Field. The Yellow Jackets were clinging to a 7–3 lead late in the game as Alabama drove for a potential winning touchdown. On fourth down at the Georgia Tech 4-yard line, Jakie Rudolph, a tiny 5'7", 155-pound defensive back, stopped Alabama running back Bobby Marlow short of the goal line. Georgia Tech won the game and went on to finish 12–0 and win the national championship.

1960: The bad feelings that surfaced in the 1961 game began the year before in Atlanta with one of the greatest comebacks in Alabama history. Georgia Tech led 15–0 at halftime and 15–6 at the beginning of the fourth quarter. Pat Trammell, Alabama's starting quarterback, had been taken out of the game as a result of injuries. Reserve quarterback Bob Skelton led Alabama to a touchdown with 8:44 left to make it 15–13. Then he drove the Crimson Tide down the field, where Richard O'Dell kicked the winning field goal from 21 yards out on the last play of the game. It was the first field goal that O'Dell had ever kicked for Alabama.

1962: Alabama returned to Atlanta after the Granning-Holt incident the year before in Birmingham. The Georgia Tech students were waiting on Bryant and the Crimson Tide. Bryant, concerned about being hit by a stray liquor bottle, donned a helmet during pregame warm-ups. Alabama was the defending national champion and ranked No. 1, but Georgia Tech upset the Crimson Tide 7–6. It was the only game Alabama lost all season and it very likely cost the Crimson Tide another national championship.

1981: Alabama was 1–0 and ranked No. 3 when it met Georgia Tech in Birmingham. It was the season opener for the Yellow Jackets, who had been 1–9–1 the year before. Trailing 21–17 late in the fourth quarter, Georgia Tech drove 80 yards for a touchdown with 3:57 left to beat the Crimson Tide 24–21 before a stunned crowd of 78,865 at Legion Field. Alabama's 50-yard field-goal attempt on the final play of the game fell short.

LSU VERSUS OLE MISS: CANNON'S 89-YARD RUN WILL LIVE FOREVER

LSU LEADS 55–37–4

It was Halloween night, 1959, and the fog that hung over LSU's Tiger Stadium only added to the eeriness of what would become a most unforgettable evening.

LSU, the defending national champion, was undefeated (6–0) and ranked No. 1 for the second straight year after an 11–0 season in 1958. Ole Miss was 6–0 and ranked No. 3. The winner would have the inside track to the SEC championship and still be in the hunt for the national championship.

With 10 minutes remaining Ole Miss was clinging to a 3–0 lead. The Rebels had so much confidence in their defense that they began punting on third down.

Billy Cannon's run in the LSU–Ole Miss game of 1959. Photo courtesy of LSU SID.

Jake Gibbs, the Ole Miss quarterback and punter, never intended to kick the ball to LSU's Billy Cannon. The ground was mushy and Gibbs figured the ball would simply slide around when it hit the ground. Instead, the kicked ball took a big hop in front of Cannon, who decided to field it on the run.

By most accounts, eight different LSU defenders touched Cannon, but none could bring him down. With each broken tackle, the roar of the LSU crowd grew louder. Gibbs was the last Ole Miss defender with a chance to bring the LSU stallion down.

"I got a hand on him," Gibbs recalled, "but he just shook me off like a puppy."

Cannon eventually lumbered 89 yards for a touchdown and a place in immortality.

Cannon's run still stands as one of the most famous plays in the history of Southern college football and the defining moment of one of the South's great rivalries.

While LSU won that famous game, the Rebels always point out that in their rematch in the Sugar Bowl they beat the Tigers 21–0. Despite the loss to LSU, the 1959 Ole Miss Rebels were later named the SEC Team of the Decade.

In the 1940s, '50s, and '60s, there was no greater rivalry in the South than LSU–Ole Miss. The most intense period of the rivalry was from 1959 to 1961, when Ole Miss could have posted three undefeated regular seasons if not for two losses and a tie to LSU. LSU had unbeaten seasons spoiled by Ole Miss in 1962 and 1969.

Here are but a few of the great moments in this rivalry:

1947: Perhaps the two greatest college quarterbacks of the era, Y.A. Tittle of LSU and Charley Conerly of Ole Miss, put together a memorable shootout in Baton Rouge on November 1. Conerly scored all three Ole Miss touchdowns and the Rebels won 20–18.

1960: Ole Miss was for the second year in a row unbeaten and in pursuit of the national championship when LSU came to Oxford with a 1–4 record. After a tough 10–7 victory over Arkansas the week before, the Rebels were flat and trailed 6–3 late in the game. Starting from his own 21-yard line, a hobbled Jake Gibbs drove the Rebels into field-goal position. Allen Green made the 41-yard field goal for the tie with only 13 seconds left in the game. Ole Miss went on to finish 10–0–1 and was declared the national champion by several services.

1961: Ole Miss was 6–0 and ranked No. 2 when it arrived in Baton Rouge to play No. 6 LSU. The Rebels led 7–3 at halftime, but in the third quarter Jerry Stovall raced 57 yards to set up a touchdown that gave LSU a 10–7 lead. That score stood up and the Tigers went on to win the SEC championship.

1964: Coach Charlie McClendon's third LSU team was undefeated and ranked No. 6 when it hosted 3–2–1 Ole Miss. The Rebels crossed into LSU territory only twice, but that was enough to take a 10–3 lead late into the game. LSU got a chance to win when Ole Miss punt returner Doug Cunningham fumbled near mid-field and the Tigers recovered. LSU scored on a 19-yard pass from Billy Ezell to Billy Masters with 3:30 left. LSU's Doug Moreau caught a tipped pass for a two-point conversion, and the Tigers won 11–10.

Ole Miss quarterback Archie Manning (1968–70) threw for 345 yards against LSU in 1969. Photo courtesy of Mississippi SID.

1969: LSU was 6–0 and appeared headed for an SEC championship when it faced 3–3 Ole Miss in Jackson, Mississippi. But the Tigers did not have an answer for junior quarterback Archie Manning of Ole Miss, who ran for three touchdowns. The Rebels knocked off the Tigers 26–23 in what would be LSU's only loss all season.

1972: LSU was 6–0 with its eyes set on another SEC championship. The Tigers trailed 16–10 in the final minutes until quarterback Bert Jones put together one of the most memorable performances of his career. Jones drove his team the length of the field, and on a play that began with 10 seconds left, Ole Miss was called for pass interference. That gave LSU a first down at the Mississippi 10-yard line with four seconds remaining. Here the controversy began, according to Marty Mule's outstanding book on LSU football, *Eye of the Tiger*.

Ole Miss fans still insist that the next play, an incomplete pass over the middle, took more than four seconds and that the game should have been over. But after Jones's pass hit the ground, one second remained on the Tiger Stadium clock.

Given one last chance, Jones hit Brad Davis out of the backfield. Davis juggled the ball and dove into the end zone for a touchdown to tie the game. Rusty Jackson added the extra point, and the Tigers won 17–16.

To this day Ole Miss fans believe they fell victim to bad time keeping. They say what Jones did, running two plays in four seconds, was impossible.

Just a few days after this historic game, a sign went up on the Louisiana-Mississippi border: "Entering Louisiana. Set your clocks back four seconds."

1979: Ole Miss jumped out to a 17–0 lead in Jackson, only to have LSU storm back to win 28–24.

1986: LSU won the SEC championship in 1986 but still lost to Ole Miss 21–19 in Baton Rouge.

2002: LSU fell behind 10–0 to Ole Miss and the Rebels still led 13–7 in the fourth quarter. But LSU intercepted an Eli Manning pass and the Tigers drove for a touchdown to win, 14–13.

2003: The largest crowd in the history of Vaught-Hemingway Stadium (62,552) turned out to watch Eli Manning play his final home game for Ole Miss. The SEC's Western Division championship was also on the line. It was a tough night for Ole Miss. With his team trailing 17–14, place-kicker Jonathan Nichols missed a 36-yard field goal that would have tied the game with 4:15 left. Manning got one more chance to win the game for Ole Miss but stumbled on a fourth-down pass. LSU won the game and went on to win the national championship.

Ole Miss coach Billy Brewer holds the Golden Egg trophy after a win over Mississippi State. Photo courtesy of Mississippi SID.

OLE MISS VERSUS MISSISSIPPI STATE: THE EGG BOWL

OLE MISS LEADS 59–39–6

Most could understand why the fans of Ole Miss wanted to celebrate after watching their team win at Mississippi A&M (now Mississippi State) in 1926. In the 23 previous meetings with their hated state rival, the Rebels had won only five times. In his book *Mississippi Mayhem*, author William George Barner III describes the scene that further fueled the rivalry and eventually led to the creation of the Egg Bowl.

When Ole Miss fans went for the goal posts after the 7–6 win, Mississippi State fans came out of the stands with cane-bottom chairs, according to Barner. Fights broke out all over the stadium until almost all of the chairs were splintered.

The war of words between the two schools continued long after the postgame scene in Starkville. Officials on both sides feared that more violence would erupt the following year. In an effort to cool the animosity between the two schools, members of Sigma Iota, an Ole Miss honor society, proposed awarding a trophy to the winning team. "The Golden Egg" a regulation-sized gold-plated football mounted on a pedestal, was designated as the trophy.

The first Battle of the Golden Egg, or Egg Bowl, as it became known, took place on Thanksgiving Day in 1927. The game was actually the 25th meeting of the two schools and Ole Miss won 20–12. This time, instead of a brawl, there was a formal ceremony where the president of Mississippi State presented the trophy to the chancellor of Ole Miss. The chancellor, in turn, handed the trophy to the Ole Miss team captain.

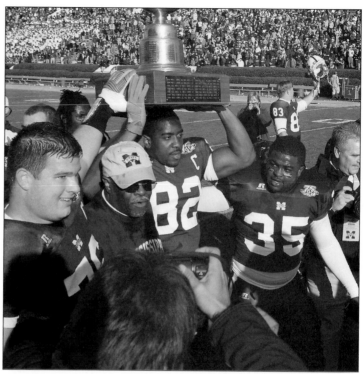

Mississippi State players celebrate with coach Sylvester Croom after they rallied to beat Ole Miss 17–14 in the 2007 Egg Bowl. Photo courtesy of Mississippi State University/Sports Information.

Over the years, the Battle for the Golden Egg has always been the highlight of the season for both schools, regardless of their respective records. Even in years when both schools were losing, an entire season could be salvaged for one of them by winning the Golden Egg.

Since 1927 the game has been played every year except 1943, when football at Mississippi's colleges was put on hold because of World War II. From 1927 to 1972, the game alternated between the campuses in Starkville and Oxford. In 1973, the game was moved to Jackson, where it remained through 1990. In 1991, the games went back to the respective campuses.

Here are but a few of the most exciting games in this heated rivalry:

1928: In the second meeting for the Golden Egg, Claude "Tadpole" Smith earned his place in Ole Miss history. Smith ran 40 yards for a touchdown and then kicked the winning extra point as the Rebels won 20–19 on Thanksgiving Day.

1941: Mississippi State won 6–0 in Oxford to claim its first and only SEC championship.

1951: Arnold "Showboat" Boykin scored seven touchdowns as Ole Miss routed Mississippi State 49–7. Boykin's performance remains one of the greatest ever in the Rebels' history.

1962: Sophomore quarterback Jimmy Weatherly missed a handoff to David Jennings late in the game, but then put the ball on his hip and ran 43 yards for a touchdown to give Ole Miss a 13–6 victory. *The Memphis Commercial Appeal* called Weatherly's play "the Goof That Laid the Golden Egg."

1983: Trailing 24–23 with only 24 seconds remaining, Artie Cosby of Mississippi State lined up to kick what would have been a winning field goal from 27 yards out. Cosby's kick appeared to be good and eyewitnesses swore the ball actually went through the upright before a gust of wind blew the ball back into the field of play. The kick was ruled no good and Ole Miss won the game.

1992: Trailing 17–10, Mississippi State ran 11 plays inside the Ole Miss 10-yard line with less than three minutes left and still could not score. The Rebels stopped a last-second drive with an interception in the end zone by Michael Lowery to preserve the seven-point victory.

1997: Mississippi quarterback Stewart Patridge hit Andre Rone for a 10-yard touchdown pass with 25 seconds left in the game to bring the Rebels to within a point, 14–13. Instead of kicking the extra point for the tie and sending the game into overtime, Ole Miss coach Tommy Tuberville showed why he would soon become known as the "Riverboat Gambler." Patridge threw to Cory Peterson for a two-point conversion and a 15–14 victory that sent Mississippi to the inaugural Motor City Bowl, its first postseason trip since 1992.

1999: The 1999 Mississippi State team earned a reputation for winning close games, and never was this more apparent than in the season finale against Ole Miss. The Bulldogs were down 20–6 midway through the third quarter but battled back to tie the game 20–20 with 27 seconds left. It appeared the game was heading into overtime, but a pass from Mississippi's Romaro Miller was intercepted and returned to the 26-yard line with eight seconds left. Mississippi State's Scott Westerfield kicked a 44-yard field goal with four seconds left, and the Bulldogs won 23–20.

2003: Jackie Sherrill hoped that his final game as the Mississippi State coach would be a win over Ole Miss. Eli Manning would have none of that as he threw for 260 yards and three touchdowns, and the Rebels won 31–0 in the 100th meeting between the two schools.

2007: Trailing 14–0 going into the fourth quarter, Mississippi State stormed back with 17 unanswered points to win 17–14. Adam Carlson kicked the last field goal of his career from 48 yards with only 18 seconds left to give Sylvester Croom his first winning season as the Bulldogs' head coach.

GEORGIA VERSUS FLORIDA:
THE WORLD'S LARGEST OUTDOOR COCKTAIL PARTY

GEORGIA LEADS 47–37–2

In 1933 officials from the universities of Georgia and Florida decided to move their annual game from the respective campuses to Jacksonville, Florida. They thought the move would bring a more festive atmosphere to the event and give both groups of fans a minivacation in the fall. Little did those men know that they were about to create one of the biggest events in all of college football.

Except for a two-year break during World War II and another two-year break (1994–95) during renovation of the old Gator Bowl Stadium, Georgia and Florida have fought their border war every year along the banks of the St. John's River.

The tickets are divided evenly between the two schools so there is no home-field advantage. Fans arrive in Jacksonville several days before the game to play golf, shop, and do a

Georgia's Bulldog drags the Florida Gator. Photo courtesy of the *Atlanta Journal-Constitution*/Calvin Cruce.

whole lot of partying. Over the years, the game became such a social event that it was finally dubbed "the World's Largest Outdoor Cocktail Party."

After the alcohol-related deaths of two students in Jacksonville, the presidents of both schools asked the media to refrain from using the term "Cocktail Party" to describe the game. But the party still goes on each year, and most of the time the fans are also treated to a pretty good game. Here are some of the best:

1964: Georgia won 14–7 when place-kicker Bobby Etter picked up a bad snap on a field-goal attempt and ran 22 yards for a touchdown.

1965: Florida quarterback Steve Spurrier threw a 32-yard touchdown pass with 41 seconds left to give the Gators a 14–10 victory.

1966: Spurrier was in the middle of his the Heisman Trophy–winning season, but more than anything he wanted to lead Florida to its first SEC title. A win over Georgia would do it. Florida led 10–3 at halftime, but in the second half the Bulldogs pounded Spurrier and won the game 27–10.

1973, 1974: Both of these games came down to a two-point conversion. In 1973 Florida made it and won 11–10. In 1974 the Bulldogs stopped the Gators and won 17–16.

1975: Florida needed a win over Georgia to nail down the first SEC championship in school history. The Gators seemed to be in good shape, leading 7–3 with 3:42 remaining. Then Georgia tight end Richard Appleby took the ball on an end-around and instead of running the ball as he had done earlier in the game, Appleby stopped, planted his foot, and threw an 80-yard touchdown pass to Gene Washington, giving the Bulldogs a 10–7 victory.

1976: Florida again needed a win over Georgia for the SEC championship, and at halftime the Gators appeared to be in control, leading 27–13. With his team still leading 27–20, Florida coach Doug Dickey decided to go for a first down on fourth and one at his own 29-yard line. Georgia stopped the play and went on to score three straight touchdowns for a 41–27 victory. The Bulldogs went on to win the SEC championship, and Dickey's "Fourth and Dumb" stuck with him the rest of his days at Florida, which weren't many. In 1979 Dickey was replaced by Charley Pell.

1980: The most famous moment in the rich Georgia-Florida rivalry, at least from the Georgia perspective, took place in 1980. Led by Herschel Walker, the great freshman running back, the Bulldogs were 8–0, ranked No. 2, and in the hunt for the national championship. Earlier in the day top-ranked Notre Dame had been tied 3–3 by Georgia Tech, so a win would have moved the Bulldogs to No. 1 in the next polls.

But with 1:03 left, Georgia trailed 21–20 and was stuck on its own 7-yard line. The Bulldogs' chance at a national championship seemed to be over. Then, on third and 11, quarterback Buck Belue hit receiver Lindsay Scott with a pass near the 25-yard line. A Florida defender slipped down and Scott raced the length of the field for the touchdown. Georgia won 26–21 and went on to beat Notre Dame in the Sugar Bowl for the national championship.

As Florida's head coach, Steve Spurrier won 11 of his 12 games against Georgia. Photo courtesy of the *Atlanta Journal-Constitution.*

1984: Florida quarterback Kerwin Bell hit Ricky Nattiel with a 96-yard touchdown pass to clinch a 27–0 victory and snap Georgia's six-game winning streak. Florida fans were so excited that they tore down a goal post and did a victory lap around the Gator Bowl.

1985: Florida was undefeated and ranked No. 1 when it arrived in Jacksonville to play a 6–1–1 Georgia team that had been tied by Vanderbilt. Tim Worley sparked the Georgia effort with an 89-yard touchdown run and the Bulldogs upset the Gators 24–3.

1990–2001: Vince Dooley retired as Georgia's head coach after the 1988 season with a 17–7–1 record against Florida. Former Heisman Trophy winner Steve Spurrier was named Florida's head coach in 1990. Spurrier had never forgotten that Georgia had knocked him out of a chance for an SEC championship in 1966 and took great joy in beating the Bulldogs. Under Spurrier Florida enjoyed its greatest run of success against Georgia, beating the Bulldogs 11 out of 12 years. Spurrier left Florida to coach in the NFL after the 2001 season.

2002: With Spurrier gone, Georgia thought its troubles against Florida were over, but the Bulldogs were wrong. Georgia was 8–0, ranked No. 3, and thinking about a run at the national championship when it played Florida in 2002. But quarterback Rex Grossman threw a 10-yard touchdown pass to give the Gators the lead in the fourth quarter, and the defense made it stand up for a 20–13 win. Georgia won the SEC championship and finished 13–1.

2003: Georgia was 7–1, ranked No. 3, and in control of its own destiny in the SEC East when it met Florida. But again the Gators found a way to win as Matt Leach kicked a 33-yard field goal with only 33 seconds left to give Florida a 16–13 victory.

2004: For the first time since 1997, and only the second time in 15 seasons, Georgia finally beat Florida as senior quarterback David Greene threw for 255 yards and three touchdowns in a 31–24 victory. It was the last Georgia-Florida game for Gators coach Ron Zook, who was fired the previous Monday but agreed to coach for the rest of the season.

2005: Georgia was 7–0 and ranked No. 3, but the Bulldogs had to play the game without quarterback D.J. Shockley, who had been injured the week before against Arkansas. Backup quarterback Joe Tereshinski did his best, but the Gators won 14–10. Georgia went on to win the SEC championship.

2007: This game featured a moment that will live forever in Georgia-Florida lore. After Knowshon Moreno scored Georgia's first touchdown, the entire Bulldogs team left the bench and ran into the end zone. A penalty was called for unsportsmanlike conduct, but the tone for the game had been set. Moreno, just a redshirt freshman, ran for 188 yards, and the Bulldogs won 42–30.

GEORGIA VERSUS GEORGIA TECH: A PEACH OF A RIVALRY

GEORGIA LEADS 59–36–5

Is it possible for a player to have his jersey retired based on his performance in just one game? Yes, if the game is big enough. And for the University of Georgia, few games have been bigger than its 1957 meeting with Georgia Tech.

The Bulldogs had very little to cheer about that season. Going into the game with Georgia Tech in Atlanta they were 2–7 and headed for their third straight losing record under coach Wally Butts. To make matters worse, Georgia was mired in an eight-game losing streak to Bobby Dodd and Georgia Tech, the longest in the history of the series for either team.

After going 10–1 in 1956, Georgia Tech (4–3–2) was also struggling when Georgia arrived at Grant Field on November 30. The winner of the game had a chance to salvage its season and get the alumni off its backs.

Georgia's Theron Sapp scores to end Georgia Tech's eight-game winning streak in 1957. Photo courtesy of the *Atlanta Journal-Constitution.*

In his book about the rivalry, *Clean Old-Fashioned Hate*, author Bill Cromartie makes it clear that if a game ever belonged to one player, the 1957 Georgia–Georgia Tech game belonged to Bulldogs running back Theron Sapp.

Sapp, a junior fullback from Macon, scored the game's only touchdown on a one-yard run late in the third quarter. From his linebacker position he recovered two fumbles. One of those set up the winning touchdown drive.

The victory touched off a wild celebration among the Georgia fans who had come to Grant Field. From that day on, Sapp became known as "the Drought Breaker" for having ended the losing streak to Georgia Tech.

Sapp went on to have a very solid career at Georgia and, in 1958, was named All-SEC. In 1959 Sapp became only the third player in Georgia history to have his jersey retired—his touchdown against Georgia Tech was that big.

Since Georgia and Georgia Tech played their first game in 1893 (won by Georgia Tech 28–6 in what Cromartie describes as a brawl-filled afternoon), this is the game that has stirred passions like few others.

The two teams stopped playing for six years (1919–25) over a disagreement that involved baseball and World War I. Cromartie writes that Georgia was in the middle of sweeping a four-game baseball series with Georgia Tech when some of Georgia's students flew a banner pointing out that in 1917–18 Georgia had not fielded a football team because of World War I while Georgia Tech, under coach John Heisman, had kept playing. Georgia Tech students and officials took offense and threatened to break off athletic relations if Georgia did not apologize. Georgia indicated that no apology would be forthcoming, and thus the schools did not play in any sport until the two sides made peace in 1925.

When Georgia Tech left the SEC after the 1963 season, the Georgia–Georgia Tech game ceased to be a conference game. Still, it has not lost any of its passion.

"Georgia has other rivals like Florida and Auburn, but Georgia Tech is the greatest of all because it's our state rival," said former Georgia coach/athletics director Vince Dooley, who was 19–6 in 25 meetings with Georgia Tech. "If you lose that one, there are a lot of people on both sides who will not let you forget it."

Dooley arrived at Georgia in 1964 just as Dodd was winding down his legendary career at Georgia Tech. Dodd retired after the 1966 season with a 12–10 record against the Bulldogs.

Here are but a few of the most memorable games in this great Southern rivalry:

1927: Georgia, 9–0 and ranked No. 1, was a heavy favorite against Georgia Tech at Grant Field. The Bulldogs knew before the game that a win would earn them an invitation to the Rose Bowl on New Year's Day. But Georgia Tech intercepted four passes, winning 12–0 and dashing Georgia's hopes of a trip to Pasadena.

1942: The week before its scheduled date, the Georgia–Georgia Tech game of 1942 was shaping up to be one of the biggest in Southern football history. Georgia, with running back Frankie Sinkwich, the Heisman Trophy winner, was undefeated and ranked No. 1 when it faced Auburn on November 21. Fans were already talking about the next week's game with Georgia Tech, which was ranked No. 2 and also unbeaten, because an invitation to the Rose Bowl would go to the winner of the game. Georgia, however, stumbled against 4–4–1 Auburn and lost 27–13. Despite the loss to Auburn, Georgia still had to bring in 8,000 extra seats for the game with Georgia Tech at Sanford Stadium. The Rose Bowl stuck with its promise that the winner of the game would go to Pasadena. It wasn't even close as Sinkwich and Charley Trippi led Georgia to a 34–0 win. Georgia (10–1) went to the Rose Bowl where it beat UCLA. Georgia Tech (9–1) went to the Cotton Bowl where it lost to Texas.

1966: The 1966 game rekindled memories of 1942. No. 3 Georgia Tech arrived at Georgia's Sanford Stadium with a 9–0 record. The Yellow Jackets were heading to the Orange Bowl on New Year's Day. Georgia (8–1) had won the SEC championship two weeks before by beating Auburn. The Bulldogs' only loss was 7–6 at Miami. Tech coach Bobby Dodd had the glamour backfield combo of quarterback Kim King and running back Lenny Snow. Georgia featured a hard-hitting defense led by All-American tackle George Patton.

Georgia's Kent Lawrence returned a punt 71 yards for a touchdown, and the Bulldogs defense simply smothered King and Snow on the way to a 23–14 victory in the 100th meeting in the series (including freshman games). Georgia went on to the Cotton Bowl, where it beat SMU, while Tech lost to Florida and Steve Spurrier in the Orange Bowl. After the 1966 season Dodd retired at Georgia Tech after 22 seasons as head coach.

1971: On a cold Thanksgiving night at Grant Field, these two old rivals played one of their most exciting games ever. Georgia was 9–1 after losing to Pat Sullivan and Auburn 12 days before. The Bulldogs were still feeling the effects of that loss as they fell behind 17–7 in the second quarter. But just before halftime Georgia quarterback Andy Johnson hit Jimmy Shirer for a 23-yard touchdown to give the Bulldogs new life. Still, Georgia Tech was leading 24–21 when Georgia took possession on its own 35-yard line with 1:29 left in the game. Then, with 57 seconds left, Georgia faced a fourth and 10 at the Georgia Tech 43. With the game in the balance, Johnson hit tight end Mike Greene for 18 yards and a first down. The Bulldogs eventually scored when running back Jimmy Poulos leaped over the top of the Georgia Tech defense from one yard out with 14 seconds left to give Georgia a 28–24 victory.

1978: Georgia fell behind 20–0 but battled back to take a 21–20 lead on Scott Woerner's 72-yard punt return for a third-quarter touchdown. But on the ensuing kickoff, Georgia Tech's Drew Hill stunned the Bulldogs with a 101-yard return for a touchdown. A two-point conversion gave Georgia Tech a 28–21 lead. Georgia got one last chance to score when it took possession at its own 16-yard line with just under six minutes left. Georgia freshman quarterback Buck Belue converted a fourth-down play to keep the drive alive. Then, on a fourth-down play at the Georgia Tech 43, Belue found Amp Arnold behind the Yellow Jacket secondary and lofted a touchdown pass with 2:25 left in the game. Belue's pass over the middle for Mark Hodge was incomplete, but Georgia Tech was called for pass interference. Given another chance, Belue pitched to Arnold for the two points and a 29–28 victory.

1984: Georgia Tech gave coach Bill Curry his first win over Georgia, 35–18 in Athens. The game snapped Georgia's six-game winning streak. Back in Atlanta, the Tech students were so excited that they broke into Grant Field and tore down the goal posts, parading the pieces up and down North Avenue.

1985: Gary Lee returned a kickoff 95 yards for a touchdown, which proved to be the winning points as Georgia Tech beat No. 20 Georgia 20–16. Georgia still had a chance to win, but quarterback James Jackson fumbled at midfield in the closing minutes.

Just to prove that the rivalry still had steam, Georgia and Georgia Tech closed out the 1990s with three of the most exciting games in the history of the series:

1997: When Charles Wiley scored on a three-yard touchdown run to give the Yellow Jackets a 24–21 lead with 48 seconds left in the game, it seemed that Georgia Tech would win. But Georgia took over on its own 35-yard line after the ensuing kickoff went out of bounds. Two quick passes to Champ Bailey and another to running back Robert Edwards put Georgia deep in Georgia Tech territory. A controversial pass interference call negated a Georgia Tech interception and gave Georgia a first down at the 8-yard line. Quarterback Mike Bobo hit Corey Allen for the touchdown with eight seconds left, and Georgia won 27–24. It was Georgia's seventh straight win over Georgia Tech.

1998: Georgia appeared to be headed for its eighth straight win over Georgia Tech, leading 19–7 going into the fourth quarter. But Georgia Tech dominated the final period, driving 74 yards for a score early in the final quarter to make it 19–15 after a two-point conversion. Brad Chambers brought the Yellow Jackets to within one, 19–18, with a 49-yard field goal with 5:01 left. Georgia Tech then drove 52 yards in the final four minutes, and Chambers kicked a 35-yard field with two seconds remaining to give the Yellow Jackets a 21–19 victory.

1999: This game will probably go down as the most controversial in the series. Georgia Tech quarterback Joe Hamilton, who would finish second to Wisconsin's Ron Dayne for the Heisman Trophy in 1999, was unstoppable. Twice he led Georgia Tech to 17-point leads in the game and twice Georgia, led by sophomore

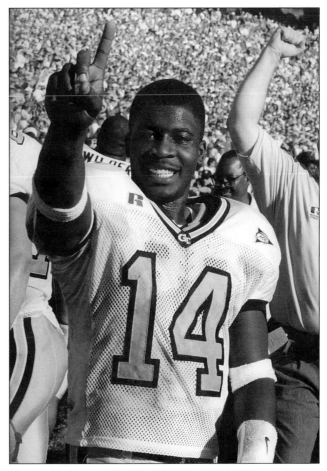

Georgia Tech quarterback Joe Hamilton led the Yellow Jackets to wins over Georgia in 1998 and 1999. Photo courtesy of the Georgia Institute of Technology/Sports Information.

quarterback Quincy Carter, fought back to tie the game. The game was still tied at 48 when Georgia started what it hoped would be the winning drive. With the final seconds ticking down, Georgia had a first down near the Georgia Tech goal line. Coach Jim Donnan instructed his team to take one shot at the end zone and then kick the field goal. But when running back Jasper Sanks was struggling for the touchdown, the ball popped loose and was recovered by Georgia Tech.

Television replays later showed that Sanks was down and that the play should not have been ruled a fumble. But the call stood and the game went into overtime. After Georgia failed to score on its possession in overtime, Georgia Tech lined up for a field-goal attempt on third down. The Bulldogs blocked the kick and Georgia fans thought that the drive was over. But Georgia Tech recovered the ball and was given another chance to kick. This time Luke Manget's 38-yard attempt was true, and the Yellow Jackets won 51–48.

The SEC officiating crew that worked the game in Atlanta was suspended after the league office reviewed the game tape.

2001–2007: After a 27–15 loss to Georgia Tech in 2000, Georgia coach Jim Donnan was fired, and Mark Richt, the offensive coordinator at Florida State, was named as the Bulldogs' new head coach. Under Richt, Georgia has won seven straight games against Georgia Tech. That ties Georgia's longest winning streak in the series.

CHAPTER 8

THE VOICES

Before television brought dozens of games into the home on multiple days of the week, and before modern transportation made getting to the games much easier, the most important link between college football and its fans was the radio play-by-play announcer.

These men did much more than just explain what was happening on the field. They were the ultimate cheerleaders and, sometimes, the most unforgiving critics. These men made no pretense of objectivity, living, dying, laughing, and crying with every first down and every last-minute play.

With their voices they were able to transport fans from every tiny hamlet in the state to that glorious stadium far, far away. Thanks to the announcers' powers of description, listeners could not only hear the band, but also they could see the band in their mind's eye. And the really good ones could take their listeners through a full range of emotions on any given Saturday afternoon.

Even some of the greatest announcers in other sports did their time in college football. Red Barber earned his fame as a baseball play-by-play announcer for the Cincinnati Reds, Brooklyn Dodgers, and New York Yankees from 1934 to 1966. But you may not know that Barber was a Florida graduate and was the voice of the Gators from 1930 to 1933.

Lindsey Nelson had a Hall of Fame career as a baseball announcer and the voice of the Cotton Bowl. But it was Nelson, the voice of Tennessee football for three seasons (1948–50), who helped form the ultrasuccessful Volunteer Radio Network in 1949.

Today, even though most games are on television, the emotional bond between Southern college football fans and their radio announcers is still very strong. In stadiums around the South, fans can be seen with radios in order to listen to their announcers while the games are in progress. They can see what happens on the field, but they need their voice to tell them what it all means. The announcer's excitement is their excitement. The announcer's joy is their joy.

Without these men, the special emotional bond between Southern college football and its fans would never have been completely cemented. Their names are synonymous with the schools they represent. Here are some of their stories.

Florida's Otis Boggs. Photo courtesy of Florida SID.

OTIS BOGGS

FLORIDA, 1939–81

Boggs was not the kind of guy you would pick out of a crowd as someone famous. He was a rotund, slightly bald, ordinary looking man who did not give the impression that he was capable of extraordinary things. But contrary to his appearance, Boggs was the valedictorian of his high school senior class and graduated from the University of Florida with a joint degree in chemistry, German, English, and history.

Boggs had the talent to do anything with his life, but he was bitten by the broadcasting bug.

What happened after Boggs graduated from Florida is a wonderful chapter in the school's football history. Boggs became a member of the Florida broadcast team in 1939, and in 1940 he took over as the Gators' play-by-play man. He stayed on the job for 43 seasons and 401 games.

Few radio voices have bonded with a group of fans the way Boggs bonded with the Gators faithful. Tom McEwen, the longtime sports editor of the *Tampa Tribune*, told a story that best illustrated the relationship between Boggs and the Florida fans. When Florida State took a 17–16 lead in the 1965 Sunshine Showdown against Florida, an FSU fan stood up in his seat, turned around, and shouted at the press box: "How you like that, Otis Boggs?" He sat down to applause and laughter.

The point of the story is that the fan would not have known Otis Boggs if Boggs had walked up and asked him to dance. But in his moment of excitement, the fan wanted to lash out at the best-known symbol of Florida football. For 43 seasons, that was Otis Boggs.

Boggs had a number of traits that endeared him to friends and foes alike. Whenever the out-of-town radio crew arrived in Gainesville, they would find a gallon of fresh-squeezed orange juice in their booth, courtesy of Otis Boggs.

In 1989 Boggs received the Distinguished Alumni Award from the university's Journalism and Communications School. In 1990 he was inducted into the Florida Sports Hall of Fame.

Boggs retired as the voice of the Gators after the 1981 season. He died on August 28, 2002, at age 82.

AL CIRALDO
GEORGIA TECH, 1954–97

For 43 unforgettable seasons, college football at Georgia Tech was best known as the time when "toe meets leather." That was the signature phrase of the late Al Ciraldo, the legendary voice of the Yellow Jackets.

Georgia Tech's Al Ciraldo. Photo courtesy of the *Atlanta Journal-Constitution.*

Georgia Tech football has always evoked memories of John Heisman, Bobby Dodd, and the Ramblin' Wreck that leads the Georgia Tech team out onto Grant Field. But it was Ciraldo who painted the picture for all the Georgia Tech fans who could not be in Atlanta to see the game for themselves.

Ciraldo, a 1948 graduate of the University of Florida, came to Atlanta in 1949 to do the radio basketball broadcasts for the University of Georgia, Georgia Tech's biggest rival. But in 1954 he joined the staff at WGST radio, the flagship station of Georgia Tech athletics. His first football broadcast for Georgia Tech was on September 18, 1954, against Tulane. Over the next 38 seasons, Ciraldo would do the play-by-play for 416 football games and 1,030 basketball games for Georgia Tech.

In 1992 Ciraldo stepped down as Georgia Tech's play-by-play announcer but remained involved in the pregame and postgame shows. In 1997 Ciraldo officially retired after a radio career that spanned 62 years. He was inducted into the National Broadcasting Hall of Fame in 1993, and today the broadcasting booth at Bobby Dodd Stadium is named after him. He is a member of the Georgia Tech Hall of Fame.

Ciraldo passed away on November 7, 1997, at age 76.

JACK CRISTIL
MISSISSIPPI STATE, 1953–PRESENT

In 1953 Jack Cristil was a 27-year-old army veteran working at a radio station in Clarksdale, Mississippi, when he sent an acetate disk of his work to Mississippi State athletics director Dudy Noble. Cristil was one of three men up for the job of play-by-play man for Bulldogs football. Cristil got the interview and the job. Then he got his marching orders from Noble.

"You tell them what the score is, who has the ball, and now much time's left, and cut out all that other bullshit," said Noble, a man known for his ability to plainly speak his mind.

Jack Cristil began broadcasting for Mississippi State in 1953. Photo courtesy of Mississippi State SID.

Cristil, now 82, is still taking that advice to heart in fall 2008, as he enters his 56th season of broadcasting Mississippi State football games. Going into the start of the 2008 season, Cristil has called 594 Mississippi State games and has endeared himself to several generations of faithful Bulldogs football fans. He has never had a contract with Mississippi State. He simply comes back each year with a promise and a handshake.

Cristil, whose father was born in Latvia and whose mother was born in Russia, knew at an early age that he wanted to be a broadcaster. As a young boy he would make up games in his head and pretend to broadcast them out loud. After he got out of the service in 1946, he hitchhiked 400 miles from Chicago to Minneapolis to take broadcasting courses at the University of Minnesota.

He began his radio career in 1948 calling minor league baseball in Jackson, Tennessee. After several years traveling around the South to call baseball games, he got the job at Mississippi State.

Cristil was named to the Mississippi Sports Hall of Fame in 1992, the first representative of Mississippi State named to the Hall who was not an athlete.

When Mississippi State wins, Cristil ends his broadcast with his signature line: "You can wrap it up in maroon and white."

GENE DECKERHOFF
FLORIDA STATE, 1979–PRESENT

Like a number of our legendary voices, Deckerhoff worked in the private sector before deciding that he could only be happy behind the microphone. An All-City basketball player in Jacksonville, Florida, Deckerhoff began calling Little League games in Palatka, Florida, in 1965.

Deckerhoff worked for Southern Bell Telephone and General Foods for several years before taking his first full-time broadcasting job in 1972 at a station in Bradenton, Florida. In 1974 he was hired by WTNT in Tallahassee, Florida, to become the basketball voice of Florida State. In the summer of 1979 he auditioned for and won the job of play-by-play announcer for Florida State football. In 2008 he will celebrate his 30th season as the voice of the Seminoles.

Deckerhoff is known as one of the hardest working people in his profession. In 1989 he added the play-by-play duties of the NFL's Tampa Bay Buccaneers to his schedule, which makes for some busy weekends during football season. In 1990 Deckerhoff started his own production company, Gene Deckerhoff Productions.

Deckerhoff wears a lot of broadcasting hats but is best known as the voice of Bobby Bowden's Florida State football dynasty.

In 2000 Deckerhoff was inducted into the Florida Sports Hall of Fame. He is in the Florida State University Athletics Hall of Fame and has been honored with the Circle of Gold Medal for outstanding service to the university.

Deckerhoff is a graduate of the University of Florida but makes no secret of his allegiance to Florida State.

The 2008 season will be Gene Deckerhoff's 30th as the voice of Florida State football. Photo courtesy of Florida State

WOODY DURHAM

North Carolina, 1971–Present

Woody Durham's love of sports began when he was a 165-pound pulling guard for Albemarle High School, the 1957 Western North Carolina champions.

"I was a terror," he recalled.

Durham loved the excitement that came with being in the arena of athletic competition, but he knew he would not be able to play football at the college level. So he searched for something that would allow him to keep that feeling of excitement.

Durham found what he was looking for in broadcasting, a career that began a week before his 16th birthday. Durham had entered a local oratory contest, and one of the judges was the manager of the town's radio station, WZKY. Soon after that contest Durham got his first job in broadcasting. Durham's mother had to drive him to his first day of work.

Woody Durham. Photo courtesy of North Carolina SID.

College football is lucky that Woody Durham was able to follow his passion. The fall of 2008 will mark Durham's 38th season of calling games on the North Carolina Tar Heel Sports Network.

Durham, a 1963 graduate of North Carolina, worked briefly at a television station in Florence, South Carolina, before joining a television station in Greensboro, North Carolina, as its lead sportscaster. In 1971, when play-by-play man Bill Currie left North Carolina, Durham was hired by Tar Heels athletics director Homer Rice.

While Durham is known nationally and internationally as the voice of North Carolina's ultrasuccessful basketball program, his work in football has always been among the best in his profession. A stickler for preparation and detail, Durham has always been able to balance his love for his school and his commitment to making every broadcast the very best it can be.

In 38 years Durham, who turns 67 in August 2008, has become one of the state's treasures and one of the most respected people in broadcast journalism. Durham has been named North Carolina Broadcaster of the Year 12 times, the latest coming in 2006. In 2005 Durham was inducted into the North Carolina Sports Hall of Fame.

Durham and his wife, Jean, have two sons, Wes and Taylor. Wes Durham followed in his father's footsteps and is now entering his 14th season as the voice of Georgia Tech. Taylor Durham is also in the radio business as the network affiliate manager for ISP Sports.

Paul Eells was the Arkansas Sportscaster of the Year 11 times. Photo courtesy of the University of Arkansas/Sports Information.

PAUL EELLS
VANDERBILT, ARKANSAS, 1967–2006

Paul Eells was born in West Branch, Iowa, and attended the University of Iowa on a baseball scholarship. But at the time of his death in 2006, Eells had endeared himself to several generations of Southerners as the football voice of Vanderbilt and Arkansas.

When it became clear that baseball would not be his profession in life, Eells enrolled in a communications class at Iowa and discovered a new passion. He was working in local television in Cedar Rapids, Iowa, when the call came from WSM-TV in Nashville in 1967.

He spent 11 seasons as the voice of the Vanderbilt Commodores and was the sports director of WSM. In 1978 Eells moved to Arkansas where he remained as the voice of the Razorbacks until his death in an automobile accident on July 31, 2006.

Eells was impeccable as a broadcaster, but he was even better known as one of the truly nice men in his profession. Eells always had time for Razorbacks fans and those who loved his work. And there were many who did.

He was named the Arkansas Sportscaster of the Year 11 times.

Eells was inducted into the Arkansas Sports Hall of Fame in February 2006, just a few months before his death. On the day of his funeral, Arkansas governor Mike Huckabee called for all state flags to fly at half-staff. Huckabee called Eells "a great man and a true Arkansas icon."

His signature phrase, and the one that will live forever in the hearts of Arkansas fans, was: "Touchdown, Arkansas! Oh my!"

JOHN FERGUSON
LSU, 1946–87

John Ferguson. Photo courtesy of LSU SID.

Marty Mule, the outstanding sportswriter for the *New Orleans Times-Picayune*, captured the essence of John Ferguson in his book on LSU football, *Eye of the Tiger.*

The year was 1942, and Ferguson had just graduated from Louisiana Tech. He stood in the office of a manager of a radio station in El Dorado, Arkansas, and asked for a job.

"What makes you think you can do this?" bellowed the manager.

"I'm better than anyone you have," Ferguson said.

That's how Ferguson got his first job in radio, which required him to work 70 hours a week for the princely sum of $17.50. Ferguson broke into the business calling baseball in the Cotton States League.

World War II interrupted Ferguson's career, but after 144 missions as an Army Air Corps transport pilot, he returned to his native Louisiana and began work on a master's degree at LSU.

In 1946 WJBO radio in Baton Rouge won the rights to broadcast LSU football games and asked Ferguson if he was available. Ferguson took the job, and on that day a 42-year-long relationship with the school and its fans began.

Over the next four decades, Ferguson's rich baritone voice brought LSU fans every heart-pounding moment of Tigers football—that is, every moment but one. Perhaps the most famous play in LSU football history was Billy Cannon's 89-yard punt return for a touchdown against Ole Miss in 1959. As fate would have it, that year Ferguson took a break from LSU football to call the Southwest Conference game of the week. He got back in the LSU radio booth to stay in 1961.

In 1984 Ferguson reluctantly moved from the radio booth to handle TigerVision, the school's cable television broadcasts. He retired in 1987.

Ferguson died on December 17, 2005. He was 86.

JOHN FORNEY
ALABAMA, 1953–97

John Forney, the voice of Alabama football during the Bear Bryant era. Photo courtesy of the University of Alabama.

Few broadcasters have timed their arrival at a major Southern school better than John Forney.

Forney graduated from the University of Alabama in 1948 and by 1953 had landed a job as a member of the Crimson Tide broadcast team. Alabama won an SEC championship that season, but coach Harold "Red" Drew left a year later, and Alabama went into a three-year tailspin.

In 1958 Alabama hired a former player, Paul "Bear" Bryant, as its football coach. Over the next 25 years under Bryant, Alabama won 13 SEC championships and six national championships. Forney was there to call every one of them as the voice of the Crimson Tide.

Forney began broadcasting at an early age. When all of the college-aged talent in Tuscaloosa was heading off to war in 1943, the manager of the local radio station needed someone who wouldn't get drafted soon. He called Tuscaloosa High School and found 15-year-old Forney, whom he hired to be a play-by-play announcer.

Forney was not only an accomplished play-by-play announcer but also a shrewd businessman. From 1948 to 1952 he learned the advertising business in New York, and when he returned to Birmingham he established his own agency, where he was a partner for 30 years.

Forney first retired in 1982, the same year as Bryant. But in 1988 he was asked to rejoin the broadcast team to help with pregame and postgame shows. He remained with the Alabama radio network until his death on July 31, 1997. He was 70.

"John will always be the voice of the Crimson Tide," says Eli Gold, who has done Alabama's play-by-play since 1988. "I may be the current custodian, but he is the man that people always have and always will associate with that title."

Forney was inducted into the Alabama Sports Hall of Fame in 1998.

BOB FULTON

SOUTH CAROLINA, 1952–94

If people have any doubt about the bond between Southern college football fans and their radio voice, consider the story of South Carolina's Bob Fulton.

Fulton had been working the Gamecocks' games for 14 years when he received an offer to move over to Georgia Tech, whose team at that time was coached by the legendary Bobby Dodd. So Fulton kept his home in Columbia, South Carolina, and commuted to Atlanta to become the voice of Georgia Tech in 1965–66.

The outcry from South Carolina fans was so great that in 1967 Paul Dietzel, in his second year as the Gamecocks' football coach and athletics director, brought Fulton back and made him a full-time employee of the athletics department. No matter who owned the radio rights to broadcast South Carolina

South Carolina broadcaster Bob Fulton. Photo courtesy of South Carolina SID.

football, the contract would stipulate that the voice would be Fulton's. Fulton remained in that position until his retirement after the 1994 season.

Given the school's relative lack of success, South Carolina' fans have to be among the most loyal in all of college football. Since 1892 the Gamecocks have posted only nine seasons of eight wins or more. That fact makes Fulton's career as the voice of South Carolina football even more remarkable.

"Our fans had a special bond with our football team," said the late Tom Price, South Carolina's long-time sports information director and the author of several books on Gamecocks athletics. "Bob had a lot to do with that."

When Fulton retired, his tenure (41 seasons) was the fourth longest with one school in NCAA Division I-A history.

A native of Ridley Park, Pennsylvania, Fulton broadcast University of Arkansas football for nine years before he came to South Carolina. In 1993 he was inducted into the University of South Carolina Athletic Hall of Fame. In 1994 he received the state's highest award, the Order of the Palmetto. In 1995 a basketball jersey bearing his name joined the retired jerseys at Carolina Coliseum. In May 2007 Fulton was honored by the South Carolina Hall of Fame for his contribution to sports.

Fulton still resides in Columbia, South Carolina.

JIM FYFFE
AUBURN, 1981–2003

Jim Fyffe's signature call was "Touchdown, Auburn!" Photo courtesy of Auburn University/Sports Information.

Jim Fyffe grew up in Paintsville, Kentucky, but it didn't take him long to become an Auburn man once he became the voice of the Tigers in 1981. And it sure didn't take him long to understand the enormity of Auburn's rivalry with Alabama.

"If you are born in the state of Alabama you can't be on the fence. You have to choose between Auburn and Alabama," Fyffe said. "And if you move to the state they make you declare. I chose Auburn. And I'm glad I did."

For 22 football seasons Fyffe's distinctive voice thrilled Auburn's fans as the Tigers enjoyed one of the most successful periods in their football history. Fyffe's signature phrase "Touchdown, Auburn!" made his voice one of the most recognizable in all of college football.

Fyffe is remembered for a series of famous calls during his career, ranging from "Bo over the top!" in a 1982 win over Alabama, to "Tillman, Tillman, Tillman!" during a 1987 win over Georgia Tech. In that game wide receiver Lawyer Tillman caught a touchdown pass with only 29 seconds left to give the Tigers a 14–10 lead. Auburn eventually won the game 20–10.

But the voice of the Tigers was silenced far too soon.

On May 14, 2003, Fyffe attended a fund-raiser in Prattville, Alabama. When he returned home, Fyffe complained of a headache and then collapsed. He was rushed to a hospital in nearby Montgomery, where it was discovered he had a brain aneurysm. He died the next morning without regaining consciousness.

"There will be other voices, but no one else will carry the excitement and enthusiasm Jim did," Auburn athletics director David Housel said at the time. "I've lost a friend. Auburn has lost a patriot."

BOB HARRIS

DUKE, 1976–PRESENT

Like a number of broadcasters, Harris fell into the profession because it was a way to stay close to the games he loved.

In Matt Fulks's book *The Sportscaster's Dozen*, Harris concedes that he did not have a lot of athletic ability. "My high school baseball coach finally told me after I had graduated that a scout was watching one of my games, and on my card beside 'speed,' he had written 'Deceptive—slower than he looks.'"

He was too small (5'9", 119 pounds) to play football or basketball, so he went to

Duke broadcaster Bob Harris. Photo courtesy of Duke SID.

North Carolina State on an academic scholarship that had been provided by his father's company. Harris's father worked for the same textile manufacturer in Albemarle, North Carolina, for 55 years.

After he graduated from college, Harris went to work for the Goodyear Tire Company, first as a salesman and eventually as a store manager. He bounced around to five different stores and finally decided that it wasn't good for his wife, Phyllis, and their two young children. He left Goodyear and moved back to Albemarle and went into the insurance business.

Still, a part of Harris wanted to give broadcasting a try. As a young boy, Harris would sit with his father listening to the great radio voices of the day like Red Barber and Bill Stern. It was something he knew he could do.

In the fall of 1967, when a local radio station needed someone to do tape-delayed broadcasts of high school games, Harris volunteered and quickly discovered his passion. In February 1968, Harris quit his insurance job and decided to pursue a broadcasting career.

For eight years, Harris toiled in relative obscurity, broadcasting high school sports in Albemarle. On Labor Day 1975 he took a job at WDNC radio in Durham as a salesman. Out of that position came an opportunity to serve as a guest commentator on Duke football broadcasts. He then moved into basketball. When play-by-play man Add Penfield experienced health problems, Harris finished the rest of the season in his spot. He has been the voice of the Blue Devils ever since.

It turned out to be the perfect marriage of man and school. While Harris is best known nationally for his work with Mike Krzyzewski's ultrasuccessful Duke basketball program, he has always taken pride in his work in football.

Harris has been named North Carolina Sportscaster of the Year twice and has received numerous other awards for this work and his contributions to broadcasting. Harris was the sports director of WDNC radio in Durham for 24 years before he left to join the Duke Radio Network in a full-time capacity. Today he is vice president of radio operations for Moore Productions. He was inducted into the North Carolina Sports Hall of Fame in May 2006.

Harris and his wife, Phyllis, are involved in local charities and have endowed an athletic scholarship at Duke.

The 2008 season will be the 33rd for Harris as the voice of the Blue Devils.

The 2008 season will be Johnny Holliday's 30th as the voice of Maryland football. Photo courtesy of the University of Maryland/Sports Information.

JOHNNY HOLLIDAY
Maryland, 1979–Present

Johnny Holliday was famous long before he became the voice of Maryland football and basketball in 1979.

A native of Miami, Florida, Holliday was named America's number one disc jockey in 1965. He was the emcee for the Beatles' last American concert in 1966.

Holliday got into broadcasting after a friend secretly entered his name in a disc jockey contest. Holliday didn't win the contest, but he discovered that radio work was something he could do and do well.

Holliday was visiting his grandfather in Georgia one summer when he was introduced to a radio station manager from Perry, Georgia, who, as it turned out, needed a disc jockey. He worked there for five months, during which he got his first play-by-play work broadcasting Perry High School basketball games. On that team was a player named Sam Nunn, who went on to become a United States senator.

Holliday worked in Georgia for five months and then bounced around from Rochester, New York, to Cleveland to New York City to San Francisco and finally to Washington, D.C., in 1969. He has been there ever since.

When Holliday became the voice of Maryland in 1979, he knew he had found a home. The 2008 season will be his 30th calling the action for the Terps.

Holliday has received every major award in broadcasting. In 2006 he received the Chris Schenkel Award from the National Football Foundation and College Hall of Fame. In 2003 he was inducted into the Radio-Television Broadcasters Hall of Fame.

Holliday is also considered one of most versatile broadcasters in sports. For 26 years Holliday has given daily sports reports on the ABC radio network. He has worked five Olympics and has been a long-time correspondent at the Masters golf tournament.

In 2002 Holliday wrote an autobiography titled *From Rock to Jock*.

CAWOOD LEDFORD
KENTUCKY, 1953–92

Like North Carolina's Woody Durham and Duke's Bob Harris, Ledford made his national reputation as the voice of a college basketball dynasty. But Ledford, like Durham and Harris, was one of radio's consummate professionals and never gave Kentucky football less than his very best.

Ledford grew up in Harlan, Kentucky, and served in the Marine Corps during World War II.

When Ledford arrived at Kentucky in 1953, Adolph Rupp was in his 23rd year of what would become a 42-year career as the Wildcats' head basketball coach. Bear Bryant was in his eighth and final season as the school's head football coach. Kentucky football struggled more often than not in his 39 seasons behind the microphone, but Ledford's sharp and clearheaded calls were always among the very best in college football.

Kentucky legend Cawood Ledford.
Photo courtesy of Kentucky SID.

Ledford possessed many strengths as a broadcaster, but he is most remembered for his exquisite use of language, which kept his listeners informed and at ease. At the same time, Ledford was anything but a houseman for the Wildcats. If Kentucky was playing poorly or giving less than its best effort, Ledford would not hesitate to report it.

"I always felt that in broadcasting your total allegiance is to the person twisting the dial and giving you the courtesy of listening to you," Ledford told the Associated Press in 1991.

Ledford was named the Kentucky Sportscaster of the Year 20 times in his 39-year career. He is one of a handful of nonplayers to be honored with a banner in the rafters at Rupp Arena.

He was inducted into the Kentucky Athletic Hall of Fame in 1987.

Ledford retired after the 1991 football and 1992 basketball seasons at age 65. He was still very much on top of his game.

"I just didn't want to stay too long," Ledford said at the time.

Cawood Ledford didn't stay too long. He left college football much too early. He died on September 5, 2001, at age 75.

LARRY MUNSON
Georgia, 1966–Present

Larry Munson has been the voice of the Georgia Bulldogs since 1966. Photo courtesy of Georgia SID.

In his 43 years as the voice of the Georgia Bulldogs Larry Munson has made no pretense of being objective. He was for Georgia and every Bulldogs fan knew it. That is why Munson remains one of the most beloved figures in school history.

Munson agonized over every opponent and worried constantly about the weaknesses of the Bulldogs.

"On the Saturday morning before the game I would be feeling pretty good about things," former coach Vince Dooley said. "And then I would run into Larry. By the time I got through talking to him I wondered if we could beat anybody."

By the time Munson arrived as Georgia's play-by-play man in 1966, he had already earned a reputation as one of the nation's best broadcasters. He had worked Vanderbilt football and basketball for 16 years and had even done a stint with the Atlanta Braves baseball team. He hosted an ultrapopular fishing show during his time in Nashville.

But as the radio voice of the Bulldogs, Munson has earned immortality. Health permitting, the 2008 season will be Munson's 43rd calling the action for yet another generation of adoring Georgia fans.

A native of Minneapolis, Munson had to earn the affection of Georgia people. For the first seven years, Georgia fans weren't too high on Munson, who replaced the very popular Ed Thilenius. First of all, he was from the North. Second of all, he seemed stiff and unemotional.

That all changed in 1973, when Georgia rallied from a 31–21 deficit to beat Tennessee 35–31. At the end of the game Munson screamed, "My God, we've just beaten Tennessee in Knoxville!" The phrase ruffled some feathers in the more strident church-going crowd, but it endeared him to the rest of the Bulldog Nation.

Munson solidified his legend during the Herschel Walker era (1980–82) when the Bulldogs won three straight SEC championships and one national championship. As he counted down the final seconds of Georgia's 19–14 win over Auburn in 1982, Munson screamed, "Look at the sugar falling out of the sky! Look at the sugar falling out of the sky!" That was his way of proclaiming that Georgia had won the SEC championship and was headed to the Sugar Bowl.

In 1980 Munson delivered the most famous call of his career in a 26–21 win over Florida in Jacksonville. With time running out and Georgia trailing 21–20, quarterback Buck Belue threw a short pass to Lindsay Scott, who outran the Florida defense for a 93-yard touchdown. At the end of the call, Munson just screamed "Lindsay Scott! Lindsay Scott! Lindsay Scott!" Georgia used that victory as a springboard to the national championship.

In 1994 Munson was inducted into the Georgia Association of Broadcasters Hall of Fame. In 1997 he was honored by the Georgia state legislature for his contributions to the university and to the state of Georgia. In 2003 he received the Chris Schenkel Award from the National Football Foundation and College Hall of Fame. In 2005 Munson was inducted into the Georgia Sports Hall of Fame.

In 2007 Munson decided that he would work only home games because it had become so difficult for him to travel. He originally planned to work Georgia's Sugar Bowl game against Hawaii but decided in late December that he could not make the trip. At the time, Munson said he still wished to broadcast Georgia's home games in 2008.

On September 22, 2008, Munson turns 86.

JIM PHILLIPS
Clemson, 1968–2003

One of the more enduring qualities of Southern college football is that once the game gets its hooks into you, no matter where you are from, you just can't leave it.

Such is the case with Jim Phillips, a native of Youngstown, Ohio, who had never set foot in the state of South Carolina when he applied in 1968 for the job to broadcast Clemson football and basketball games. He remained the voice of the Tigers for 36 years until his death on September 9, 2003.

Phillips had a remarkable career, which included the historic 12–0 run to the national championship in 1981. One of his frustrations is that he was unable to call Clemson's Orange Bowl win over Nebraska, which clinched the national title, because NBC had exclusive television and radio rights to the game.

At age 69 he was the only play-by-plan man in the ACC to call all his school's games in football, men and women's basketball, and baseball. Phillips broadcast over 2,000 events for Clemson.

Clemson broadcaster Jim Phillips. Photo courtesy of Clemson SID.

Phillips earned the respect from legions of fans as well as his fellow broadcasters because of the credibility he brought to his broadcasts. He was enthusiastic about Clemson but always believed in giving the opponents their due. "You should always tell it like it is, because you lose credibility if you don't," Phillips said in 1992. "Everyone I have admired in this business over the years has used that approach."

Phillips was chosen South Carolina Sportscaster of the Year five times, and in 1992 Clemson bestowed its highest honor on Phillips by naming him to the school's Athletic Hall of Fame. Phillips also received the Marvin "Skeeter" Francis Award, which is awarded for outstanding service and dedication to the ACC.

Phillips had just broadcast his 400th Clemson football game when he suffered an aortic aneurysm at his home and passed away. He was 69.

John Ward, Tennessee's longtime radio voice. Photo courtesy of Tennessee SID.

JOHN WARD
TENNESSEE, 1968–98

Ward completed his 31st and final year as the voice of Tennessee football with a broadcaster's dream: a perfect 13–0 season and a national championship.

Ward thought that his retirement from broadcasting would take place without a lot of fanfare. He was wrong.

"If you're not from Tennessee, you won't understand this," said Jeff Hall, the place-kicker on that national championship team. "But John Ward is more important to Tennessee football than any player or coach we've ever had. From the time I was a little boy, he *was* Tennessee football. He was the man we trusted."

Ward didn't start out to become a broadcasting legend. While getting a law degree from Tennessee, he picked up extra cash by doing play-by-play of high school football. He went to work at an advertising agency and then was given the opportunity to become the voice of the Vols.

Because the bulk of his income came from his successful advertising business, he would always call his radio work a hobby. But it was a hobby he performed with passion, a passion that was shared by several generations of Tennessee fans.

Ward is best known for a series of phrases, or "Wardisms," that have become his trademarks. Here are a few:

"It's football time in Tennessee!" (Right before every kickoff)

"He's at the 10, 5, 4, 3, 2, 1. Give him six. Touchdown, Tennessee!"

"The kick is up. Ladies and gentlemen, that kick is gooooooooood!"

As a broadcaster, Ward was never flashy. He believed he was there to paint a picture of the game, and the focus should never, ever be on him. On June 3, 1998, he announced that the coming season would be his last as the radio voice for Tennessee football. At a press conference called for the announcement, Ward was short and to the point.

"I have a prepared statement, and I am going to read it," Ward told the assembled media. "It's time."

And with that, Ward sat down.

"You cannot measure what John Ward did for Tennessee football," said coach Phillip Fulmer after Ward had called his last game.

Ward was named Tennessee's Sportscaster of the Year 27 times and is a member of the Tennessee Sports Hall of Fame.

EPILOGUE

Why the Game Will Last

You've now met the men who, as players and coaches, formed the building blocks of Southern college football as you know it today. You've visited the towns and enjoyed the unique traditions that have made the game so special for generation after generation of fans.

You've relived the games and remembered those special moments that will be talked and argued about today, tomorrow, and long after we are all gone.

But no story about Southern college football would be complete without an examination of the one thing that above all else keeps the college football fans coming back to campus year after year.

It is the thing keeps the Internet chat rooms buzzing for 365 days a year.

It is the thing that causes 92,138 people to show up at Alabama for a spring game.

It is the thing that drives a father to take his children on a tour of his old campus and share some precious memories.

Father and sons: Archie Manning (left) of Ole Miss, son Peyton Manning (middle) of Tennessee, and son Eli Manning of Ole Miss. Archie and Peyton photos courtesy of the *Atlanta Journal-Constitution*/Eli photo courtesy of Nathan Latil.

It is the thing that encourages friends who are busy and scattered across several states to find a way to coordinate their schedules so that they can meet on one of those brilliant fall Saturdays.

It is love.

While other sports inspire excitement, enthusiasm, anger, and happiness, in the South college football is the only one that generates an emotional attachment that goes to the very core of who we are. Southerners enjoy many other sports, but college football is the one we will always love, and this love can take on many forms.

The love of family, for one. Many Southerners use college football as the vehicle to bring their far-flung families together several times each year. Unlike the potentially stressful reunions at Christmas and Thanksgiving, college football games give family members a chance to actually relax and enjoy each other.

"When you go to a game in the South, you're likely to see four generations together," says Frank Broyles, the former athletics director at Arkansas. "It's part of our heritage, and that heritage is passed along from generation to generation. It means something very important to our people."

The love of school is another. No matter how successful we may become, our college campuses will always tug at our hearts. They are where we grew up, where we suffered our first major triumphs and disappointments, where we fell in love (at least once). Football gives us the chance to come back and, for a little while, be young again—to remember those days when all of life's possibilities were still ahead of us.

Georgia's Porter Payne (left) and his son Billy in 1948. Photo courtesy of Georgia SID.

Friends, you just don't get these feelings watching the NFL.

Because Southerners love college football, it is much more than just mere entertainment or just a way to pass the time on Saturdays in the fall. In the South we have a sincere, long-term emotional investment in college football, and each year it pays huge dividends.

If you still think this is just a game when there is so much evidence to the contrary, then consider this:

For Southerners, the passing college football seasons are not just a record of games played. Oh, no. They are the markers that serve to connect the important events of our lives.

"In Alabama people won't say, 'my child was born in 1972,'" says Roy Kramer, the former commissioner of the SEC. "They'll say, 'my child was born the year Auburn blocked two punts and beat Alabama.' That's how ingrained the sport is in our culture."

In the South the arrival of the college football season each September is the return of a long-lost friend. Regardless of how

Georgia's Billy Payne (right), the future chief of the 1996 Atlanta Olympics, with dad Porter Payne in 1968. Photo courtesy of Georgia SID.

The sons of Georgia Tech All-Americans (left to right): Harvey Hardey (Harvey Jr.), Bill Healey (Rob), and Ray Beck (Tommy), all signing with former coach Bobby Dodd in 1968. Photo courtesy of the *Atlanta Journal-Constitution.*

Former Ole Miss great Charlie Conerly in 1987. Photo courtesy of the *Atlanta Journal-Constitution.*

bad other things may be in our lives, we know that each fall the leaves will turn, the temperatures will finally drop, and college football will be back. There's a lot of comfort in that thought.

And there's some additional comfort in this: when things are going badly in our lives we can, thanks to college football, think back to a special Saturday afternoon, and it makes us feel better.

One of Tennessee's biggest wins under coach Johnny Majors (1977–92) was a 35–7 upset over No. 2 Miami in the Sugar Bowl on January 1, 1986. Miami was in the middle of a great dynasty, which saw the Hurricanes win four national championships from 1983 to 1991. Oddsmakers didn't give Tennessee a chance in the game. That's why the victory was so sweet and still remains such a pleasant memory today.

Several years after that game, Majors was on the road for a speaking engagement. After his speech a man walked up to him. "He told me that whenever he is feeling down and out, he just watches the

In the South, college football fans get an early start. Here, young Ashley Green roots for the Bulldogs at a Georgia game in 1985. Photo courtesy of the *Atlanta Journal-Constitution*/Joey Ivansco.

videotape of that game," Majors says. "And it makes him feel better. That's how much that one game meant to the Tennessee people."

No other sport creates that kind of emotional bond with its fans.

So the celebration of college football in the South is ultimately a celebration of love. Love of family, love of school, the love of beautiful fall afternoons with friends. It is the very best of life in the South today, just as it was over 100 years ago.

Bill Curry said it best at the beginning of this book. In the South, college football is not just a game. It's who we are.

And all of us are better for it.

SOURCES

Adventure Quest, Inc. *The Heisman: Sixty Years of Tradition and Excellence.* Bronxville, NY: Adventure Quest, Inc., 1995.

Attner, Paul. *The Terrapins: Maryland Football.* Huntsville, AL: The Strode Publishers, 1975.

Bradley, Bob. *Death Valley Days: The Glory of Clemson Football.* Marietta, GA: Longstreet Press, 1991.

Bradley, Bob, Sam Blackman, and Chuck Kriese. *Clemson, Where the Tigers Play: The History of Clemson University Athletics.* Champaign, IL: Sports Publishing, Inc., 1999.

Browning, Al. *Bowl, Bama, Bowl, 1926–88: A Crimson Tide Tradition.* Sterrett, AL: Five Points South Productions, 1998.

Clarkson, Julian. *Let No Man Put Asunder: Story of a Football Rivalry.* Ft. Myers, FL: Hillsboro Printing and Lithographing Co., 1968.

Cromartie, Bill. *Clean Old-Fashioned Hate.* Atlanta, GA: Gridiron Publishers, 1984.

Dunnavant, Keith. *Coach: The Life of Paul "Bear" Bryant.* New York: Simon and Schuster, 1996.

Dye, Pat, with John Logue. *In the Arena.* Montgomery, AL: Black Belt Press, 1992.

Forney, John, and Steve Townsend. *Talk of the Tide: An Oral History of Alabama Football.* Birmingham, AL: Crane Hill Publishers, 1993.

Fulks, Matt. *The Sportscaster's Dozen: Off the Air with Southeastern Legends.* Chicago: Masters Press, 1998.

Fulmer, Phillip, with Jeff Hagood. *A Perfect Season.* Nashville: Rutledge Hill Press, 1999.

Givens, Wendell, with Arthur Ben and Elizabeth N. Chitty. *Ninety-Nine Iron.* Birmingham, AL: Seacoast Publishing, 1992.

Hester, Wayne. *Century of Champions: The Centennial History of Alabama Football.* Birmingham, AL: Seacoast Publishing/Birmingham News, 1991.

Hester, Wayne. *Where Tradition Began: The Centennial History of Auburn Football.* Birmingham, AL: Seacoast Publishing/Birmingham News, 1991.

Mule, Marty. *Eye of the Tiger.* Marietta, GA: Longstreet Press, 1993.

Mule, Marty. *Rolling Green: A Century of Tulane Football.* New Orleans: Tulane University Athletic Department, 1993.

Price, Tom. *A Century of Gamecocks: Memorable Football Moments*. Columbia, SC: Summerhouse Press, 1995.

Price, Tom. *The '84 Gamecocks: Fire Ants and Black Magic*. Columbia: University of South Carolina Press, 1985.

Scherer, George. *Auburn-Georgia Football: A Hundred Years of Rivalry*. Jefferson, NC: McFarland and Company, Inc., Publishers, 1992.

Smith, Derek. *Glory Yards: Georgia vs. Florida*. Nashville: Rutledge Hill Press, 1993.

Smith, Loran. *Between the Hedges: 100 Years of Georgia Football*. Marietta, GA: Longstreet Press, 1992.

Smith, Loran, with Lewis Grizzard. *Glory, Glory*. Atlanta, GA: Peachtree Publishers, 1981.

Spurrier, Steve, with Norm Carlson. *Gators: The Inside Story of Florida's First SEC Title*. Orlando, FL: Tribune Publishing, 1992.

Thilenius, Ed, and Jim Koger. *No Ifs, No Ands, And a Lot of Butts: 21 Years of Georgia Football*. Atlanta, GA: Foote and Davis, Inc., 1960.

Wells, Larry. *A Century of Heroes: One Hundred Years of Ole Miss Football*. Marietta, GA: Longstreet Press and Oxford, MS: The University of Mississippi Athletic Department, 1993.

Wenzell, Frank, and Rita Cantrell Wenzell. *The Fanatic's Guide to SEC Football*. Pensacola, FL: LightSide Productions, Inc., 1993.

Whitten, Don. *The Dog Comes Home: Ole Miss Football in 1983*. Oxford, MS: Yoknapatawpha Press, 1984.

Wilkinson, Jack. *Focused on the Top: Georgia Tech's Championship Story*. Marietta, GA: Longstreet Press, 1991.

Woody, Larry. *A Dixie Farewell: The Life and Death of Chucky Mullins*. Nashville: Eggman Publishing, 1993.

Vaught, John H. *Rebel Coach*. Memphis: Memphis State University Press, 1971.

ABOUT THE AUTHOR

The 2008 college football season will be Tony Barnhart's 32nd as a reporter for newspapers, television, and radio.

The 1999 Georgia Sportswriter of the Year, Barnhart began his newspaper career at the *Union* (South Carolina) *Daily Times* in 1976. He then spent seven years at the *Greensboro* (North Carolina) *News & Record* before joining the *Atlanta Journal-Constitution* in 1984.

In addition to his newspaper work, Barnhart spent 10 seasons as a reporter for ESPN, including seven seasons with its award-winning *College Game Day* show. In 2004 Barnhart became a regular contributor to the *College Football Today* show on CBS.

In 1996 Barnhart was the screenwriter for *The Southern Game*, a documentary on Southern college football produced by Georgia Public Television. The documentary was one of three finalists for a Southern Regional Emmy Award.

Barnhart is a past president of the Football Writers Association of America and the United States Basketball Writers Association. He is a former member of the National Football Foundation and College Hall of Fame's Honors Court, an 11-member panel that selects each year's incoming class to the College Football Hall of Fame.

In July 2006 Barnhart received the Jake Wade Award from the College Sports Information Directors of America. The award is given to a member of the media "who has made a significant contribution to the coverage of college athletics."

In March 2007 Barnhart received the Fred Russell Award from the All-American Football Foundation. The Russell Award recognizes sportswriters who have made a significant contribution to college football.

Barnhart has written three books: *Southern Fried Football*, first published in 2000; *What It Means to Be a Bulldog*, published in 2004; and *Dooley: My 40 Years at Georgia*, published in 2005.

A 1976 graduate of the Henry W. Grady School of Journalism at the University of Georgia, Barnhart lives in Atlanta with his wife, Maria. Their daughter, Sara Catherine, is a 2008 graduate of the University of Georgia School of Law.

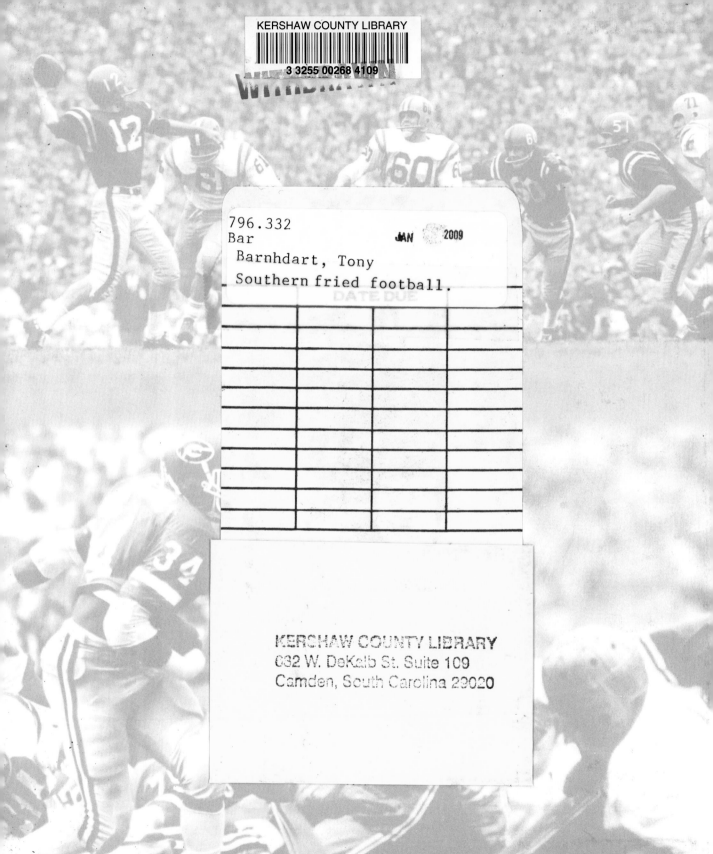